Anthropology of Policy

Anthropology of Policy argues that policy has become an increasingly central organizing principle in contemporary societies, shaping the way we live, act and think.

This book shows how anthropological approaches to policy can provide insights into a range of contemporary issues, from equal opportunities in Sweden and health care policies in Norway and Denmark, to conflicting discourses on AIDS policy in Africa, and Thatcherite housing policy in Britain. Other chapters include European Union audiovisual policies aimed at creating 'European consciousness', the Canadian government's covert policy for redefining Canadian national identity, and the management of modern Americans. Despite the importance of policy as a key institution of modern society, it remains curiously under-theorized and lacking in critical analysis.

By problematizing 'policy' as language, as cultural agent, and as political technology, and by drawing attention to its links with discourse, power and subjectivity, the authors outline an approach that reconceptualizes the field of anthropology and sets a new agenda for anthropological theory and methods. They also provide an ethnographic challenge to those normative models, popular among practitioners, which depict policy as a neat, linear, rational process.

Cris Shore is lecturer in Social Anthropology at Goldsmiths' College, London and **Susan Wright** is lecturer in Social Anthropology at the University of Sussex.

European Association of Social Anthropologists

The European Association of Social Anthropologists (EASA) was inaugurated in January 1989, in response to a widely felt need for a professional association which would represent social anthropologists in Europe and foster cooperation and interchange in teaching and research. As Europe transforms itself in the 1990s, the EASA is dedicated to the renewal of the distinctive European tradition in social anthropology.

Other titles in the series:

Conceptualizing Society
Adam Kuper
Revitalizing European Rituals
Jeremy Boissevain
Other Histories
Kirsten Hastrup
Alcohol, Gender and Culture
Dimitra Gefou-Madianou
Understanding Rituals
Daniel de Coppet
Gendered Anthropology
Teresa del Valle
**Social Experience and
 Anthropological Knowledge**
Kirsten Hastrup and Peter Hervik

Fieldwork and Footnotes
*Han F. Vermeulen and Arturo
 Alvarez Roldan*
Syncretism/Anti-Syncretism
Charles Stewart and Rosalind Shaw
Grasping the Changing World
Václav Hubinger
Civil Society
Chris Hann and Elizabeth Dunn
Nature and Society
Philippe Descola and Gísli Pálsson
The Ethnography of Moralities
Signe Howell
Inside and Outside the Law
Edited by Olivia Harris

Anthropology of Policy

Critical perspectives on
governance and power

Edited by Cris Shore and
Susan Wright

London and New York

First published 1997 by Routledge
11 New Fetter Lane, London EC4P 4EE

Simultaneously published in the USA and Canada
by Routledge
29 West 35th Street, New York, NY 10001

Typeset in Times by Routledge
Printed and bound in Great Britain by
Creative Print and Design (Wales), Ebbw Vale

British Library Cataloguing in Publication Data
A catalogue record for this book is available from the British Library

Library of Congress Cataloging in Publication Data
Anthropology of Policy: critical perspectives on governance and power
/edited by Cris Shore and Susan Wright.
p. cm.
Includes bibliographical references and index
1. Anthropology–Methodology. 2. Policy sciences. 3. Public
policy. 4. Social policy. I. Shore, Cris, 1959– . II. Wright,
Susan, 1951– .
GN33.A45 1997
320'.6–dc21   96–51859
                                                                    CIP

ISBN 0–415–13220–7 (hbk)
ISBN 0–415–13221–5 (pbk)

Contents

Contributors   ix
Preface and acknowledgements   xiii

Introduction

1 Policy: A new field of anthropology   3
Cris Shore and Susan Wright
Towards an anthropology of policy   3
Anthropology and the art of government   10
Rethinking political anthropology   12
Reconceptualizing 'the field': Methodological
    implications for anthropology and policy studies   14
Policy as language: Discourse and power   18
Policy as cultural agent: Constructing national identity   24
Policy as political technology:
    Governmentality and subjectivity   29
Epilogue   34

Part I Policy as language and power

2 Writing development policy and policy analysis
plain or clear: On language, genre and power   43
Raymond Apthorpe
The writ of language   44
Radical realism and ideal ruralism   46
Institutions and mechanisms   53
Policy language   54

3 **The implications of 'medical', 'gender in development' and 'culturalist' discourses for HIV/AIDS policy in Africa**   59
Gill Seidel and Laurent Vidal
Introduction   59
Theoretical frameworks   60
Medical discourse   61
Epidemiological discourse about risk groups   64
Gender and development discourse   66
Culturalist discourse   71
Effects of the culturalist discourse in Côte d'Ivoire   73
Conclusion   77

4 **Patients' bodies and discourses of power**   88
Helle Ploug Hansen
Policy in a hospital setting   88
The hospital as a negotiated order   90
The hospital policy document   90
The clinical praxis   91
The daily round and its interpretation   93
Discourses of power   99
Conclusion   101

Part II Policy as cultural agent

5 **Free to make the right choice? Gender equality policy in post-welfare Sweden**   107
Annika Rabo
Welfare state with a human face   109
Policies of equality between women and men   111
Higher education, policies of sexual equality and issues of gender   116
Reactions to a government bill   119
A state-commissioned report   123
'We are all different'   126
Conclusions: Sexual equality policy, higher education and 'free choice'   131

6 **The cultural politics of populism: Celebrating Canadian national identity**   136
Eva Mackey
Multiculturalism, constitutional crisis and celebrations   138
Key aspects of celebratory policy   141

Non-political patriotism and civil society as
    diagnostics of power   143
Naturalizing imagery, celebratory taboos and
    invented symbols   145
Which people?   147
Coexisting discourses   148
'The people' at the Wallaceford Pumpkin Festival   150
Populism and locality at the Brookside
    Raise-the-Flag day   154
Legitimacy and common sense   159

7 **Governing Europe: European Union audiovisual policy**
   and the politics of identity   165
   Cris Shore
   Anthropology, identity and the politics of communication   165
   Audiovisual policy and European integration   167
   Television without frontiers: From 1984 Green Paper
       to 1989 Directive   169
   Creating a 'Community of Europeans': The politics of
       media policy   172
   Beyond the nation state? EU audiovisual policy and
       supranationalism   177
   Using TV as the cultural arm of nation-building: Flaws
       in EU strategy   180
   Conclusion   186

Part III Policy as political technology: Governmentality and
subjectivity

8 **Reform and resistance: A Norwegian illustration**   195
   Halvard Vike
   Introduction   195
   Moral economy and policy   197
   The plan   199
   The context: A Norwegian industrial community   202
   Decision-making and the labour party ideology   204
   Marx and Weber on modernity   207
   Political resistance   209
   Conclusions   213

 9 **Poverty in a 'post-welfare' landscape: Tenant management
    policies, self-governance and the democratization of
    knowledge in Great Britain**   217
    Susan Brin Hyatt
    From government of *the poor to government* by *the poor*   217
    *Subsidized housing and the rise of 'the social' in
      Great Britain*   220
    Democratizing knowledge and the policing of communities   224
    *Housing policy and poverty under the regimes of advanced
      liberalism*   231

10 **Managing Americans: Policy and changes in the meanings of
    work and the self**   239
    Emily Martin
    Kinds of power   241
    Work and life   244
    Persons, groups and their interfaces   245
    Corporate selves   248
    Sane and insane selves: Attention deficit disorder   252

Epilogue

11 **Anthropology and policy research: The view from Northern
    Ireland**   261
    Hastings Donnan and Graham McFarlane
    Policy-orientated anthropology seen from above and below   261
    The context for policy research in Northern Ireland   263
    *Anthropologists and policy-related research in
      Northern Ireland*   266
    *Getting to know Northern Irish farm households:
      Anthropology marginalized*   270
    *'Truncated' anthropology and policy research in
      Northern Ireland*   274
    *Anthropology, policy and the mutual suspension of
      disbelief*   277

    Index   282

Contributors

Raymond Apthorpe has long experience of researching and consulting on development issues for international development agencies. He is currently an independent researcher working for the United Nations Development Programme in Malawi and is Visiting Professor in the field of Relief and Development Policy Evaluation at the National Centre for Development Studies, ANU Canberra, Australia. Recent publications include 'Policy anthropology as expert witness', *Social Anthropology* 4 (2) 1996: 163–79 and *Arguing Development Policy: Frames and Discourses* (co-edited with Des Casper), London: Cass (1996).

Hastings Donnan is Reader in Social Anthropology at Queen's University, Belfast, Northern Ireland. Among his most recent publications are co-edited books on *Islam, Globalization and Postmodernity* (London: Routledge 1994), *Border Approaches: Anthropological Perspectives on Frontiers* (1994), and *Family and Gender in Pakistan* (1996). He was editor of *Man. Journal of the Royal Anthropological Institute* from 1993–5.

Helle Ploug Hansen is Dean and Associate Professor at the School of Advanced Nursing Education, University of Aarhus, Denmark. She has a PhD in anthropology and a background in nursing. Her book *I Grænsefladen mellem Liv og Døg. En kulturanalyse af sygeplejen pa en onkologisk afdeling* (*Between Life and Death. A Cultural Analysis of Cancer Nursing Care*) is published by Gyldendal: Copenhagen (1995).

Susan Brin Hyatt is an Assistant Professor of Anthropology at Temple University, Philadelphia, USA. Her doctoral fieldwork, for which she received her PhD from the University of Massachusetts, was based on two years of fieldwork conducted on council housing estates in Bradford, in northern England. Her interest in grassroots movement and urban policy grew directly out of her seven years' experience as a community organizer in Chicago. She is currently working on articles on feminist anthropology and activism and on the political significance of women's friendship networks in poor communities.

Graham McFarlane is Senior Lecturer in Social Anthropology at Queen's University, Belfast, Northern Ireland. He has been working on issues of identity in Northern Ireland, and has recently extended this research to Greece as a consequence of his involvement as coordinator of a project on Greek and Irish farming households. Among his publications are *Social Anthropology and Public Policy in Northern Ireland* (co-edited with Hastings Donnan, Aldershot: Avebury, 1989). He is currently co-editing (with Hastings Donnan) a collection of essays entitled 'Culture and policy in Northern Ireland'.

Eva Mackey is currently a postdoctoral research fellow at the Centre for Cultural Risk Research, Charles Sturt University, Australia. She received her Doctorate in Social Anthropology from the University of Sussex in 1996 for her research on cultural pluralism and national identity in Canada. Her publications include 'Postmodernism and cultural politics in a multicultural nation', *Public Culture* (1995).

Emily Martin is Professor of Anthropology at Princeton University, USA. Her work on ideology and power in Chinese society was published in *The Cult of the Dead in a Chinese Village* (Stanford University Press 1972), *Chinese Ritual and Politics* (Cambridge University Press 1981) and, with Hill Gates, *The Anthropology of Taiwanese Society* (Stanford University Press 1981). Beginning with *The Woman in the Body: A Cultural Analysis of Reproduction* (Beacon Press 1987), she began work on the anthropology of science and reproduction in the USA, in particular on how gender stereotypes shape medical language, and popular conceptions of the immune system. *Flexible Bodies: Tracking Immunity in America from the Days of Polio to the Age of AIDS* (Beacon Press 1994), analyses how the concept of 'flexibility' in immune discourse is implicated in transforming notions of health and business practices. Her current work concerns theories of normalization and the evolving constitution of selfhood in contemporary society.

Annika Rabo is Assistant Professor, Department of Social Anthropology, University of Linköping, Sweden. She has carried out fieldwork on development and education issues in Syria, Jordan, and more recently in teacher colleges in Sweden. Recent publications include 'Gender, state and civil society in Jordan and Syria' in C. Hann and E. Dunn (eds) *Civil Society. Challenging Western Models*, London: Routledge (1996) and 'Evaluations as modern rituals' in B. Rombach and K. Sahlin-Andersson (eds) *Modern Evaluations in the Public Sector*, Stockholm (1995).

Gill Seidel is Fellow/Honorary Reader in the Africa Research Unit, Department of Social and Economic Studies, University of Bradford. She has specialized in racist and anti-racist discourses and the construction of marginality. Her current research interests are discourse, gender and development with special reference to STDs/HIV/AIDS. Her publications include *The Nature of the Right. A Feminist Analysis of Order Patterns* (edited) Amsterdam/Philadelphia: John Benjamins (1988); 'The discourses of HIV/AIDS in sub-Saharan Africa: discourses of rights/empowerment vs. discourses of control/exclusion', *Social Science and Medicine* 36 (3) 1993; and 'Confidentiality and HIV status in KwaZulu-Natal, South Africa: implications, resistances, challenges', *Health Policy and Planning* 11 (4) 1996.

Cris Shore is Lecturer in Social Anthropology at Goldsmiths' College, London. His first major research explored the relationship between local and national politics in post-war Italy through an ethnographic study of the Italian Communist Party (*Italian Communism*, London: Pluto, 1990). Current research interests include the European Union, its policies, institutions and personnel. He is former editor of *Anthropology in Action* and co-editor of *The Anthropology of Europe* with Victoria Goddard and Josep Llobera, Oxford: Berg (1994) and *The Future of Anthropology: Its Relevance to the Modern World* with Akbar Ahmed, London: Athlone Press (1995). He is currently writing a book on the cultural politics of

European integration and co-editing (with Stephen Nugent) a collection of essays entitled *Anthropology and Cultural Studies*.

Laurent Vidal is an anthropologist at the Institut Français de Recherche Scientifique pour le Développment en Coopération (ORSTOM) in Paris. Since 1990 he has worked in Côte d'Ivoire on representations of AIDS and its effects on institutions and families. His research interests also include ethical and methodological issues in anthropological research on AIDS. He is co-editor of *Les sciences sociales face au sida. Cas africains autour de l'exemple ivoirien* (with J. Dozon, Paris: ORSTOM, 1995). Other publications include 'Le temps de l'annonce. Séropositivités vécues à Abidjan', *Psychopathologie Africaine* 26 (2) 1994: 265–82, 'L'anthropologie, la recherche et l'intervention sur le Sida en Afrique. Enjeux méthodologoques d'une rencontre', *Sciences sociales et santé* 13 (2) 1995: 5–27 and *Le Silence et le Sens*, Paris: Anthropos-Economica (1996).

Halvard Vike obtained a PhD in social anthropology from the University of Oslo in 1996. He currently works as a researcher at the Telemark Research Institute, Norway. Among his research interests are political anthropology, history and anthropology, sociolinguistics and symbolism. His PhD thesis is titled 'Conquering the Unreal: Politics and Bureaucracy in a Norwegian Town' (Department and Museum of Anthropology, University of Oslo, 1996).

Susan Wright lectures in social anthropology at Sussex University. Her research interests are the changing ideas of citizenship and systems of governance in Iran and Britain. After a government-commissioned study of rural decision-making in Britain, as a community worker, she researched people's interactions with state and voluntary organizations in ex-mining villages in north-east England. In the same area, she was commissioned by the county council to make an ethnographic evaluation of their corporate policy to develop an 'empowering' local state. Recently, she has resumed, after twenty years, a study of tribespeople's responses to changing systems of governance in Iran. Recent publications include *Anthropology of Organizations* (edited, Routledge, 1994) and *Power and Participatory Development* (co-edited with Nici Nelson, Intermediate Technology Publications, 1995).

Preface and acknowledgements

Policy studies receive input from numerous disciplines – politics, public administration, social policy, organization studies, international relations – among which a few writers would now include anthropology. However, the scope and implications of anthropology's contribution have rarely been explored. The inspiration for an 'anthropology of policy' stems, in some measure, from our encounter with the present, and the experience of living in Britain throughout the 1980s and 1990s – a period characterized by the rise of neo-liberal discourses and practices of government. This book takes up and extends debates about the impact of policy by exploring its mechanisms, disguises, and its implications for cultural practices in different societies. What unites these essays is their shared concern with investigating the connections between policy, power, subjectivity and changing forms of government. They argue that an anthropological approach to policy treats the models and language of decision-makers as ethnographic data to be analysed rather than as frameworks for analysis. By excavating the prescriptive tones and normative assumptions that underlie policies, they examine how policy discourses 'work' to control political agendas, and the complex ways in which policies construct their subjects as objects of power.

The origins of this edited collection of essays began with a workshop organized by Anthropology in Action at the 1994 Conference of the European Association of Social Anthropologists (EASA) held in Oslo. We are grateful to Goldsmiths' College and Sussex University for providing travel grants that made attendance at that conference possible. As editors, we wish to thank both EASA and Anthropology in Action for supporting this project, as well as those contributors to the workshop who made it such a success, and whose papers helped to sharpen the ideas and focus of the present volume. Some of the original contributors to that panel are represented in this volume, other chapters by Emily Martin, Annika Rabo, Eva Mackey, Hastings Donnan and Graham McFarlane, Raymond Apthorpe, Gill Seidel and Laurent Vidal were specifically commissioned.

A special debt of gratitude is owed to Delphine Houlton for proofreading the introduction and for her excellent editorial advice, to Dean Powley for her Herculian labours in sub-editing the manuscript and to Roger Goodman for his encouragement and patience on behalf of the EASA Committee. We would like to thank the 1996 cohort of third-year anthropology students on the Policy and Power course at Sussex University whose creative discussions provided a catalyst for thinking critically about the themes covered in the text. Finally, we would like to thank all the contributors for their work, and for their patience, tolerance and enthusiasm in responding to our comments and suggestions; we hope that the result has been worthwhile.

Cris Shore and Sue Wright
November 1996

Introduction

Chapter 1

Policy
A new field of anthropology

Cris Shore and Susan Wright

TOWARDS AN ANTHROPOLOGY OF POLICY

> Europeans feel increasingly cynical, powerless and frustrated about government. They see public policy made under the anaesthetic of corporate influence, political information organized through spin doctors and a media which constantly feeds them on a diet of pap and consensus. People simply do not have the tools to participate in public life.
>
> (White 1996: 14)

> (Comment by Aidan White, Brussels-based general secretary of the International Federation of Journalists and chair of the European Commission Information Society Forum working group on democratic and social values, discussing the state of decision making in the European Union.)

This book sets out to chart a new domain of anthropological enquiry, the *anthropology of policy*. We ask: how do policies 'work' as instruments of governance, and why do they sometimes fail to function as intended? What are the mobilizing metaphors and linguistic devices that cloak policy with the symbols and trappings of political legitimacy? How do policies construct their subjects as objects of power, and what new kinds of subjectivity or identity are being created in the modern world? How are major shifts in discourse made authoritative? How are normative claims used to present a particular way of defining a problem and its solution, as if these were the only ones possible, while enforcing closure or silence on other ways of thinking or talking?

One aspect of the background against which this book arises, as the above quotation from Aidan White suggests, is the concern that citizens are becoming alienated from an increasingly remote and commercialized policy-making process. A second aspect, as demonstrated by many of the chapters, is that the frontiers of policy are expanding. We argue that policy has become an increasingly central concept and instrument in the organization of contemporary societies. Like the modern state (to which its growth can be linked), policy now impinges on all areas of life so that it is virtually impossible to ignore or escape its influence. More than this, policy increasingly shapes the way individuals construct themselves as subjects. Through policy, the individual is categorized and given such statuses and roles as 'subject', 'citizen', 'professional', 'national', 'criminal' and 'deviant'. From the cradle to the grave, people are classified, shaped and ordered according to policies, but they may have little consciousness of or control over the processes at work. The study of policy, therefore, leads straight into issues at the heart of anthropology: norms and institutions; ideology and consciousness; knowledge and power; rhetoric and discourse; meaning and interpretation; the global and the local – to mention but a few. These issues are addressed in this introductory section and in the three subsequent sections which focus on policy as language and power, policy as cultural agent, and policy as political technology – governmentality and subjectivity.

As neo-liberal ideas and practices have come to supplant the post-war model of the welfare state, the ways in which policies are used as an instrument of power for shaping individuals – or, to use Foucault's terminology, as a political technology – are related by many of our contributors to a more global phenomenon of changing patterns of governance. The emphasis is mainly, but not exclusively, on Europe and North America. However, through international structural adjustment programmes and Western training schemes for 'Southern' policy makers, neo-liberal models of the state and patterns of governance are being exported to the Third World. Our aim is to provide anthropological insights into the new structures through which policy operates and the discourses and agencies through which it is articulated. By examining policy, we hope to shed light on changing styles and systems of governance and how these are reconfiguring the relationship between the individual and society.

This book represents a continuation of the anthropological work on organizations initiated in the 1980s by BASAPP (British Association for Social Anthropology in Policy and Practice) which culminated in the volume edited by Wright (1994). BASAPP, renamed Anthropology in Action, organized a session on 'Policy, Morality and the Art of Government' at the 1994 Oslo conference of the European Association of Social Anthropologists. Papers given at that session form the basis of several chapters in this book. One key point to emerge was that organizations exist in a constant state of *organizing*, and that process revolves around the concept of policy. From universities and schools to public agencies and large corporations, policy is increasingly being codified, publicized and referred to by workers and managers as the guidelines that legitimate and even motivate their behaviour. To adapt a metaphor from Arthur Koestler (1967), policy is the ghost in the machine – the force which breathes life and purpose into the machinery of government and animates the otherwise dead hand of bureaucracy. This capacity to stimulate and channel activity derives largely from the objectification of policy – that process through which policies acquire a seemingly tangible existence and legitimacy. However, the objectification of policy often proceeds hand in hand with the objectification of the subjects of policy. Like Victorian photography or the 'panopticon' prison (or the alienated Europeans whom White says are fed on a diet of pap), the objectified person 'is seen but he does not see; he is the object of information, never a subject in communication' (Foucault 1977: 200).

On closer examination, however, policy fragments – it becomes unclear what constitutes 'a policy'. Is it found in the language, rhetoric and concepts of political speeches and party manifestos? Is it the written document produced by government or company officials? Is it embedded in the institutional mechanisms of decision-making and service delivery? Or is it (*pace* Lipsky 1980) whatever people experience in their interactions with street-level bureaucrats? A policy may differ enormously in these various manifestations. Much of the work of organizing is to make these fragmented activities appear coherent, so it can be claimed that an intention has been realized and a successful result achieved.

An instrumentalist view of government conceptualizes policy as a tool to regulate a population from the top down, through rewards and sanctions. According to this conception, policy is an intrinsically technical, rational, action-oriented instrument that decision makers use to solve problems and affect change. As Titmuss stated, policy denotes 'the principles that govern action directed towards given ends' (Titmuss 1974: 23). Policy has a more diffuse impact when, through metaphors of the individual and society, it influences the way people construct themselves, their conduct and their social relations as free individuals. We use 'governance' to refer to the more complex processes by which policies not only impose conditions, as if from 'outside' or 'above', but influence people's indigenous norms of conduct so that they themselves contribute, not necessarily consciously, to a government's model of social order. In other words, to use Graham Burchell's (1993: 267) description, governance is 'a more or less methodical and rationally reflected "way of doing things", or "art", for acting on the actions of individuals, taken either singly or collectively, so as to shape, guide, correct and modify the ways in which they conduct themselves'. In this sense, governance is understood as a type of power which both acts *on* and *through* the agency and subjectivity of individuals as ethically free and rational subjects: 'it presupposes rather than annuls their capacity as agents', as Colin Gordon (1991: 5) states. This can be witnessed, for example, when British subjects begin to reform themselves into 'responsible, independent citizens' according to a Thatcherite ideology of enterprise and associated moral discourses on the 'enterprising self', the 'sovereign consumer' and the 'active citizen' (Heelas 1991). Similarly, it can be seen when, as a result of policies designed to expose the legal profession to market forces, changes are induced in the self-definition of lawyers, who increasingly see themselves as entrepreneurs, suppliers of a commodity to consumers in the market place, rather than instruments of justice (Stanley 1991).

Our argument is that policy has become a major institution of Western and international governance, on a par with other key organizing concepts such as 'family' and 'society'. However, whereas social scientists have treated the latter as ideological and politicized concepts and explored their operation in depth, 'policy' is still frequently treated as if it were politically and ideologically neutral, and has scarcely been analysed or theorized by anthropologists. By problematizing 'policy', we aim to chart a new territory for social, and particularly political, anthropology. Some *de facto* anthropology of policy already exists, but, lacking a clear identity, it is often called something else. On the one hand, pioneering analyses of complex power systems have been carried out effectively through studies of policies, but have not been labelled as such. For example, anthropological analyses of the 1984 Warnock Report and the 1990 Human Embryology and Fertilisation Bill in Britain shed light on the ways developments in medical science have unsettled concepts of kinship, family, parenthood and personhood which underpinned the moral, ethical and social order (Rivière 1985; Cannell 1990;

Strathern 1992a, 1992b; Edwards et al. 1993). On the other hand, anthropologists working on policy-making and evaluation in fields as various as health and medicine, community care, family, environment and development, have tended to confine publications to the substantive concerns of the particular policy being examined. Training manuals on policy ethnography, such as Van Willigen and Dewalt (1985), concentrate on how to study policy as a 'given'. Despite recognition that 'the idea of policy is as central to the development of applied anthropology as the concept of culture has been to the anthropological profession as a whole' (Chambers 1985: 37–8), anthropologists have rarely turned their analytical gaze towards policy as a concept or cultural phenomenon. Nor, in the main, have they exploited the insights that the structures, discourses and agencies through which policy operates can offer on the workings of power.[1] We propose that a focus on policy provides a new way of formulating these issues, which is essential if anthropologists are to understand those shifting political and cultural orders that Appadurai calls 'global ethnoscapes' (1991).

If anthropology has saliency for understanding policies as political and administrative processes, the converse is also true. Policies are inherently and unequivocally *anthropological* phenomena. They can be read by anthropologists in a number of ways: as cultural texts, as classificatory devices with various meanings, as narratives that serve to justify or condemn the present, or as rhetorical devices and discursive formations that function to empower some people and silence others. Not only do policies codify social norms and values, and articulate fundamental organizing principles of society, they also contain implicit (and sometimes explicit) models of society. Like Malinowski's notion of 'myth' and its function in Trobriand society, a policy can serve as a guide to behaviour and 'charter for action' (Malinowski 1926). There are parallels between the pragmatic uses of policy and those of history which, as Buckley notes, function in at least three distinct ways: 'as a rhetorical commentary that either justifies or condemns; as a "charter" for action; and as a focus for allegiance' (Buckley 1989: 184). In many respects, therefore, policies encapsulate the entire history and culture of the society that generated them. To use Mauss's concept (1954), policies can be studied as 'total social phenomena' as they have important economic, legal, cultural and moral implications, and can create whole new sets of relationships between individuals, groups and objects.

Policies may also be analysed as examples of what Turner (1967), in his study of Ndembu ritual, labelled 'dominant symbols' or what Schneider (1968), in his study of American kinship, called 'core symbols' – analytical keys to understanding an entire cultural system and its underlying elements. For Schneider, conjugal sexual intercourse was the core symbol at the heart of American kinship as sex within marriage expressed most succinctly the symbolic opposition between the two basic components of American kinship reckoning, namely 'nature' and 'law'. With its religious and familial overtones, conjugal sex was a symbol and moral charter which set up parameters of thinking and acting in other domains (such as the legal, political and economic). Policies can work in a similar way to reveal the structure of cultural systems. For example, America's post-war policy of 'containment' towards communism, summed up in the Truman Doctrine of March 1947, provides an exemplary illustration of core symbols and moral charters in action. President Truman's speech to the US Congress, in which he declared that 'it must be the policy of the USA to support free peoples who are resisting subjugation by armed minorities or outside pressures' (Truman 1948: 8491), persuaded Congress to pledge economic and military aid to Greece and Turkey (and later to the whole of Europe through the Marshall Plan) and helped to trigger the Cold War. This policy of 'containment' used Manichean language to frighten and 'educate' the American public about the dangers of communist ideology (Gaddis 1972: 317). A metaphor more commonly associated with contagious disease, containment became the idiom for rethinking not only US defence and foreign policy, but also internal political control (as witnessed in McCarthyism). It was subsequently instrumental in redefining what it meant to be American. Thus, acting as a core symbol, the idea of containment spilled over into, and restructured, many different domains.

Policies are most obviously political phenomena, yet it is a feature of policies that their political nature is disguised by the objective, neutral, legal–rational idioms in which they are portrayed. In this guise, policies appear to be mere instruments for promoting efficiency and effectiveness. This masking of the political under the cloak of neutrality is a key feature of modern power. Foucault identified 'political technologies' as the means by which power conceals its own operation. As Dreyfus and Rabinow (1982: 196) sum up: 'political technologies advance by taking what is essentially a political problem, removing it from the realm of political discourse, and recasting it in the neutral language of science'. Central to this process is the use of 'expert' knowledge in the design of institutional procedures. For example, the modern prison relies on a host of detailed architectural and organizational mechanisms for ordering people through control of time and space. Constant surveillance of each inmate, in cells and corridors, parade grounds and exercise yards, as well as through daily rotas and drills is an efficient way of simultaneously physically disciplining each individual body and ordering the whole system (Dreyfus and Rabinow 1982: 156). The same surveillance techniques provide the knowledge necessary for experts to establish classifications of deviancy and criminality, and to locate each individual within this normative grid. Having internalized these categories, other kinds of expert knowledge (supplied by sociologists, criminologists, psychologists, religious ministers, behaviour therapists, medics and anthropologists) help inmates to act upon and reform themselves. The effectiveness of these political technologies relies on a combination of external 'subjection' and internal 'subjectification' (Rabinow 1984). That is, individuals constitute themselves in terms of the norms through which they are governed so that although ' "imposed" on individuals, once internalized, [these norms] influence them to think, feel and act in certain ways' (Lukes 1973: 15).

Such 'techniques of the self', involving the self-regulating capacities of subjects 'normalized' through the powers of expertise, have become key resources for modern forms of government and have established crucial conditions for governing in a liberal democratic way (Miller and Rose 1990). Liberalism renders its political subjects 'governable' by requiring that they become self-activating and free agents (Burchell 1991: 119). Taking this argument further, Nikolas Rose argues that the idea of 'freedom' acts as an instrument of government control by creating new subjects of power and new intermediaries who intervene in the social. Thus to construct a 'free society' and 'free market' entails:

> a variety of interventions by accountants, management consultants, lawyers, industrial relations specialists and marketing experts in order to establish the conditions under which the 'laws of supply and demand' can make themselves real, to implant the ways of calculating and managing what will make economic actors think, reckon and behave as competitive, profit seeking agents, to turn workers into motivated employees who will freely

strive to give of their best in the workplace, and to transform
people into consumers who can choose between products.

(Rose 1992: 2–3)

The ethnographic studies in this volume explore further the way
that new kinds of 'neo-liberal' rationalities of conduct have come to
underpin the conception of how these new 'political subjects'
should be ruled, and the political technologies and moralities associated with such systems.

ANTHROPOLOGY AND THE ART OF GOVERNMENT

Looked at anthropologically, the relationship between policy and
morality sheds interesting light on the art of government. Both
policy and morality attempt to objectify and universalize ideas.
Both are guided by broader sets of cultural ideals (or rather, by an
underlying philosophy and rationality). Both are also located in the
realm of ideas, outside the individual yet manifest in individual
thoughts and actions. However, whereas morality is explicitly
concerned with ethics, policy purports to be more pragmatic, functional and geared to efficiency. The way it achieves an appearance
of being purely instrumental, and nothing to do with morality, politics or ideology, is lampooned in Jonathan Lynn and Antony Jay's
satirical caricature of the archetypical civil servant, Sir Humphrey
Appleby, who constantly tutors his Minister on the finer points of
public administration. 'Government isn't about morality,' he says,
without even a hint of irony, 'it's about stability. Keeping things
going, preventing anarchy, stopping society falling to bits. Still
being here tomorrow . . . Government isn't about good and evil, it's
only about order and chaos' (Lynn and Jay 1983: 116).

Another way policy and government achieve this illusion of
standing above morality is by objectifying and universalizing political decision-making. Objectifying decision-making serves to
collectivize responsibility for decisions adopted, and even to deny, at
times, the roles of human agency and politics in the policy process.
This can be seen, for example, when governments blame their
country's recession and high unemployment on the global economy
rather than on their own domestic economic strategies, or when
they dismiss arguments for greater state intervention with the ritual-
istic and fatalistic response that they cannot 'buck the market' or
interfere with the 'laws of nature'. A classic example of reliance on

impersonal 'laws' resulting in immoral action was when the British government used Thomas Malthus' 'Essay on the Principle of Population' to justify a policy of non-intervention during the 1840s Irish famine. Malthusian population theory, 'the crudest, most barbarous theory that ever existed' according to Friedrich Engels (cited in Flew 1986: 51), nevertheless appealed to British government policy makers and was given further 'scientific' credibility by Charles Darwin. Writing on his 'conversion' to Malthusian theory and its explanation for why disease and famine would naturally weed out 'lesser fitted' individuals from a population, Darwin wrote in his autobiography:

> Then it flashed upon me that this self-acting process would necessarily improve the race, because in every generation the inferior would inevitably be killed off and the superior would remain – that is, the fittest would survive . . . I had at last found the long-sought-for law of nature that solved the problem of the origin of species.
>
> (cited in Flew 1986: 51)

As these examples suggest, policies – and the iron laws they purport to rest upon – often function as a vehicle for distancing policy authors from the intended objects of policy (Wright and Shore 1995: 29). Equally, perhaps, policy serves as a mechanism for disguising the identity of decision makers. Hence, defining a course of action as 'official policy' of the government (or organization) serves to make decision-making more generalized, more impersonal, bureaucratic and anonymous. Like bureaucracy (of which it is a major accessory), policy can serve to cloak subjective, ideological and arguably highly 'irrational' goals in the guise of rational, collective, universalized objectives.

Policies also have a legitimizing function. Not only do they outline the course of action to be taken, they also serve to fix that course within the framework of a wider and more universal set of goals and principles. This works to lend further 'authority' to the decisions taken. It also functions to rule out disagreement – for challenges to policy can be construed by the powerful as a challenge to the principles upon which their policy decision was putatively founded (for example, respect for tradition, the rule of law, Christianity, individual choice or free trade). Thus, for example, tough management decisions about who is to be made redundant or promoted, or why lucrative pay deals are awarded to executives and managers when other company employees are given a pay-freeze, can be justified in the context of the rational policy goals outlined in a company's Mission Statement. There are parallels here with the 'formalized codes' and linguistic rituals described in Bloch's study of political oratory and power in traditional societies (Bloch 1975). Although Bloch's notion has been criticized as too deterministic, it nonetheless adds a significant dimension to understanding how such formalized codes work as instruments of power. They shift the discourse on to a sacred plane where users are obliged to draw upon limited, and highly ritualized, sets of metaphors, references and images. The effect is to buttress the authority of rulers by rendering opposition virtually impossible – as one cannot successfully argue against the 'proper order of things'.

RETHINKING POLITICAL ANTHROPOLOGY

By formulating a more coherent anthropology of policy, and by rethinking policy as a cultural category and political technology, we aim to give a new impetus to political anthropology. We do this by drawing on a number of strands of anthropology. First, we examine the concept of policy and the language through which it is manipulated politically. The anthropological literature on political language, successfully used by Bloch (1975) and others for analysing oratory and power in 'traditional' (i.e. non-Western) societies, has rarely been developed to explore the rhetorical constructions of policy (with a few notable exceptions such as Lloyd-Jones (1981)). Policy language and discourse, we suggest, provides a key to analysing the architecture of modern power relations. It also helps us question whether the new discourses documented throughout this book, with their characteristic emphases on liberalism, individualism, markets and management, are evidence of a decisive change or 'epistemological break' in the way government is conceptualized and practised. Second, following this, we probe the relationship between governance, policy and subjectivity, analysing the ways in which new subjects of power are constituted by, and through, policies.

Third, we use policy as an analytical concept to take forward a new agenda originally developed for political anthropology in the 1970s, but which has not adequately progressed, often for lack of appropriate conceptual tools. Political anthropologists tried to conceptualize traditional small-scale societies within larger state and international systems. Bailey's work on 'encapsulation' (1970), Barth's transactional theory (1959) and Schwartz and Turner's concept of ever-widening 'fields' of political activity (Schwartz 1968) were attempts to find a more appropriate framework for studying political systems as *systems*, and units within a wider context. Marxist anthropology provided further impetus, first under the influence of Althusser and structural Marxism, with its arcane preoccupation with the levels and numbers of modes and forces of production, and later inspired by Gramsci's ideas about power and hegemony, as well as Wallerstein's theory of the 'modern world system' and its impact on peripheries (1974). One central problem for anthropology was how to move away from a conceptualization of the local and the national, or village and state, as two separate polities with 'relations' mediating between them. This dualism, bequeathed from classical sociological thinking, was reinforced in numerous classificatory schemas. These all attempted to explain how modern mass industrial society 'evolved' by contrasting it with its ideal-typical opposite: small, rural, face-to-face community life, variously described as *Gemeinschaft* (Tönnies 1951) 'folk society' (Redfield 1955), where relations are more feudal (Marx and Engels 1968), 'particularistic' (Parsons 1951) and 'patron-client' like (Weber 1966) and where 'multiplex' relationships flourish (Gluckman 1955). For anthropology, the difficulties of combining micro and macro levels within a single field of analysis are as much methodological as theoretical. Some notable studies made headway by locating local sites of mining and other industries within international capitalist systems (Nash 1979; Taussig 1980; Mintz 1985). More recently, the focus has been on 'resistance', especially examining the weapons of the weak (Scott 1985) and the small acts of defiance in the practices of everyday life (de Certeau 1984). However, traces of this macro/micro dualism persist. As Abu-Lughod points out, scholars' convergence on resistance not only romanticizes the creativity of the human spirit in refusing to be dominated by large systems of power, it also treats such power as exterior to the local polity which is seen as the source of residual freedoms (1990: 52). Her argument, which this book endorses, is that anthropologists are in a unique position to understand the workings of multiple, intersecting and conflicting power structures which are local but tied to non-local systems (1990: 42). In other words, a focus on policy provides a new avenue for studying the localization of global processes in the contemporary world. To borrow from Caplan's observation on the significance of 'disputes', the study of policy 'enables us not only to see social relations in action, but also to understand cultural systems' (Caplan 1995: 1).

RECONCEPTUALIZING 'THE FIELD': METHODOLOGICAL IMPLICATIONS FOR ANTHROPOLOGY AND POLICY STUDIES

If policies are typically used as tools of government, they are equally tools for *studying* systems of governance. Thus, the immediate answer to the question 'Why an anthropology of policy?' is that policy provides a powerful conceptual tool for analysing the processes and agencies of government described above. It also offers the potential for a radical reconceptualization of 'the field'; not as a discrete local community or bounded geographical area, but as a social and political space articulated through relations of power and systems of governance. In one sense, an anthropological approach to policy can be absolutely traditional. That is, it is standard anthropological practice to focus on a concept that appears, to the people concerned, to be axiomatic and unproblematic, and to explore its different meanings and how it works as an organizing principle of society. However, by focusing on policy, the field of study changes. It is no longer a question of studying a local community or 'a people'; rather, the anthropologist is seeking a method for analysing connections between levels and forms of social process and action, and exploring how those processes work in different sites – local, national and global. This is not confined to 'studying up' in Nader's (1972) sense of focusing on corporations, elites and centres of power as an antidote to the traditional emphasis on 'studying down'; it is what Reinhold (1994: 477–9) calls 'studying through': tracing ways in which power creates webs and relations between actors, institutions and discourses across time and space.

The sheer complexity of the various meanings and sites of policy suggests they cannot be studied by participant observation in one face-to-face locality. The key is to grasp the interactions (and disjunctions) between different sites or levels in policy processes. Thus, 'studying through' entails multi-site ethnographies which trace policy connections between different organizational and everyday worlds, even where actors in different sites do not know each other or share a moral universe. However, unlike the postmodernist emphases on the 'poetics' and 'polyphony' of 'multi-locale ethnographic texts' (Marcus and Fischer 1986: 94) – which offer only a spurious equality to disenfranchised voices (J. Marcus 1990) – this approach treats 'policy communities' as not just rhetorical, but contested political spaces. From the prism of different perspectives on any particular policy issue, the questions addressed are 'Whose voices prevail?' and 'How are their discourses made authoritative?' (Wright 1995: 79).

Treating policy as a new anthropological field means not only working in various sites, but also with new kinds of materials. Among the most important are policy documents. There is a long anthropological tradition of treating historical materials as a valuable source of ethnographic data. The same approach can be taken in analysing policy documents as 'cultural texts'. They can be treated as classificatory devices, as narratives that serve to justify or condemn the present, or as rhetorical devices and discursive formations that function to empower some and silence others. This is clearly shown, for example, in Seidel's analyses of racist discourses in Europe and HIV/AIDS discourses in Africa (Seidel 1987; 1993; and this volume).

We have discussed how a policy focus can help reconceptualize the 'field' of anthropology, but this approach can also contribute to current developments within policy studies. Critics within policy studies argue that their discipline is still largely dominated by a rational systems model which, according to Gordon, Lewis and Young, has a 'status as a normative model and as a "dignified" myth which is often shared by the policy-makers themselves' (1993: 8). According to this model, policy is represented as a neat linear process of 'problem identification', 'formulation of solutions', 'implementation' and 'evaluation'. Rather than employing this linear model as an analytical device, many practitioners and policy academics have tended to treat it as a prescriptive framework so that a normative tone about how policy *should* be made, implemented and assessed creeps into the analyses. Various models of policy-making have tried to manage a complicated interplay of factors by making them appear to follow a logical sequence of linear steps. For example, some models focus on decision-making as 'bounded, purposive calculated, and sequential events which the actors perceive to have significant consequences' (Weiss 1986: 221). This has been criticized as a 'highly stylized rendition of reality' (Weiss 1986: 223) because it is rare to be able to identify a clear-cut group of decision makers, or an event which can be pinpointed as the moment when the decision was made. Other models are 'incremental'. They treat policy as arising from a continuous bustle of activity in which people do not perceive themselves as making policy but 'over time, the congeries of small acts can set the direction, and the limits, of government policy. Only in retrospect do people become aware that policy was made' (Weiss 1986: 222). Weiss tries to encompass all possibilities in all situations by breaking the incremental policy-making process down into a classification of eight types of behaviour: reliance on custom, improvization, mutual adjustment, accretion, negotiation, move and counter move, implementing pet remedies prior to identification of a problem, and indirection.

Some policy studies analysts share the dissatisfaction of anthropologists that classifying particular actions as one or other of these strategies does not explain what is happening in these 'congeries of small acts'. Instead of simplifying policy processes in terms of systematic and tidy ideal-types, they are looking to anthropology to explore the characteristic complexity and messiness of these processes (Czarniawska-Joerges 1992). However, an even more promising approach is adopted in Ball's study of education policy in modern Britain (1990a). Ball deconstructs the discourses and rhetoric of policy to expose the way that a new rationality and ideology – and with them, a new form of managerial power – have been systematically introduced into the education system. He analyses the complexity, discontinuities and contradictions to reveal how '[p]olitical, ideologically-loaded decisions are choked by bureaucratic-administrative systems and [how] attempts are made to displace issues of moral and cultural identity with the imperatives of administrative efficiency' (Ball 1990b: 154). By looking at policy as a field we can ask, echoing Ball, 'Efficiency for whom?' and 'What new subjects and relations of power do such policies create?'

Our aim in reconceptualizing the field and analysing the links between policy, subjectivity and governance is to develop what Richard Fox (1991) calls an 'anthropology of the present': one that can rise to the challenge of diagnosing and understanding the increasingly complex processes and institutions that shape contemporary societies. However, whereas Fox presents this project largely in terms of recapturing anthropology's waning authority, and reappropriating those concepts 'imperialized [*sic*] by other disciplines or misconstructed in the world' (Fox 1991: 13), we propose a different agenda.

The task for an anthropology of the present, we argue, is to unsettle and dislodge the certainties and orthodoxies that govern the present. This is not simply a question of 'exoticizing the familiar'. Rather, it involves detaching and repositioning oneself sufficiently far enough from the norms and categories of thought that give security and meaning to the moral universe of one's society in order to interrogate the supposed natural or axiomatic 'order of things'. Standing outside one's own conceptual schemas is always difficult. As has often been pointed out in anthropological studies of language, native speakers are usually quite unconscious of the metaphors and rules that make up what D'Andrade (1984) has called their 'cultural meaning systems' or the normative cognitive structures that shape their reality.

The problem is how to make these opaque structures visible, or to use Burchell's metaphor (1993: 277), how to discern the contours of the 'goldfish bowl' we inhabit. That is, how to become aware of the historical contingency and inventedness of our taken-for-granted present. Burchell proposes a solution based on Foucauldian methods of analysis. This entails first examining the 'historically conditioned emergence of new fields of experience' and new ways of objectifying ourselves as subjects in relation to new practices of government (1993: 277). Second, the 'historian of the present' then *re-problematizes*, that is to say, engages in an activity which dismantles the coordinates of his or her starting point and indicates the possibility of a different experience, of a change in his or her way of being a subject or in his or her relation to self – and so also, of a change of others' selves' (1993: 277). This endeavour is seen as an experiment with no pre-set methodology, and a risky experience which may transform one's consciousness and sense of self. Burchell calls this an 'historico-transcendental criticism of actuality' or an 'undoing' of 'constituted standpoints' from a *'non-identitarian'* posture (1993: 277). Stripped of its jargon, this approach has much in common with the 'anthropology of the present' suggested above, both being concerned with diagnosing the rationalities and mentalities that structure our contemporary world. In anthropology, this kind of distanciation and methodological flexibility has always been an integral yet problematic aspect of studying *other* cultures. Reconceptualizing the 'field' of anthropological enquiry enables us to use this approach in an anthropology of the present and to see how our discipline itself is positioned within, and contributing to, rationalities of governance (Donnan and McFarlane 1989: 5–6;

Wright 1995: 87–8). The chapters in this book depart from, and extend, Foucault's analysis by exploring these processes from ethnographic and cross-cultural perspectives.

POLICY AS LANGUAGE: DISCOURSE AND POWER

Part I examines the language and discourses of policy. Pioneering anthropological work on political language in the 1970s 'discovered' that while anthropologists had conducted their work *through* language, they had seldom made studies *of* language. This work, summarized by Grillo (1989) and Parkin (1984), focused on the rhetorical devices and tropes that politicians used to persuade and control audiences. These are important for the study of policy, but there are further essential dimensions, especially the analysis of *written* policy documents. Apthorpe is among the few anthropologists who have examined how such devices are deployed in development policy documents.

The introduction of the concept of 'discourse' took this debate in new directions. Although anthropologists have privileged the oral, this analytical concept can equally be applied to written material. Discourse is notoriously difficult to define. One agreed starting point is that discourse embraces all aspects of linguistic organization at, or above, the phrase level (Grillo 1989: 17–18). Seidel (this volume) says that discourses are ways of thinking which may overlap and reinforce each other and close off other possible ways of thinking. We define discourses as configurations of ideas which provide the threads from which ideologies are woven. This definition highlights the fact that language is socially constituted and not an autonomous domain, and that our anthropological interest in discourse concerns the 'politics of discursive practice' (Grillo 1989: 17). A key concern is who has the 'power to define': dominant discourses work by setting up the terms of reference and by disallowing or marginalizing alternatives. Policies enable this to happen by setting a political agenda and giving institutional authority to one or a number of overlapping discourses. In the process of a new discourse being formulated, certain 'keywords' undergo shifts in use and meaning. Raymond Williams (1976: 12–13) noted that after the Second World War 'culture' was being used in new settings with new tones, rhythms and meanings as part of the struggle towards new ways of seeing culture and society. Tracking the historical semantics of 'culture' revealed that changes in the meaning of a keyword invariably entailed changes in its 'habitual grouping' with associated terms. For example, in the eighteenth century 'culture' shifted from associations with agriculture ('cultivation') to become part of a cluster including 'art', 'civilization', 'development', 'science' and 'community' (Williams 1976: 87–93). Interestingly, the major semantic shifts that Williams records coincide with the period that Foucault identified with the birth of modern power. We suggest that these semantic shifts provide 'fingerprints' for tracing more profound transformations in rationalities of governance.

The important point, however, is that keywords accumulate meanings historically and that whereas one meaning may dominate at any particular moment, previous meanings, although eclipsed, can always be resurrected. This is true of the term 'policy'. From the Greek *polis* ('city') and its *polites* ('citizens'), to the Latin *politia* came two associated meanings: 'polity' (meaning civil organization, form of government and constitution of the state), and 'policy' (the art, method or tactics of government and regulating internal order (Partridge 1958: 509)). This last constellation of meanings split. With the formation of Robert Peel's 'new police' in 1829, administration of internal order became a domain of 'policing', notionally separate from policy (although as Hyatt, this volume, shows, neo-liberal government has re-introduced this association between policy and policing). The meaning of policy as 'art of government' has also changed. Initially a pejorative term associated with 'stratagems', 'trickery', 'cunning', 'deceit', 'hypocrisy', policy has now been 'made respectable' (Pick 1988: 97) in its contemporary guise as 'a course of action adopted and pursued by a government, party, ruler or individual' (Oxford English Dictionary 1961). A host of other, subaltern, meanings also evolved over the centuries and are still occasionally utilized. For example, 'the improvement of an estate' or the 'polishing or refining of manners' (see Martin, this volume).

Some keywords never have a permanent, fixed or definite meaning: they are always, in Gallie's terms (1956), 'essentially contested concepts'. One such is 'individual', which became a keyword during the introduction of neo-liberal rationalities of government in Britain. 'Individual' was used to convey an image of how people should relate to each other, to government, and to themselves. In the mid-1980s the Conservative Party struggled over the meaning of 'individual', particularly in contrast to 'active citizen' and in battles with the Labour Party, which attempted to form an alternative image of social relations and governance through the word 'community' (Andrews 1991: 12). When such keywords succeed, not only in competitions within the 'political field' (Bourdieu 1991), but also in attracting mass popular support, we term them 'mobilizing metaphors' (Wright 1993). Mobilizing metaphors become the centre of a cluster of keywords whose meaning extend and shift while previous associations with other words are dropped. Their mobilizing effect lies in their capacity to connect with, and appropriate, the positive meanings and legitimacy derived from other key symbols of government such as 'nation', 'country', 'democracy', 'public interest and the rule of law'.

Thus 'individual' became part of a cluster including 'freedom', 'market', 'enterprise' and 'family' and previous associations with 'society', 'public' and 'collective' were diminished. During this period, Reinhold studied how a struggle to promote 'positive' images of gay and lesbian people in Harringay, London, was taken up nationally as part of the New Right's attempt to give 'family' a narrow definition and to marginalize and demonize alternatives. This ethnography of a policy process shows how struggles over keywords were occurring in several sites simultaneously (in parliament, the press, and locally) until new meanings and association were brought together in New Right discourse which was given authority through legislation. Thus 'promoting positive images of homosexuality' was recast as 'promoting homosexuality' and subverting the family – the fabric of the nation.

All three chapters in Part I explore policies as sites of contestation. They identify the different resources (linguistic and non-discursive) political actors bring to bear on policy processes to make their discourse prevail. However, although some discourses are deeply embedded in institutional policy and practice, these chapters reveal how they are constantly contested and sometimes fractured.

Apthorpe is concerned with the language and writing style of policy documents and policy research. He describes policy as a form of wording and willing with language intended more to please and persuade than inform and describe. A policy document sets out an exemplary position in a style chosen to attract; it establishes goals in language which uplift and inspire allegiance; or it sets out 'clearly' what inescapably ought to be done and 'stands to reason', and cannot be negotiated or bargained over. He argues that part of a policy's purchase on events comes from its 'style' or, in Foucault's term, 'gaze' – a focus which is selected and pursued. The success of a policy, he claims, depends on its style not being noticed. That policy documents are scrutinized for the content of their words, rather than their writing style, is to neglect an important aspect of how policy creates affect and effect. Similarly, policy researchers who focus only on the content of their reports to policy makers, and do not examine their style may lose an opportunity for their policy writing to persuade readers and influence policy decisions.

To illustrate this argument, Apthorpe draws on his experience in the 1970s as one of a global team of researchers evaluating the impact of high yielding hybrid grain varieties introduced in the Green Revolution for the United Nations Research Institute for Social Development (UNRISD). A parallel set of studies was conducted by the International Rice Research Institute (IRRI). The two research teams disagreed with each other fiercely, and the UNRISD research had a lesser impact on the policy makers. Apthorpe initially thought the disagreement was over research methods. UNRISD researchers took a 'radical realist' approach – a critical, bottom-up, small-scale and empirical perspective. They accused IRRI researchers of substituting ideal types and binary oppositions (rural/urban, traditional/modern) for 'actual lived reality'. While UNRISD concluded that the new technology increased small farmers' dependency, IRRI celebrated the new technology and modernization. Each denied the other's objectivity and each claimed the other adopted a politically inspired perspective.

Apthorpe now realizes that the dispute concerned more than methodology. The two approaches have very different *styles* of writing. The dominant language of development is 'scientistic rationalism' to which the law-like generalizations of IRRI's 'ideal ruralism' approach appealed. Imbued with their own conceit, the radical realists could not see their style as others saw it: a genre as selective in its perspective and in what it excluded, described, and prescribed as its opponent's.

In one sense, the language of policy-making seems to endorse realism by presenting 'problems' as if they could be solved by filling knowledge gaps with new, objective data. But these gaps are not voids. They are crowded spaces already filled with moral values and preconceptions. They require prescriptive language which says what is *needed*, rather than descriptive accounts 'telling it as it *is*'.

Whereas Apthorpe focuses on the persuasive power of language in policy-making and policy research, Seidel and Vidal focus on discourse. Their definition of discourse highlights its essentially political role in policy-making: discourse is 'a particular way of thinking and arguing which involves the political activity of naming and classifying, and which excludes other ways of thinking'. They examine how two discourses ('medico-moral' and 'culturalist') about HIV and AIDS in Africa overlap and reinforce each other, but are contested by a third 'gender and development' discourse which sets up very different parameters for thinking and acting. As they illustrate, because dominant policy discourses shape ways of classifying people and defining problems, they have serious material consequences.

While epidemiological models of infection spread and categories of 'risk groups' and 'disease vectors' purport to be scientific and value-free, they are far from neutral. The definition of 'risk group' focuses attention not on mobile men who are called 'migrant workers' but their female counterparts who are labelled 'prostitutes'. It is women who are maintaining fragile household economies through complex arrangements in which sex is one of the things exchanged, who are considered 'vectors' of disease, rather than their partners. This medical discourse overlaps with and reinforces a moral discourse which associates the disease with sexual sinners. Women are blamed for the disease and can become subjects of violent abuse, either from partners or as a 'class', when they are rounded up for testing, targeted for education or hounded in a neighbourhood which wants to be cleansed.

A further 'culturalist' discourse constructs 'Africa' as an undifferentiated whole. This identifies 'risk cultures' in terms of assumed uniform 'cultural traits' such as refusal to use condoms, absence of male circumcision, or the practice of levirate marriage. These are depicted as 'cultural obstacles' to the adoption of preventative measures which had been effective in Western contexts. According to Seidel and Vidal, this discourse draws on colonial representations of 'Africa' as sexually promiscuous and a reservoir of infection, to create a vision of Africa as a breeding ground for AIDS. This culturalist discourse portrays culture as the only explanatory factor, and cultural practices as if they are uniform and immutable. 'Africa' is constructed as if incapable of change and 'doomed'.

These medico-moral and culturalist discourses are occasionally fractured by a gender and development discourse and activism challenging normative assumptions where the male is the measure of all things. The problem is shifted from women on to social relations by focusing on gender, defined as relations of power (including violence) between the sexes. This exposes the inappropriate and damaging effects of policies derived from the dominant discourses. The main policy aims at prevention (not care) and concentrates on HIV testing of pregnant women in antenatal clinics who are instructed to inform their male partners of the test result and persuade them to wear condoms. Seidel and Vidal explain why this strategy has been unsuccessful from positions of gender inequality.

The gender and development discourse reveals that policy makers and practitioners working within the medico-moral and culturalist discourses miss, on the one hand, universals like women's physiology and gender relations. On the other hand, assumptions about 'risk groups' and 'risk cultures' cause them to miss the detail of individuals' actual practices, their constraints, resources, and capacity to innovate and change. Although activists have sometimes challenged policies and practices derived from scientific and moral explanations of disease spread, the medico-moral discourse still predominates in the international organizations which fund and influence AIDS policy.

Hansen's study of a Danish hospital explores connections between discursive and extra-discursive activity in the daily round of an oncology ward. The hospital has written documents which reflect national policy on providing patients with information, achieving good patient–nurse–doctor communication, and nurse–doctor cooperation. In the hospital round, nurses, doctors and some patients appeal to these shared policy goals. In Bourdieu's terms, they interact in a 'field', a site where parties compete for symbolic capital – the policy goals – whose value they share. Since communication, information-giving and cooperation between staff can be achieved momentarily but cannot be acquired once and for all, they continually strive for this symbolic capital.

Hansen's ethnography highlights three discourses: patients' discourse of lived experience of the body–self; nurses' discourse of caring and doctors' medical discourse based on their professional gaze and technology. Patients, nurses and doctors have competing interpretations of the hospital policy's goals and compete in a struggle for power over the definition and treatment of the sick body. Both discursive and extra-discursive activities are involved. Hansen uses Bateson's definition of communication as encompassing verbal and non-verbal acts, silence and passivity. Whereas doctors control the timing of the round and do most talking, the

waiting, passivity and silence of nurses are also ways of communicating. Their extra-discursive activities, pointing to particular places
in the notes, or positioning themselves by the door in the patient's
room all influence decisions about the patient's treatment. What
Hansen illustrates is how a policy document concerning the
patient's 'body-politic' is translated into everyday action in a daily
round which, she concludes, may be understood as performing the
art of government.

POLICY AS CULTURAL AGENT: CONSTRUCTING
NATIONAL IDENTITY

If the language of policy provides anthropologists with a lens for
exploring how political systems work at the level of discourse and
power, and as systems of *meaning*, examination of particular policies can provide unique avenues for analysing wider issues of
governance, including various ways particular governments attempt
to manufacture consent. A basic problem confronted by all political
systems, democratic or totalitarian, is how to consolidate the legitimacy and authority of the party in office. More successful regimes
engineer conditions so that, seemingly, consent of the public comes
'naturally'. That is, by extending hegemony over a population and
'naturalizing' a particular ideology as common sense, it becomes
incontestable, inviolable and beyond political debate. Anthropology,
with its sensitivity to the actors' points of view and the ways these
contradict or clash, combined with its capacity for problematizing
the taken for granted (including its own theories and models), is
particularly suited to analysing how ideologies infiltrate the institutions and practices of everyday life. Reconfiguring basic categories
of political thought to create new kinds of political subjects is one
of the most effective strategies governments can employ to achieve
this hegemonic power. In post-1980s Britain, such categories are
conveyed in epithets and shibboleths such as 'the moral majority',
'citizen's charter', 'consumer sovereignty', 'the property-owning
democracy', 'popular capitalism', 'tax payers' rights', 'stake-
holders' and 'active citizenship'. Whole populations can be
constructed as new kinds of 'citizens' and subjects of power, often
in ways of which they are not fully conscious. It seems increasingly
necessary, and possible, for governments in modern industrial societies to employ ever more sophisticated strategies for profoundly
reshaping the citizen's constructions of the 'self'.

The three chapters in Part II examine the state's attempt to construct and infuse national identity among populations in different ethnographic settings: Canada, Sweden and the European Union. Each case study highlights the crucial yet contradictory role played by intellectuals and elites – particularly government officials – in nation-building. Using a multi-site ethnographic approach, Eva Mackey assesses the way the Canadian federal government, under the Progressive Conservative Party, exploited Canada's 125th anniversary as a vehicle for inculcating a new, populist model of Canadian national identity. While the rest of America, in different ways, marked 1992 as the quincentenary of Columbus's 'discovery' of the New World, Canada's government chose instead to promote a massive celebration of 'Canadianness' by coordinating private-sector sponsorship of small-town festivals which would extol the virtues of being Canadian. As Mackey notes, the 'Canada 125' policy originated against a background of declining government popularity and deepening constitutional crisis involving, *inter alia*, a backlash against multiculturalism, and growing xenophobia and hostility toward the political gains made by ethnic minorities. Yet, to reap maximum political advantage from this mobilization of Canadian patriotism, the government had to disguise the extent of its own involvement in the celebrations: to be effective, these had to be perceived as authentic local initiatives by 'the people'. If, as Foucault argues, the effectiveness of power lies in its ability to mask itself and 'hide its own mechanisms' (1978: 86), then the Canadian government pursued this maxim a step further. It not only disguised its intervention behind local festivities, but tried to pretend that 'Canada 125' did not have the status of a policy. The tactic involved making civil society, constructed as 'the public' and 'ordinary Canadians', appear to be the dynamic, autonomous agent and architect of supposedly unprompted or spontaneous cultural initiatives.

However, closer inspection reveals that this government-led conception of 'the people' was highly selective, partisan and sanitized. Canada is characterized by a long history of state intervention in culture and of state attempts to forge a national identity based on the idea of Canada as a tolerant, multicultural society. Under the Progressive Conservative Party, this idea shifted as the government tried to champion the cause of 'the people' *against* the Canadian state. This otherwise familiar conservative attack on 'big government' was novel in the way the government invited Canadian multinational corporations to assist in promoting its nationalist campaign at local levels. The result was that the hierarchy of Canadianness, which under multiculturalism had been understated, came to the fore in local festivals. It appears that 'true' Canadians (or 'Canadian Canadians') are descended from the 'Founding Nations' of Britain and France, and are upright, honest, local, white folk. Mackey's ethnography indicates that the government's radical ideological agenda has effectively appealed to a version of national identity which privileges 'Canadian Canadians', but which constructs them as socially conservative and non-political.

Contradictions inherent in official government policy, and conflicts over the use of symbols of national identity, are also themes analysed by Annika Rabo. She argues that gender equality ('*Jämställdhet*') is a key concept and integral aspect of Swedish national identity. Government rhetoric proclaims that, in terms of sexual equality, Sweden is the most progressive country in the world. Yet, while most Swedes see this principle as an axiomatic component of the Swedish welfare model and 'Swedishness' itself, in practice there is little gender equality in the labour market and women remain grossly under-represented in most institutions and organizations of power. The policy of *Jämställdhet* has thus been grafted on to reluctant organizations dominated by men. Taking higher education, Rabo shows how contradictions in the thinking of Sweden's policy experts have become increasingly evident as Sweden replaces its welfare state with a more *laissez-faire* model of society in which the 'market' provides the dominant metaphor for relations between citizens and state. But the ideology that underlies the new rhetoric of deregulation and 'free choice' merges uncomfortably with Sweden's traditionally corporatist and centralized style of government. Swedish political elites regard education as vital for economic development, but they cannot abandon the habits of managerial intervention or the language of social engineering. Thus, at a time of chronic recession, the government is creating hundreds of new jobs to promote *Jämställdhet* in education. However, the explanations given by these policy makers as to why so few teachers are men, or why few women occupy influential university positions, conspicuously fail to take gender issues or politics into consideration. Instead, these 'experts' perpetuate uncritical norms and assumptions about male and female differences and their reflection in supposed male and female competencies, values, knowledge and disciplines.

Shore's study of conflicts over European Union audio-visual

policy continues the analysis of how political elites utilize policy as an instrument for forging large-scale social identities. A study of the development of the European Commission's controversial *Television Without Frontiers* directive provides a focus for examining the many different political interests and agendas at work and rival visions concerning the future of Europe. For European federalists (and many European Union officials), the creation of a 'European audio-visual space' is seen as a means for furthering European integration by strengthening Europe's competitiveness and promoting 'European values' and 'European culture' against Japanese and American cultural imperialism. The idea is that film and television, as communication technologies, might do for the European Union what the novel and the newspaper once achieved for the nation state: namely, lay the foundations for the construction of a 'European' public. The invention of an 'imagined community of Europeans' would lend much needed legitimacy and authority to the political institutions of the European Union.

Examination of European Union reports and policy documents highlights the flaws in these arguments. It suggests that policy-making in Europe is a messy business involving compromises and conflicts between competing 'players' at all levels of the European political arena. It also shows how the boundaries between 'culture' and commerce are constantly being manipulated for political ends and how discourses and metaphors concerning the 'European interest' are frequently mobilized to disguise the national interests and *raison d'état* of member states. Shore concludes that audio-visual policy represents one of several new cultural battlefields over which national governments, interest groups and ideologies compete to shape the European agenda.

Despite talk of a 'post-nationalist' era shaped by transnational processes and the eclipse of nation states, these chapters show that nation states continue to play a decisive role in the governance of their populations. However, that *style* of governance has shifted in important ways. Significantly, they suggest that 'national culture', 'citizenship' and 'personal freedom' are becoming increasingly important and sensitive issues for governments. We are witnessing transformations in the power and nature of old nation states. Their authority is being challenged both from 'above', by international organizations and institutions (including the European Union, the North Atlantic Free Trade Association, the World Trade Organization and the international money markets), and from 'below' by regionalist and separatist movements. Together with the erosion of economic sovereignty brought by increasing globalization, these pressures have resulted in governments giving far greater prominence to the politics of 'culture' and 'identity'. National identity has become politicized in unprecedented ways. As Anthony Smith observes, 'national identity today determines not only the composition of the regime's personnel, but also legitimates and often influences policy goals and administrative practices that regulate the everyday lives of each citizen' (Smith 1991: 144). But these chapters also vividly demonstrate how 'culture' is an increasingly important domain of governance through which modern states try to organize and control civil society. The scope of government and the techniques of governance have expanded notably into the 'cultural sector' precisely at the moment that the nation state's powers to control its own economic and political space have dwindled.

These chapters also reveal the ways competing visions of governance vie for supremacy. Stripped to its essentials, what is being witnessed is a struggle between an old social democratic model – based on a paternalistic, bureaucratic, welfarist approach to government – and a neo-liberal model in which the power of government is mediated and disguised by *laissez-faire* economics and flanked by an ethos of individualism. The former was most closely associated with the Keynesian, 'Labourist' approach of early post-war governments that supported the welfare state and the idea of full employment. The latter originates from the 1980s assault on this model pioneered by politicians and economists of the 'New Right', most notably Margaret Thatcher, Ronald Reagan, and the gurus of monetarist economics, Friedrich Von Hayek and Milton Friedman. The intellectual basis of 'New Right' politics represents an alliance between economic liberal and conservative theory. Its philosophy can be briefly stated: in economic affairs, the state should promote private economic enterprise and encourage markets – introducing them even where no markets exist. In cultural and moral affairs government should sustain 'traditional' values in education and family life (King 1987).

While the social democratic model is often depicted in terms of 'big government' and 'proliferating bureaucracy', and neo-liberalism as 'rolling back the frontiers of the state', in practice neo-liberal reforms do not mean less government. Rather, the result has been an increase in more subtle methods of intervention and technologies of governance based on ideas of 'freedom', 'enterprise', 'management' and the market – all of which function to make the regulatory power of the state more diffuse and less visible. Neo-liberalism has achieved a new system of governance in which power and account-ability have become, in Foucault's words, simultaneously more 'individualizing and totalizing', impinging much more directly on the individual as a conscious, self-activating agent. As Rose (1992: 7) states, an 'ethic of private improvement and responsibility' has been articulated into a public ethic of social order by 'locking each "free" individual' into a 'play of normative gazes' and 'throwing a web of visibilities, of public codes and private embarrassments over personal government'.

POLICY AS POLITICAL TECHNOLOGY:
GOVERNMENTALITY AND SUBJECTIVITY

Part III explores further the idea of policy as a vehicle for intro-ducing neo-liberal or post-social rationalities of governance. The chapters deal with policy, not so much as political discourse or as an instrument for forging large-scale collective social identities, but rather as a form of power which works upon the individual's sense of *self*. These authors are united by a common concern to analyse the processes by which new norms of conduct – often actively engi-neered and promoted by government and organizations – come to be adopted and internalized by individuals. The focus here is on how 'techniques of the self' work to produce new subjects of power.

The ways in which individuals conspire in their own subjectifica-tion by uncritically embracing the values of their political masters have long been a topic of interest to critical sociologists, from Marx and Engels' (1964) writing on ideology and consciousness, to Gramsci's 'Modern Prince' and 'hegemony in civil society' (1971) and Althusser's 'ideological state apparatus' (1971). From a non-Marxist perspective, Durkheim also analysed this issue:

> The coercive power that we attribute to the social fact represents so small a part of its totality that it can equally well display the opposite characteristic. For, while institutions bear down upon us, we nevertheless cling to them; they place constraints upon us, and yet we find satisfaction in the way they function, in that very constraint.
>
> (Durkheim 1982: 47, n.4).

Anticipating Foucault by seventy years, Durkheim highlighted that while external norms may indeed constrain us, they are nonetheless just as likely to be experienced as constitutive and liberating to the individual as they may be coercive.

However, it is Foucault's work on madness, civilization, discipline and deviancy that provides the most sophisticated conceptual armoury for analysing the relationship between power, normalization and subjectivity. Foucault's analysis of the rationality of government (or what he calls 'governmentality') provides a useful starting point for understanding how modern systems of power work (Foucault 1991). Briefly, he argues that there was a major shift in the rationality of government during the middle of the eighteenth century – that is, in the conceptualization of the space to be governed and the nature of government itself. Whereas in the pre-modern era government had mainly been confined to maintaining sovereignty over a given territory, by the 1840s the 'population' had replaced the principality as the main object of government. The birth of the modern era for Foucault is marked by the onset of a new regime of power in which the 'problem of population' (its health, wealth, fertility, education, moral conduct) and control over the human body become central foci of state discipline and surveillance. The rationality of modern liberal government became the art of applying principles of economy to the management of populations. It is above all a normative rationality: 'self-contained and nontheoretical, geared to efficiency and productivity' (Rabinow 1984: 20). The invention of statistics and the development of economics as a distinctive level of reality were key instruments that made this transformation possible. From a model of good government, the family comes to be considered as an instrument of government (Foucault 1991: 99). As Foucault (ibid.: 92) states, modern government became a question of 'how to introduce economy – that is to say, the correct manner of managing individuals, goods and wealth within the family . . . into the management of the state'.

Through the period of the development of modern power, the rationality of government has shifted a number of times. Since the mid-twentieth century in Western Europe and North America there have been two competing conceptualizations of the space to be governed and the appropriate modes of governing. These have been given various labels but, as noted above, the ones adopted here are 'social democratic' and 'neo-liberal'. The shift in each direction can be discerned most clearly in the political technology which came to prominence during this time – policy. In the former, government was not only to be of society, but through society (Hyatt, this volume). In Britain, this approach to governance through the social was codified in the Beveridge Report (Rose 1992: 13). Social insurance schemes aimed to encourage individuals to see themselves as part of a national society – to view themselves across the span of their own life, connected to the lives of contemporaries and linked across generations. Security was simultaneously for each and for all, individualized and totalized. But the operation of policies was not always successful in encouraging individuals to see their personal identity and interests in terms of the collective. As Hyatt argues the social was a domain to be purposefully planned and regulated for the public good. Environments were engineered to produce a certain kind of person. In British housing estates, the layout and design of houses, and the detailed regulation and policing of behaviour, were attempts to reconfigure the poor from the top down. Policies for large-scale redesign of the urban environment and improvement of living standards were drawn up by professionals who previously had been at arm's length from government but were now brought into the bureaucracy. However, some supposed beneficiaries of these reforms experienced them as oppression. Where they felt manipulated, the link was lost between ideology and consciousness, or professional knowledge and private, self-interested improvement. And when people failed to identify with the policies of their rulers, the normative power of modern government lost its ideological grip.

This is clearly exemplified in Halvard Vike's chapter. In the Norwegian context of well-established social democratic government, a policy for totally reorganizing care for the elderly was introduced. This heralded a major shift in governance in which expert knowledge was prioritized over political participation. Vike views the Elderly Care Plan as a symbol. Administrators represented the elderly in figures and charts made up of units (clients, beds, units of service) and flows (of resources and spending). Essential stereotypes of 'sickness' and 'poverty' were attributed to the elderly. Through a decontextualized logic of means and ends, elderly care was to be radically reorganized to meet needs better and solve a budget crisis. The plan exemplified Foucault's definition of a political technology which recast a political problem in the neutral language of a science.

The new form of governance represented by this policy met with resistance. Administrators held information meetings and presented their plan as 'expert knowledge', positioning themselves as producers performing to lay consumers. The protesters rejected the concept of 'expert competence' based on converting relationships and values into figures and charts, objectifying them within a rationalizing and controlling gaze. They refused to accept that without expert knowledge they lacked authorized language. They argued in meetings, converted professional language into everyday terms, changed figures and flows back into relationships and told stories about their own lives. The protesters rejected the administrators' rational decision-making – which made no connection with their lives – by refusing to produce alternative financial plans for elderly care. They claimed such a task was 'administration' and should not dominate the political process. Lacking an alternative plan, the policy to reorganize elderly care was passed by the Municipal Assembly. However, the protesters had made their point that this technology introduced a new rationality of government which they experienced as oppression. Their link to a pre-existing moral and political order through which they had gained their identity and contributed to governance had been broken.

Hyatt's analysis of Conservative government housing policies in Britain represents a shift in the opposite direction towards governance as 'technologies of the self'. The neo-liberal government not only rejected 'governing through society', but claimed that society itself was a product of welfare benefits, social work and other government interventions (Burchell 1993: 274). The aim was to dismantle this edifice. 'Too many people', Mrs Thatcher asserted, 'are casting their problem on society. And, you know, there is no such thing as society. There are individual men and women, and there are families. And no government can do anything except through people, and people must look to themselves first' (*Women's Own* 1987: 10). Market metaphors helped reconceptualize the space to be governed, even turning government itself into a form of enterprise organized through pseudo-markets. Schools, hospitals, general practitioners, housing estates, even railways were remodelled as 'free', independently managed, competitive, quasi-enterprises (but within state-funded systems subject to complex regulation (Burchell 1993: 274)). Individuals were offered similar responsibility to take over and manage issues previously the province of government, providing that subsequent audits found they had used their freedom properly. Hyatt's analysis of housing policies from the perspective of a local authority housing estate in Bradford elaborates this point. These 'council estates', once icons of 'governing through the social', were run down by the 1980s and a third of the houses in the Bradford estate needed rebuilding. Lacking alternatives, residents responded to government policies to take over the ownership and management of their own estate. These policies aimed to improve the quality of life in derelict estates by empowering tenants to become active citizens, to exercise choice in their own interests, and to experience freedom through self-management.

Three changes in tenants' access to and ownership of expert knowledge were central to these attempts to govern through freedom. First, indigenous knowledge, which experts had disregarded, was revalued. Second, local authority information on maintenance costs, repairs and lettings was made available to tenants, now deemed partners in housing management for the first time. Third, new state-funded experts in self-management trained tenants in the profession of housing management and the skills of empowerment. These transfers of knowledge were considered essential for forging the hero of New Right ideology (in Hyatt's phrase) – the self-reliant, self-governing, self-managing tenant.

Women on this Bradford estate dealt successfully with the authorities and achieved the housing redevelopment in the way they wanted. However, the changes in their lives that this entailed were met with ambivalence. The women acquired a new sense of authority in their dealings with experts, but at the expense of turning rooms in their houses into offices, operating without a basic administrative infrastructure, and devoting hundreds of hours of voluntary labour to campaigning and local organizing. The stumbling block was not just burn-out among people already over-burdened with poverty. They decided not to become self-managing tenants when they realized that being practitioners of policy also involved policing. They refused to collect each other's rents and monitor their neighbours' behaviour. If tenants did not incorporate attainment of norms and continuous improvement into their sense of self, no government apparatus existed to make them into responsible citizens. As Rose argues, governing through freedom was only possible because the welfare state's disciplinary technologies had instilled habits of private improvement, rationality and civilized sensibility (Rose 1992: 6). In the absence of technologies of normalization, self-management for the tenants meant not government through the free choices of self-fulfilling individuals but lawlessness and chaos.

If rationalities of governance embody images of how subjects relate, first, to each other, second, to government, and third, to themselves, Martin's chapter explores this last dimension. The private-sector management policies that she studied in the United States have been the well-spring of many neo-liberal concepts and technologies of governance. Whereas Bradford tenants sought discipline and normalization from external agencies to complement their own activities, US 'flexible workers' relied not on normative grids but on internally generated motivation. Martin associates docile bodies held in minutely ordered time and space with the total institutions and mass production systems of the early twentieth century. In the 1990s, by contrast, companies which were continuously adapting production to consumer demand aimed to create self-managed workers who could operate in frequently changing teams, repeatedly re-skilling themselves in ever-shifting environments. Unstable environments require a new kind of subject: not passive or docile, but active, flexible workers who freely and continuously draw on their capacities and develop their potential to make themselves anew.

There are no longer predictable career patterns or standard categories, and no point of reference stays still long enough for there to be any norms. What was once classified as abnormal, hyperactive behaviour – such as Attention Deficit Disorder (ADD) – is being redefined as exhibiting the ideal qualities of the self-managed worker: a distorted sense of time and space, an exaggerated sense of urgency when engaged with a task, always changing, bored by routines, easily frustrated, risk-taking, scanning the environment, dealing with the outside in creative and innovative ways – in a word, (self-)driven.

Martin suggests that company policy, articulated through its 'corporate culture', invests itself 'inside' the worker, as an inner manager of the self. The boundary between organization and self, between management and self-management, has collapsed – but in a way that the worker experiences as gaining agency. When Foucault was unmasking the operation of modern power in the 1970s, 'flexible accumulation' and the reorganization of production were barely starting. What Martin reveals is that this neo-liberal rationality is associated with the emergence of a new kind of subject regulated by a new form of power.

EPILOGUE

The concluding chapter by Donnan and McFarlane assesses the pitfalls and potential of anthropology's contribution to policy research by reviewing recent examples of policy-oriented anthropological research in Northern Ireland. Despite the apparent success of anthropologists in obtaining research work and grants in the policy field, they argue that the written product seldom achieves standards the discipline expects elsewhere. They state that 'anthropologists have adapted pragmatically by compromising theoretical concepts, epistemological principles and methodological rigours that they would otherwise take for granted in more academic arenas'. This is evidenced particularly in the ways non-anthropological definitions of 'culture' – as a relatively discrete collection of essential beliefs, attitudes, assumptions, values and behavioural orientations – are uncritically reproduced in policy literature. As a result, anthropologists are accomplices in reproducing a vision of the world which, elsewhere, they would normally criticize. The dangers of culture being relegated to a residual category – and anthropology to a mere methodology – are all too apparent.

Exploring this problem further, Donnan and McFarlane argue that policy research necessarily involves simplifying the world to render it comprehensible in fairly positivistic ways. Policy makers are not unaware of this, but the nature of their work requires them to produce summary accounts and generalizations. Their conclusion, that anthropologists may have to do likewise if they want their reports to be read, vividly illustrates the point that involvement in the policy field obliges anthropologists to think about the way their discipline is positioned within the policy process. However, their study suggests that such involvement may itself be changing anthropology by subtly influencing – and perhaps subverting – its academic agenda and the production of anthropological knowledge.

Finally, our contributors show how innovative approaches in political anthropology can illuminate the operationalization of policy in various new domains. In so doing, they advance the frontiers of anthropological enquiry to reveal how policies work as instruments of governance, as ideological vehicles, and as agents for constructing subjectivities and organizing people within systems of power and authority.

NOTE

1 Apthorpe is one exception who has kept his 'anthropological eyes' focused on the way the discourses and practices of the development projects in which he has been involved help to reproduce relations of power in the modern world system. As Kuper observes, however,

Apthorpe, like most applied anthropologists, has had difficulty in maintaining an anthropological audience (Kuper 1983: 190–1).

REFERENCES

Abu-Lughod, Lila (1990) 'The romance of resistance: tracing the transformations of power through Bedouin women', *American Ethnologist*, 17 (1): 41–55.

Althusser, Louis (1971) *Lenin and Philosophy*, London: New Left Books.

Andrews, Geoff (ed.) (1991) *Citizenship*, London: Lawrence and Wishart.

Appadurai, Arjun (1991) 'Global ethnoscapes: notes and queries for a transnational anthropology', in Richard Fox (ed.) *Recapturing Anthropology. Working in the Present*, Santa Fe: School of American Research Press.

Bailey, Frederik G. (ed.) (1970) *Stratagems and Spoils: A Social Anthropology of Politics*, Oxford: Blackwell.

Ball, Stephen J. (1990a) *Politics and Policy Making in Education*, London: Routledge.

—— (1990b) 'Management as moral technology', in S. J. Ball (ed.) *Foucault and Education: Disciplines and Knowledge*, London: Routledge.

Barth, Fredrik (1959) *Political Leadership among the Swat Pathan*, London: Athlone Press.

Bloch, Maurice (ed.) (1975) *Language and Oratory in Traditional Society*, London: Academic Press.

Bourdieu, Pierre (1991) *Language and Symbolic Power*, Cambridge: Polity Press.

Buckley, Anthony (1989) 'We're trying to find our identity: uses of history among Ulster Protestants', in Elizabeth Tonkin, Maryon McDonald and Malcolm Chapman (eds) *History and Ethnicity*, London: Routledge.

Burchell, Graham (1991) 'Peculiar interests: civil society and governing "the system of natural liberty"', in Graham Burchell, Colin Gordon and Peter Miller (eds) *The Foucault Effect*, Hemel Hempstead: Harvester Wheatsheaf.

—— (1993) 'Liberal government and techniques of the self', *Economy and Society*, 22 (3): 267–82.

Cannell, Fanella (1990) 'Concepts of parenthood: the Warnock Report, the Gullick debate and modern myths', *American Ethnologist*, 17: 667–86.

Caplan, Pat (1995) 'Introduction', in P. Caplan (ed.) *Understanding Disputes: The Politics of Argument*, Oxford: Berg.

Chambers, Erve (1985) *Applied Anthropology: A Practical Guide*, Englewood Cliffs NJ: Prentice-Hall.

Czarniawska-Joerges, Barbara (1992) *Exploring Complex Organisations. A Cultural Perspective*, London: Sage.

D'Andrade, Roy (1984) 'Cultural meaning systems', in Richard Schweder and Robert Levine (eds) *Culture Theory: Essays on Mind, Self and Emotion*, Cambridge: Cambridge University Press.

De Certeau, Michel (1984) *The Practice of Everyday Life*, Berkeley: University of California Press.

Donnan, Hastings and McFarlane, Graham (eds) (1989) *Social Anthropology and Public Policy in Northern Ireland*, Aldershot: Avebury.

Dreyfus, Hubert and Rabinow, Paul (1982) *Michael Foucault: Beyond Structuralism and Hermeneutics*, Brighton: Harvester Press.

Durkheim, Emile (1982) *The Rules of Sociological Method*, London: Macmillan.

Edwards, Jeannette, Franklin, Sarah, Hirsch, Eric, Price, Francis and Strathern, Marilyn (1993) *Technologies of Procreation. Kinship in the Age of Assisted Conception*, Manchester: Manchester University Press.

Flew, Antony (1986) 'Introduction to Thomas Malthus', *An Essay on the Principle of Population*, Harmondsworth: Penguin.

Foucault, Michel (1977) *Discipline and Punish*, Harmondsworth: Penguin.

—— (1978) *The History of Sexuality*, Harmondsworth: Penguin.

—— (1991) 'Governmentality', in Graham Burchell, Colin Gordon and Peter Miller (eds) *The Foucault Effect: Studies in Governmentality*, Hemel Hempstead: Harvester Wheatsheaf.

Fox, Richard (1991) 'Introduction: working in the present', in R. Fox (ed.) *Recapturing Anthropology. Working in the Present*, Santa Fe: School of American Research Press.

Gaddis, John Lewis (1972) *The United States and the Origins of the Cold War, 1941–1947*, New York: Columbia University Press.

Gallie, W. B. (1956) 'Essentially contested concepts', *Proceedings of the Aristotelian Society*, 56: 167–98.

Gluckman, Max (1955) *The Judicial Process among the Barotse of Northern Rhodesia*, Manchester: Manchester University Press.

Gordon, Colin (1991) 'Government rationality: an introduction', in Graham Burchell, Colin Gordon and Peter Miller (eds) *The Foucault Effect: Studies in Governmentality*, Hemel Hempstead: Harvester Wheatsheaf.

Gordon, Ian, Lewis, Janet and Young, Ken (1993) 'Perspectives on policy analysis', in Michael Hill (ed.) *The Policy Process*, Hemel Hempstead: Harvester Wheatsheaf.

Gramsci, Antonio (1971) *Selections from the Prison Notebooks*, Quintin Hoare and Geoffrey Nowell Smith (eds), London: Lawrence and Wishart.

Grillo, Ralph (ed.) (1989) *Social Anthropology and the Politics of Language*, London: Routledge.

Heelas, Paul (1991) 'Reforming the self: enterprise and the characters of Thatcherism', in Russel Keat and Nicholas Abercrombie (eds) *Enterprise Culture*, London: Routledge.

King, Desmond (1987) *The New Right: Politics, Markets and Citizenship*, London: Macmillan.

Koestler, Arthur (1967) *The Ghost in the Machine,* London: Hutchinson.

Kuper, Adam (1983) *Anthropology and Anthropologists: The Modern British School*, London: Routledge and Kegan Paul.

Lipsky, Michael (1980) *Street-level Bureaucracy: Dilemmas of the Individual in Public Services*, New York: Russel Sage Foundation.

Lloyd-Jones, David (1981) 'The art of Enoch Powell: the rhetorical structure of a speech on immigration', in Robert Paine (ed.) *Politically Speaking*, Philadelphia: Institute for the Study of Human Issues.

Lukes, Stephen (1973) *Émile Durkheim. His Life and Work*, Harmondsworth: Penguin.

Lynn, Jonathan and Jay, Antony (1983) *Yes Minister. The Diaries of a Cabinet Minister*, London: BBC.

Malinowski, Bronislaw (1926) *Myth in Primitive Psychology*, London: Kegan Paul.

Marcus, George and Fischer, Michael (1986) *Anthropology as Cultural Critique*, Chicago: University of Chicago Press.

Marcus, Julie (1990) 'Introduction: anthropology, culture and postmodernity', *Social Analysis*, 27: 3–16 (Special Issue) *Writing Australian Culture: Text, Society and National Identity*.

Marx, Karl and Engels, Friedrich (1964) *The German Ideology*, London: Lawrence and Wishart.

—— (1968) *The Communist Manifesto*, London: Lawrence and Wishart.

Mauss, Marcel (1954) [1925] *The Gift*, London: Cohen and West.

Miller, Peter and Rose, Nikolas (1990) 'Governing economic life', *Economy and Society*, 19 (1): 1–31.

Mintz, Sidney W. (1985) *Sweetness and Power: The Place of Sugar in Modern History*, Harmondsworth: Penguin.

Nader, Laura (1972) 'Up the anthropologist – perspectives gained from studying up', in Dell Hymes (ed.) *Reinventing Anthropology*, New York: Random House.

Nash, June (1979) *We Eat the Mines and the Mines Eat Us*, New York: Columbia University Press.

Parkin, David (1984) 'Political language', *Annual Review of Anthropology* 13: 345–65.

Parsons, Talcott (1951) *The Social System*, New York: Free Press.

Partridge, Eric (1958) *Origins. A Short Etymological Dictionary of Modern English*, London: Routledge and Kegan Paul.

Pick, John (1988) *The Arts in a State*, Bristol: Bristol Classical Press.

Rabinow, Paul (1984) *The Foucault Reader*, Harmondsworth: Penguin.

Redfield, Robert (1955) *The Little Community*, Chicago: Chicago University Press.

Reinhold, Susan (1994) 'Local Conflict and Ideological Struggle: "Positive Images" and Section 28', University of Sussex: unpublished D.Phil. thesis.

Rivière, Peter (1985) 'Unscrambling parenthood: the Warnock Report', *Anthropology Today*, 1 (4): 2–7.

Rose, Nikolas (1992) 'Towards a critical sociology of freedom', inaugural lecture, Goldsmiths' College, University of London, 5 May.

Schneider, David (1968) *American Kinship: A Cultural Account*, Englewood Cliffs NJ: Prentice Hall.

Schwartz, Marc (ed.) (1968) *Local Level Politics. Social and Cultural Perspectives*, London: University of London Press.

Scott, James (1985) *Weapons of the Weak. Everyday Forms of Peasant Resistance*, Newhaven/London: Yale University Press.

Seidel, Gill (1987) 'The white discursive order. The British New Right's discourse on cultural racisim with particular reference to the Salisbury Review', in Iris M. Zavala, Teun van Dijk, Myriam Diaz-Diocartz (eds) *Approaches to Discourse, Poetics and Psychiatry*, Amsterdam/ Philadelphia: John Benjamins.

—— (1993) 'The competing discourses of HIV/AIDS in Sub-Saharan Africa: discourses of rights and empowerment vs discourses of control and exclusion', *Social Science and Medicine*, 36 (3): 175–94.

Smith, Anthony (1991) *National Identity*, Harmondsworth: Penguin.

Stanley, Christopher (1991) 'Justice enters the marketplace: enterprise culture and the provision of legal services', in Russel Keat and Nicholas Abercrombie (eds) *Enterprise Culture*, London: Routledge.

Strathern, Marilyn (1992a) *Reproducing the Future: Anthropology, Kinship and the New Reproductive Technologies*, Manchester: Manchester University Press.

—— (1992b) *After Nature: English Kinship in the Late Twentieth Century*, Cambridge: Cambridge University Press.

Taussig, M. (1980) *The Devil and Commodity Fetishism in South America*, Chapel Hill: University of North Carolina Press.

Titmuss, Richard (1974) *Social Policy. An Introduction*, London: Allen and Unwin.

Tönnies, Ferdinand (1951) *Community and Society*, New York: Harper and Row.

Truman, Harry (1948) 'Speech to the US Congress', *Keesing's Contemporary Archives*, VI: 8491–4.

Turner, Victor (1967) *The Forest of Symbols: Studies in Ndembu Ritual*, Ithaca: Columbia University Press.

Van Willigen, John and Dewalt, Billie (1985) *Training Manual in Policy Ethnography*, Washington: American Anthropological Association.

Wallerstein, Immanuel (1974) *The Modern World System*, New York: Academic Press.

Weber, Max (1966) [1922] *Economy and Society*, Cambridge MA: Harvard University Press.

Weiss, Carol (1986) 'Research and policy-making: a limited partnership', in F. Heller (ed.) *The Use and Abuse of Social Science*, London: Sage.

White, Aidan (1996) 'Exposing Europe's decision-makers to public scrutiny', *European Voice*, 2 (16): 18–24.

Williams, Raymond (1976) *Keywords*, London: Fontana.

Woman's Own (1987) 'AIDS, education and the year', Douglas Keay's interview with Mrs Thatcher, 31 October.

Wright, Susan (1993) 'Mobilising metaphors: contested images of "individual" and "community" in contemporary British politics', unpublished paper, Sociology and Social Anthropology seminar, Hull University, 20 January.

—— (ed.) (1994) *Anthropology of Organisations*, London: Routledge.

—— (1995) 'Anthropology: still the uncomfortable discipline?', in Akbar Ahmed and Cris Shore (eds) *The Future of Anthropology: Its Relevance in the Modern World*, London: Athlone Press.

Wright, Susan and Shore, Cris (1995) 'Towards an anthropology of policy', *Anthropology in Action*, 2 (2) (Summer): 27–31.

Part I

Policy as language and power

Chapter 2

Writing development policy and policy analysis plain or clear

On language, genre and power

Raymond Apthorpe

> He struck the tips of his fingers together. He had found the right words:
> clear, practical, superior. She would not, with her clumsy vocabulary,
> dare answer him.
>
> (Canetti 1982)

The language and the writing of policy and research on policy function as a type of power.[1] Often the primary aim of policy language is to persuade rather than inform, yet rarely is it subject to critical scrutiny. Anthropology, with its concern with genres, performances and agencies, can contribute crucially to scrutiny of policy and analysis of policy through its language.

The 'power of language' arises from congruencies (and other relations) of social, political and cultural institutions with linguistic mechanisms. Therefore policy in its announced (written or spoken) expression requires both institutionalist and mechanist examination. Its purchase on events comes from somewhere in between the linguistic and extra-linguistic, that is, it draws from wording and willing as vocabulary and grammar, and language as ceremony and office.

It is useful to think of policy writing as a 'genre'. Genre makes a written artefact analysable. It provides 'a counterpart at the textual level of the concept of sociological boundaries thereby defending inquiries from the danger of degenerating into purely [mechanist] technical, linguistic, analyses' (Green 1983: ix). Genre is 'a broadly conceived textuality . . . realized in the dialogic engagement of particular people and particular utterances with one another (rather than in the timeless and placeless notion of Saussureian *langue*)' (Baxter and Fardon 1991: 4, 7). Genre comes from somewhere in between the structural and the functional, the institutional and the mechanical. Its power of agency is owed to this relative indeterminacy of origin and effect.

In anthropology as well as power, in policy analysis as well as in policy, rehearsal of what is and ought to be done and why and how, distracts our attention from genre (Green 1988). This chapter treats the writing of policy and of policy analysis as susceptible to, and deserving of, critical attention. A particular case of a global development policy research is considered: Why, despite its empiricism and geographical scope, did this research not make the difference to development policy it sought? But first a few generalities.

THE WRIT OF LANGUAGE

Language as policy and power is exercised through genres or, as we will also say, 'styles' of expression. Modes, genres or styles in this sense are some of the forms of practices which are properly subject to analysis in part as stylistics. By 'style' here is meant not literary style but something akin to Foucault's 'gaze' according to which a focus is selected and pursued. One example is when the power of some policy statements depends on being plain, and better still, absolutely plain, in gaze and style. In this case, from lack of clarity, a certain sense of purpose and identity can be drawn, and a symbolic force achieved. The power of other statements may depend on being clear, rather than plain, the former as in 'the clear truth', the latter as in 'the plain truth'. Clarity comes from something being taken away (e.g. 'being economical with the truth'), while plainness comes from nothing being added.

A second example is goal language. Where the primary purpose of charters, constitutions and creeds is ideological, the first requirement is that they be in a form and style of goal language which inspires, uplifts, persuades, gains support, defines parameters, gives a badge to wear (Thompson 1985).

As a third example consider, for instance, from everyday life the assuring and reassuring 'See you'. 'See you at this same time next week', the television announcer smiles straight into the lens of the camera which with its back-up paraphernalia transmits her or his image to your home. It is your favourite programme and announcer. You are touched, warmed – and entirely apt to overlook the fact that (through the medium of television) your announcer hasn't actually seen you – or even your image – this week or ever. 'See *you* next week', unpacked, comes down to 'see *me* next week'. In this instance, the message sent is completely contrary to the information given. This is characteristic of intent to persuade not only you or me but *everyone*. A friend or acquaintance saying 'see you' to another on parting without any time element or other qualification, sends a definite message, but the information is completely open-ended and vague. The same technique is used in policy as well as everyday speech.

A fourth example of style in policy writing is a focus on what Williams (1983) called 'keywords' or Baumann (1987) called 'key words'. Such words, of which there are various types, depend on context as well as text, on perspectives as well as objectives, performing as winsome, winning or weasel words. Then power comes as much from the barrel of a phrase or sentence as a gun. Winning (and losing) words have moral ways, and political effect, all of their own.

Where policy may fail as practice, it may succeed as composition and code. But where the socio-semiotic facts of life depend for their grip on not being noticed as artefacts, undoubtedly the reasons for this success will be elusive to pin down. For example, and however paradoxically, the writing and style of policy analysis is usually less seriously examined than the wording and writing of policy. This is why this chapter takes up a case of research and policy analysis by way of illustration.

'Policy' as in 'policy statement' and 'policy studies' involves the presentation of a position that is held to be exemplary in some way, and in a style chosen mainly to attract, please and persuade you (though later it may be applied to you). This is the shine of 'policy' on show, on parade. What is thus announced may be justified both as what 'is known', as well as what 'stands to reason'. It is most unlikely to be said to depend on a weighing of positions and evidence, hard bargaining, drastic exclusions and the like. Rather it must be something simply plain or clear. Bitter evidence may be more refutable as well as exposing of what is judged to be best kept out of the public eye. Typically the perennial speech of policy involves utterance about things which inescapably ought to be done and which, at the same time, we are assured can and will be done once 'the policy' is 'in place'.

Hearing, seeing, saying no evil. A fourth wise monkey would *write* no evil. But little policy writing is the work of a fourth wise monkey. The plainer (as in one genre), or the clearer (as in another), a policy is painted, the more it is driven by evasion and disguise. The more writing sets out to please those who desire to be pleased by it, the more it is constitutive of what it is meant to allay, promise or punish. Unexamined styles of language practice, then, divert policy statements and policy studies from making a difference to policy. Wording policy in its utterances and communiqués is a craft and fine art in itself. Much time and effort will have been spent on wording (unless it came 'naturally', that is by practice and habit). Until the right form of willing and wording is found, we may be waiting, as well as wanting, for policy and policy analysis. In the end, as in the beginning, is the word. Leaving wording – and writing and reading – unexamined leaves a good part of the agenda that was set with the aid of it unexamined also.

RADICAL REALISM AND IDEAL RURALISM

To illustrate the achievement of genre and the power of writing in development policy research, we may consider by way of a particular case the set of 'green revolution' studies carried out by many researchers (including the present writer) in the 1970s. This global research project was managed by Andrew Pearce. He overviewed its findings and recommendations in a final publication *Seeds Of Plenty, Seeds Of Want* (1980; see also, Pearce et al. 1977). All these studies were meant by their authors to stand, as we might put it now, as realist and radical studies of people's livelihoods.

The project of realism is the epitome of plain style – 'to tell it as it is'. By 'radical' we (literally) meant getting to the roots (including 'grassroots') of institutions and technologies. 'Radical' also meant something close to 'critical': few rural development studies at that time were empirical field studies so what the field had to tell, as it were, had therefore not been told. The empirical philosophy is that to be empirical is to be realist, and being realist about policy and policy analysis is to be radical.

The expression 'green revolution' referred to high-yielding grain hybrids. The purpose of our study (known as Global-2 to its UN sponsors and the United Nations Research Institute for Social Research which devised and executed it) was to assess the social and economic results of the hybrids bred for their high yield capacities which to some seemed much less rosy than it was supposed they would be. The organizing concept selected and defined by Andrew Pearce for these studies was 'rural livelihood', a multiplex idea comprising a series of coincident concerns with technologies and institutions, description and prescription, diagnosis and prognosis. The research guidelines he circulated to all the case study researchers referred also to the matter of the state and its powers and tendencies of incorporation. Ultimately, however, what was written up was not the effect of these tendencies for both rural livelihoods and the state but only for the former. Our terms of reference called for descriptive and diagnostic research. The lead assumption was that if you were a peasant or a small farmer, you would be seeking your living mainly from the land, and this would be a meagre living only. All the odds – what Andrew came to call biblically 'the talents effect' – would be against anything better.

It was, then, a premise from the outset that, in the rural areas selected for study, 'something was wrong'. This was not simply research to close an 'ethnographic gap' – research for the sake of research – it was research to evaluate rural development policy. Nevertheless, 'peasant farming' was not envisaged as being in such great difficulty as to have reached or be reaching a terminal stage. It was not supposed that this particular mode of livelihood should be allowed or induced to disappear altogether and replaced by another. Perhaps it was for this reason that the research design did not include scope for comparison of peasant farming with other types of farming. (Precedent may have played a greater part than selective choice, however, as UNRISD's earlier studies of co-operatives – including mine – neglected to include comparison with non-co-operatives.)

At all events, 'peasant farming'[2] stood not only as the actual problem to be investigated, it was also the solution to be found, in the sense that a reformed peasant farming, not something different in kind like collectivization or corporatization, was the scenario to be considered. While, at first sight, therefore 'rural livelihood' may appear to stand as a seemingly innocuous and neutral device for the marshalling of descriptive data, it proves on further inspection to be a coalescence of all sorts of considerations. This is the first issue to note critically.

Is this to go too far with an analytical unpacking of what was announced as something that would serve simply as a rallying point for the making of field observations? Possibly, yet while it did serve usefully in this role, this was not research seeking description of village and farm life for its own sake alone. Therefore, it would be odd if the chosen unit of descriptive account were unrelated to the project's ultimate objective, which was evaluation and prescription.

In 1973, when the project was well under way and reaching tentative conclusions, a meeting in Manila was convened jointly by the

United Nations Research Institute for Social Research (UNRISD)[3] and the International Rice Research Institute (IRRI) in the Philippines (whose parent organization elsewhere had pioneered the type of hybrid botanical research concerned). At that time, both institutes were undertaking rural studies on the social and economic consequences of the new cereal varieties. The purpose of the meeting was scientific, for each institute to take note of the work of the other, to make comparisons and perhaps some mutual adjustments accordingly. But on those few occasions when both sides actually bothered to turn up at a particular session, there was nothing like any such meeting of minds or exchange (except of abuse).

IRRI branded UNRISD's objectives as (hopelessly) 'leftist'. UNRISD sought to maintain that while it was indeed very much in the business of political economy, (hopefully) that was not the same thing as 'leftism' at all. UNRISD called IRRI's approach 'technicist'. IRRI said UNRISD was 'subversive'. Each label was equally vigorously repudiated. Neither side would concede any degree of objectivity, of 'science', to the other. No area of common concern, let alone agreement (including agreement to differ), emerged whatever.

Some years after that non-event, a joint master's thesis in development studies at the Hague's Institute of Social Studies compared and contrasted the two organizations' research approaches and findings. Among its conclusions, the following stand out:

UNRISD's concept of development was more encompassing; it viewed development in terms of welfare, structural and normative aspects. Through these perspectives, UNRISD addressed itself to problems relating to the entire (rural) economy. In effect, [its] postulates on the impact of agricultural technology are similar to some of those of both modernization and dependency. In contrast, the postulates of IRRI are confined to those of modernization alone . . . IRRI states that as a result of increase in real income, farmers have moved up to a higher rung on the agricultural ladder . . . UNRISD on the other hand . . . very much addressed itself to the social imbalances and economic disparities that already exist and are attributable largely to the fact that social policy and reform have not kept pace with the spread of the technology. While IRRI views the commercialization of agriculture positively (as an index of modernization),

UNRISD on the other hand deplored it, because it aggravates the dependency of small peasants. Land distribution is skewed in most developing countries, and small peasants generally live from 'subsistence farming', lacking the necessary ability and resources required for the adoption of the new technology.

(Lorenzco and Maranan 1980)

These generalizations sum up well the differences between the two research institutes in relation to their respective green revolution studies. Where perspectives are considered to be so different, objectives can hardly be similar.

As it may be put now, decades later, in contention were two styles of genre in analysis. These could be labelled respectively as UNRISD's *plain* realist and IRRI's *clear* idealist. What UNRISD defined as the enemy (of its own 'radical realism', as this chapter terms it) was what it saw as an 'ideal ruralism'. This was 'ideal' because, as a syndrome of abstract conceptions, it made for preoccupation not with any actual pattern of rural livelihood but only an ideal type. Radical realism says it is uncomfortable with such abstraction. It complains that ruralism revels too much in it, and turns too much to 'technical' terms (which it brands 'jargon'). This is a good portrait and can to a fair extent be recognized by its sitter. Such deductive and formal abstraction is meant by those who practise it, however, precisely to ensure that they avoid falling into the 'local bias' of which realist case studies are accused.

Radical realism's case against its idealist rival can be summarized as follows. Ideal ruralism relies on only negative characterization even for 'positive' targets. For instance, the rural poor are described as landless, stockless, feckless, or whatever negatively else. Ideal ruralism is ahistorical and deductive in its prescriptions as to policies and its ways of problem identification and formulation; it sharply contrasts 'rural' with 'urban', including for instance, recommending land reform as a policy prescription only for rural and not for urban situations. Social ruralism neglects non-farm (and even off-farm) activities; it strongly distinguishes between private and public enterprises in binary and exclusive favour of (at the time of these studies) the latter.[4]

The following is how radical realism would characterize its own style of speech. (The bracketed quotes are from Linda Nochlin's study of realism in fine arts and literature (1971) – they apply equally in social science.) Radical realism positively values:

meticulous, small scale, and contemporary observation ('truthful, objective and impartial representation of the real world'); a poverty and middle-class focus ('the poor . . . hardly had been granted a fair share of serious artistic attention before the advent of realism – nor had the middle classes who were the dominant forces in society'); perspectives from below ('No one has ever done monuments or houses from below, beneath, up close, as one sees them by going by in the street, said Degas'); implicit, non-programmatic, social engagement ('Realism did not necessarily involve any overt statement of social aims or outright protest against intolerable political conditions. But the mere intention to translate the appearances, the customs, of the time implied a significant involvement in the contemporary social situation and might then comprise a threat to existing values and power structures as menacing as throwing a bomb').

At the time, and this is a further crucial issue, we UNRISD researchers considered our professional research as distinct from our personal political, engagement (just as our rivals, in their turn, considered their own positions to be professional not personal). We saw it as unprogrammatic, not programmatic intellectual engagement. Occupied with political economy though we were, *our* version and justification of this was that it was not politics but realism. But this, as noted already, was not at all how we and our objectives and perspectives were seen by IRRI's researchers. Indeed, they saw them diametrically differently. Their objectives and ours were seen to be substantively opposite, and what one side took in formalist fashion to be objectives were taken by the other not to be objectives but perspectives.

In retrospect, and in the terms of the present discussion on stylistics, it (at last) becomes perfectly understandable to me that not only our detractors' perspectives, but also our own, were open to political criticism of an essentially similar sort. For one thing, as every version of realism may know, the human personality is mutilated by a dichotomous division into public and private (Lukács 1964: 9). Certainly our version was aware of this – indeed we accused our rival of among other things making a mistaken division. What we failed to see was that realism's contrary view was just as much a matter of politics, realist politics, as a disciplinary view of political economy.

Radical realist case studies seldom elicit serious consideration by management, by whom after all they may have been commissioned and for whom they have been carried out and written up. Certainly, the green revolution studies did not. Why? Of course this is a complex question, deserving multiple types of answer (one of which, in its shortest form, is simply that they were radical and were directed to a management that was not). Nevertheless, some of this lack of power over policy is identifiable through stylistic analysis of one's own language, and that of one's rival. The point is that, even where it is possible to draw a hard and fast line between the two (which is not often), style can be as menacingly powerful as substance (so where really is the line between them to be drawn?). Policy management wants guidance that is clear, not plain.

From the outset we at UNRISD saw the contest as being principally with a form of developmentalism which was unacceptable to us. Our style was radical/empiricist. We believed the enemy's to be completely different – technocratic/developmentalist. From the beginning we recognized that any contest of a realist with an idealist, deductive, conceptualization of rural life would be an uneven contest (because then, as now, the latter is dominant as ideology and style in the ruling development discourses).

What in our determination and diligence to be empirical we failed to recognize was that there were hardly fewer problems with regard to our position, than with theirs. That radical realism is as rigorous in its exclusions and as selective in its perspectives, as ideal ruralism is, did not come within our own concept then of what was problematic in research *beyond* research method: namely what was being done through writing and text was itself a constitutive realm through its diacritical marks and turns.

To rehearse just a few observations with the benefit of hindsight and discourse stylistic analysis, one is that radical realism can be so much preoccupied with local substantive details that theory and policy become seemingly inseparable from this focus. Another is the often related eventuality that where policy is believed to have detached itself from small-scale observations made from within and below in local situations, it is likely to be utopian. One damaging implication and result of utopian policy is with regard to the roles and staffing of operational and research agencies alike. Taking the view that blame for poverty attaches not to peasants but planistrators, radical realism argues that such offices must be restaffed or even abolished. This has very little appeal for the officers concerned.

A third, then, is realism's conceit that it is not a style at all, not just one perspective on reality, but what amounts to a style-less style. Realism says it lets substance – reality – show and write itself as if it had no perennial and internal dilemmas of its own. Yet this is very far from being true. Realism's internal dilemmas (whether in science or art, as more quotes from Nochlin (1971) indicate) are that it is neither empirical only, nor empirical enough, to realize its project unmitigatedly and guilelessly (realism 'is in a . . . highly ambiguous relation to the highly problematical concept "reality"'). Moreover, realism claims to be objective and comprehensive ('claims to be all-inclusive in subject-matter and aims to be objective in method, though this objectivity is hardly ever achieved in practice'); and it is selective in what it chooses to describe and prescribe ('is didactic, moralistic, reformist').

Depending on whether such inner tensions are perceived or not, and managed or not, they cannot fail to influence the ways in which an approach to research is planned, done, presented and received. Realism's style is particularist, specific. This ill-suits development policy's characteristic concerns with transferability and replicability (also pedagogy's concerns with teachability). Being justificatory of the conventional role of 'development experts' and the like is another power of law-like idealist over realist approaches. Thus MacIntyre says, 'If social science does not present its findings in the form of law-like generalisations, the grounds for employing social scientists as expert advisers to government or private corporations become unclear and the very notion of managerial expertise is imperilled' (1981: 85).

Developmentalism's dominant language is a scientistic type of rationalism, closely associated with neoclassicism as in orthodox economics and other disciplines. Rationalistic models of policy (such as the 'policy cycle' model) exaggerate policy as 'problem-solving' and 'decision-making' as policy is presented in other than bureaucratic and technocratic constructions. But if it is to bureaucracy and technology that anthropology and other social sciences would commit themselves, it must to a significant extent be written or at least played in the same key.

Anthropology of rationalism can usefully borrow from another area and discipline, and take the view that the question is 'not (to) ask . . . what reasons do, and then answer that they persuade. Rather we want to know how it is that reasons *can* persuade . . . the reason does not constitute the feature, it displays the feature by making reference to the concern which provides for it' (McHugh et al. 1974: 84).

To sum up, as empiricism, realism passes too readily from instance to case. It has its own recourse to 'types': 'realism ... without realizing the difference between description and prescription ... tries to reconcile the two in the concept of "type"' (Rene Welleck, cited in Duke 1984). Its own inherent tendency is to overshoot its proclaimed 'simply descriptive' aims. Determinedly descriptive in their styles of observation and representation – as case studies in the realist genre typically are – they are received, as they are written, also as didactic positions which far from putting an end to controversy take it into new areas. At issue were, after all, two sides each buttressed by their own case studies. The difference was not that IRRI eschewed, while UNRISD pursued, field research. Rather, it was the preference of one for plain realism, and of the other for clear idealism.

INSTITUTIONS AND MECHANISMS

The vocabulary of development aid is a clue to the institutional (and ideological) power of language. The vocabulary of development 'projects' (and other instruments) is a clue to the mechanical (and organizational) power of language.

The vocabulary of 'aid', whether from governmental or non-governmental agencies, is virtuous as well as donative and promissory. It depends for much of its effect on the sweetest and seemingly entirely unproblematic of words, 'cooperation'. In the actual conduct of methods of aid and development, this sugar coats many a bitter pill. But, for aid agents, the good word 'cooperation' goes on its merry way nevertheless. 'Community' (and 'participation') are other sure-fire winning words (again governmental and non-governmental organizations differ very little in recourse to them), living blameless lives of their own in language, policy and analysis of whatever hue – red, blue or green (or imperial purple or Himalayan yellow). Thus Raymond Williams (1983) points out how unusual community is as a political term. It is the one type of term, along with, for example, 'cooperation' and 'participation' which has never been used in a negative sense. People never, from any position, want to say they are against community, or against the community. Like Williams, while we might be glad this is so, we should also be suspicious of a term which is agreed among so many people, which everybody likes, and which everybody is in favour of. One crucial characteristic of these sorts of keywords is that they do not require an opposite word to give or enhance their meaning. They acquire much of their winning warmth from their popular meanings in everyday usage. A further characteristic is that, as a rule, they are not ever put to serious empirical test – or if they are, and they fail, they continue to circulate in good currency nevertheless. The projects they herald may be evaluated, and whether they are winners or not is another matter.

Much the same is the case as regards empirical testing with development policy's mechanist vocabulary of technical/jargon (not everyday) words, which work more at the level of aid instruments – projects – than on the plane of aid principles – conditionalities. Take, for example, 'informal sector' (a term contributed to development vocabulary by Keith Hart in an ILO World Employment Programme consultancy report). Originally this term was supposedly empirically descriptive of a state of employment, averring 'easy access' (and several other features). However, when it was put to real empirical test (e.g. Hannerz 1985), it was found to be far from accurately descriptive of the state of 'informal' employment for which it was devised. Indeed, for the purpose for which it was coined, it proved to be false. Yet it continues to be in standard circulation in development policy and study nevertheless (though I understand Hart himself abandoned it eventually).

Why isn't bad description driven out by the good? Lisa Peattie (1987) says the term 'informal sector', whether it is true or false, serves to give development economics and policy an entrée to an area of actual conduct which it lacked before. Therefore, 'to relinquish the term would mean to relinquish the entree' (ibid.). A second type of reason has to do with the mechanism of a word's place being guaranteed – or at least insured – by a binary bind with an opposite 'polar word' (Arnold 1937: Ch. V *passim*) whose standing is bad not good. Here, performance (coming from somewhere in between structure and function) is all. Persuasive power in the public text is strongest where descriptive power is weakest. Rebuttal (McHugh et al. 1974) is forestalled by decoying attention from the good uttered, to the evil implied.

POLICY LANGUAGE

Policy language, then, is itself a form and source of policy power. Policy discourse tries more to persuade than describe; genre and style are integral to policy paradigms, not adornments to be dispensed with if they do not please. It is not through its language alone that the general nature (if there is any such thing) of policy or a policy analysis can or ought to be comprehended. But language policy undoubtedly has distinctive and consequential styles of practice (for some initial remarks on stylistics of religious writing, newspaper reporting and legal documents, see Crystal and Davy 1969). They can easily be recognized though they may be difficult to define.

While policy language presents policy as being data-driven, complaining at times therefore about 'lack of data', this masks the extent to which it is data-driving (lack of 'appropriate' data), choosing the data it prefers. By 'data' in policy and policy analysis is meant what is wanted and what can be handled, through measurement perhaps. Where measurement is sought, however, is where institutional meaning and significance is caught by number. Little depends alone on what it is technically possible to count.

The language and styles of policy reflect cultural values and moral systems (cf. Wright and Shore 1995, and in this volume) as well as cognitive style. So, too, do those of anthropology and policy analysis, with legitimizations that are promiscuous, shared and ceremonial. And always part of the message to be conveyed has to do with ceremony, with ritual that is procedure if you will, even where it goes with great determination for the instrumental.

The languages of policy and policy analysis seek power through characteristically uttering policy problems as though they could be solved by 'closing gaps' in research information by the provision of new and appropriate neutral data. But what are called information 'gaps' are not only that. They also represent some making, and taking, of social, cultural and political distance. Being not just empty, they are therefore not merely awaiting to be closed by 'science'. The same is true of so-called 'gaps' between 'theory' and 'practice'.[5] They are not voids, but already crowded spaces of moral practices and biases, so to say 'full' already of pre-, con- and mis-conceptions – without which of course life and policy would be unwriteable (and unreadable).

Empirical development policy research, especially in the use of case studies, however earnestly it engages with policy, does not find acceptance because it documents real life concretely and neutrally. In research, as in policy and politics, measure is taken of battles of fact by the style and objectives of war. To concentrate on the battles only is to neglect the broader setting, which is the war. This broader frame and perspective of disputation is what makes matters important enough to be worth fighting over. It deserves, therefore, much more attention than it usually gets. In policy analysis, as in policy, concern with objectives and objectivity cover concern with perspectives and perspectivity. Policy or research may fail to make a difference either by failing to reach its own standards, or, even more tellingly, by disregarding those of its competition.

NOTES

1 This paper draws on a lecture in the series 'Making policy analysis matter: to commit social anthropology to current public issues', given at the École des Hautes Études en Sciences Sociales, Paris, July 1995, at the kind invitation of Jean-Claude Galey. It links closely with others in that series, published as 'Policy anthropology as expert witness' (1996a), and 'Reading development policy and analysis: on framing, naming, numbering and coding' (1996b) and 'On UNDP's human development reporting and social anthropology' (forthcoming). See also, Des Gasper and Raymond Apthorpe (1996) 'Discourse analysis and policy discourse'. Some earlier work subsumed in this chapter includes my 'Agricultures and strategies: the language of development policy' (1984a), 'Development policy discourse' (1986b), 'Development indicators: some relativities of objectivity and subjectivity' (1984b) and 'Social labelling and agricultural development' (1986a). I am most grateful to Sue Wright and Cris Shore for their invitation to contribute this chapter, and for their editorial directions, plain and clear, which made a great difference.

2 It is as 'small farmer' that 'peasant' is used principally in the UNRISD oeuvre, largely to avoid 'modes of production' connotations of 'mentality' or 'precapitalism' in 'transition to' (or 'from') 'socialism'. But of course with 'small farmer' there are other difficulties, arising particularly from capture of the term by 'capitalism'. Of these, some are 'cross cultural' as with 'household ' and 'family' seen ethnocentrically as 'Western' (and lumpishly as units rather than processes): see, for example, Russell (1993).

3 At that meeting I represented Global-2. Earlier Andrew and I had visited Brian Fegan in his Philippines field research site (where he was working on a related topic).

4 Since the early 1970s, in a new orthodoxy in development policy, there has been a reverse with 'private' taking the esteemed place in sectoral discourse. But in mainstream development economics and related arguments, the dichotomous nature of the private–public distinction remains as a – indeed often *the* – pivotal divide for making ideology, policy and strategy.

5 Charles Gore taught me about these gaps that are not gaps in the early 1980s (at Swansea, where and when the case analysis in this paper was first written – for a book that never came about).

REFERENCES

Aijmer, G. (1985) 'Applied anthropology and the informal sector: a sense of direction?' in H. O. Skar (ed.) *Anthropological Contributions to Planned Change and Development*, Gothenburg Studies in Social Anthropology 8, Acta Universitatis Gothoburgensis.

Apthorpe, R. (1984a) 'Agricultures and strategies: the language of policy discourse' in E. Clay and B. Schaffer (eds) *Room For Manoeuvre In Public Policy*, London: Heinemann Educational Books.

—— (1984b) 'Development indicators: some relativities of objectivity and subjectivity' in J. G. M. Hilhorst and M. Klatter (eds) *Social Development and Social Planning*, Aldershot: Croom Helm.

—— (1986a) 'Social labelling and agricultural development', *Land Use Policy*, October, London: Butterworth.

—— (1986b) 'Development policy discourse', *Public Administration and Development* 6 (4): 377–89, London: Wiley for Royal Institute of Public Administration.

—— (1996a) 'Policy anthropology as expert witness', *Social Anthropology* 4 (2): 163–79, Cambridge: Cambridge University Press.

—— (1996b) 'Reading development and development policy: on framing, naming, numbering and coding' in R. Apthorpe and D. Gasper (eds) *Arguing Development Policy: Frames And Discourses*, London: Cass. (Also published as a Special Issue of *European Journal of Development Research* 8 (1): 16–35.)

—— (forthcoming) 'On UNDP's human development reporting and social anthropology', *Social Anthropology*.

Arnold, T. (1937) *The Folklore Of Capitalism*, New Haven: Yale.

Barthes, R. (1973) *Mythologies*, London: Paladin.

Baxter, P. W. T. and Fardon, F. (1991) 'Genre as a middle term' in P. W. T. Baxter and F. Fardon (eds) *Voice Genre Text: Anthropological Essays in Africa and Beyond*, Bulletin of John Rylands University Library of Manchester 73 (3): 3–10.

Baumann, G. (1987) *National Integration and Local Integrity: The Miri of the Nuba Mountains in the Sudan*, Oxford: Clarendon Press.

Canetti, E. (1982) *Auto de fe*, London: Cape.

Crystal, D. and Davy, D. (1969) *Investigating English Style*, London: Longmans.

Duke, M. S. (1984) 'Chinese literature in the post Mao Era: the return of "critical realism" ', *Bulletin of Concerned Asian Scholars* 16 (3) 2–4.

Gasper, D. and Apthorpe, R. (1996) 'Discourse analysis and policy discourse' in L. Apthorpe and L. D. Gasper (eds) *Arguing Development Policy – Frames and Discourses*, London: Cass.

Green, B. S. (1983) *Knowing the Poor: A Case Study in Textual Reality Construction*, London: Routledge and Kegan Paul.

—— (1988) *Literary Methods and Sociological Theory: Case Studies of Simmel and Weber*, Chicago: Chicago University Press.

Hannerz, U. (1985) 'The informal sector', in H. O. Skar (ed.) *Anthropological Contributions to Planned Change and Development*,

Gothenburg Studies in Social Anthropology 8, Acta Universitatis Gothoburgensis.

Lorenzco, E. T. and Maranan, R. G. (1980) 'The Impact of Green Revolution in South and South East Asia Based on the Studies of Unrisd and Irri', unpublished joint Master's thesis, Hague: Institute of Social Studies.

Lukács, G. (1964) *Studies In European Realism: A Sociological Survey of the Writings of Balzac, Zola, Tolstoy, Gorki and Others*, New York: Grosset and Dunlop.

McHugh, P., Raffel, S., Foss, D. C. and Blum, A. (1974) *On the Beginnings of Social Inquiry*, London and Boston: Routledge and Kegan Paul.

MacIntyre, A. (1981) *After Virtue: A Study in Moral Theory*, Notre Dame IN: University of Notre Dame.

Nochlin, L. (1971) *Realism*, London: Penguin.

Peattie, L. (1987) 'An idea of good currency and how it grew: the informal sector', *World Development* 15 (7): 851–60.

Pearce, A. (1980) *Seeds of Plenty, Seeds of Want*, Oxford: Clarendon Press.

Pearce, A. et al. (1977) 'Technology and peasant production: a discussion', *Development and Change*, 8 (3).

Russell, M. (1993) 'Are households universal? On misunderstanding domestic groups in Swaziland', *Development and Change* 24: 755–85.

Skar, H. O. (1985) 'Questioning three assumptions about the informal sector in view of some data from Lima, Peru', in H. O. Skar (ed.) *Anthropological Contributions to Planned Change and Development*, Gothenburg Studies in Social Anthropology 8, Acta Universitatis Gothoburgensis.

Thompson, G. (1985) 'The bewitchment and fall of a village politician' in R. G. Abrahams (ed.) *Villagers, Villages and the State in Modern Tanzania*, Cambridge African Monograph 4, Cambridge: African Studies Centre.

Williams, R. (1983) *Keywords*, London: Fontana.

Wright, S. and Shore, C. (1995) 'Towards an anthropology of policy: morality, power and the art of government' in *Anthropology in Action* 2 (2): 17–31.

Chapter 3

The implications of 'medical', 'gender in development' and 'culturalist' discourses for HIV/AIDS policy in Africa

Gill Seidel and Laurent Vidal

INTRODUCTION

This chapter sets out three discourses (medical, gender in development and culturalist) on HIV/AIDS in sub-Saharan Africa. Each of the discourses is a particular 'way of thinking and arguing' about the epidemic and the reasons for its spread which excludes other ways of thinking. Discourses involve naming and classifying. This is a political activity. As such, it is not merely symbolic, but has material outcomes that impinge on people's lives. In particular it is gender relations – power relations between the sexes – that are marginalized in both the medical and culturalist discourses, and which have serious effects on women.

Discourses are not purely symbolic resources and arguments, but resources that may be politically invested by social actors (such as government, or non-government organizations) to particular ends. Familiar examples include discourses that construct 'the nation' at different times in history, with exclusions of 'race', ethnicity, gender, and of different sexualities (Capitan 1988, 1993). Responses to AIDS everywhere have been moralizing and stigmatizing (Treichler 1987; Watney 1988, 1989; Patton 1992). Long before AIDS, different groups were blamed and scapegoated for disease (Ranger and Stack 1992). Inappropriate categorizations or ways of classifying that derive from specialized and still hegemonic discourses, like epidemiology, may lead to further victimization and blaming of vulnerable populations. These discourses when translated and mobilized through forms of action, including through policy, may lead to challenging rights and access to resources of all kinds to 'out groups'. These political and ideological battles are fought out through discourse as well as in extra-discursive activity.

Discursive practices also involve the use of metaphors. The difficulty arises when in a monologic or non-argumentative situation it is taken for granted that metaphors have a single, univocal interpretation. Sontag has deplored the tendency for illness to be used as a metaphor (Sontag 1979). A poignant example is that pertaining to 'blood': 'bad blood' or 'dirty blood', standard symbolism used by doctors in some parts of Africa to convey to patients that they are HIV positive in a post-test situation (Collignon et al. 1995). This has had particular consequences, as we identify below. Dominant discourses and particular semiotic practices, because they are univocal, tend not to differentiate between other 'voices', subjectivities and experiences and, when they inform policy and practice, lead to inappropriate and at times disastrous interventions.

This work on discourses, policy and materialities draws on extensive fieldwork in East, West and southern Africa, and on secondary sources.[1] In these parts of Africa, where HIV spread is primarily heterosexual, and where women are held as responsible for the health of their families, the dominant paradigm is one that constructs women as largely responsible for HIV spread.

THEORETICAL FRAMEWORKS

The general discursive framework as applied to AIDS is developed elsewhere (Seidel 1993a). It is an extension of earlier work on racist and sexist discourses (Seidel 1988), and of the culturalist discourse and projects of the New Right (Seidel 1984, 1987). It has been shaped by largely French post-structuralist work dating from the mid-1970s. Although multi-disciplinary, it has been influenced in particular by the work of Michel Foucault, but tempered by an encounter with feminist epistemology.[2] In the UK, anthropological critiques of linguistic studies' focus on the individual were important (Bloch 1975; Parkin 1984; Grillo 1989), as was post-structuralist anthropological work inspired by new social movements (Escobar 1992).

All have a shared concern with power relations and the multiple sites of power and, with different emphases, with the persistent dissymmetries and exclusions around gender, 'race' and class, as well as the marginalization of particular cultures and languages (Seidel 1988; Wodak 1988; Van Dijk 1990; Michard 1997).[3] The work on culturalist discourse, its theorization and exemplification in relation to AIDS has been illuminated in particular by Vidal from his anthropological studies in anti-tuberculosis centres in Abidjan, Côte d'Ivoire (Vidal 1993, 1994).

MEDICAL DISCOURSE

AIDS in Africa has been constructed as a predominantly medical matter. Although the virus is a bio-medical phenomenon, the conditions and reasons for its spread are clearly social. Yet social processes figure little in dominant discourses. Reasons for the medical emphasis include the structural dominance and prestige of the medical profession, the power invested in bio-medical culture in Africa, as elsewhere, and in health bureaucracies. This power was enhanced by the Global AIDS Programme set up by the World Health Organization (WHO GPA) (since 1996 reduced to a mere UN AIDS initiative) which collaborated not with NGOs (non-government organizations) but with health ministries accustomed to vertical modes of communication. This cooperation resulted in financial and purely quantitative methodological packages for medically designed 'AIDS control' programmes.

The critical social sciences have been marginalized (Seidel 1994) and underfunded, with serious consequences. In particular, the discourse and practices of epidemiology, seen as altogether scientific and value-free, have targeted, cajoled and harassed particular groups of women, with little understanding of the constraints in which they live their lives (Schoepf 1993a, 1993b), or of their models of disease and illness.

The WHO classified the global epidemic into three patterns, but effectively into just two. In Pattern 1 countries (USA, the industrial West, Australasia, and Latin America) the spread was seen as primarily homosexual (the medical terminology). In Pattern 2 countries (East, Central and southern Africa, and the Caribbean) it was heterosexual. (Pattern 3, about which little was known at the time, included Asia, eastern Europe and the Pacific). Attention has been paid to the effects of the clash of institutional cultures and its effects in the United States. Meanwhile the pattern classification (Frankenberg 1989) has also had an impact on women, and in itself is a simplistic dichotomy and simplified view of human sexuality. These classifications, shaped by the early history of the epidemic in the States, meant that case definitions for women with AIDS, as well as children, supplied by the CDC (Centres for Disease Control in Atlanta, Georgia) were not forthcoming until the second decade;

and even then were altogether inadequate, as acknowledged in a WHO meeting and subsequent report (Carael 1990; Merson 1990). These definitions, their sidelining of women-specific conditions, and hence the invisibility of women living with HIV/AIDS, continue to be contested (ACT UP 1990; Denenberg 1990; Levin 1990; Berer and Ray 1993).

The impact of this classification has been fourfold. First, it has marginalized the African continent as a Pattern 2 country (defined in relation to the US and northern norm). Second, it fuelled the dangerous myth that AIDS was exclusively a 'gay disease' in the North, thereby suggesting that heterosexuals in the North were 'naturally' immune from HIV infection. Third, it assisted the construction, not through explicit naming, but through overlapping and reinforcing meanings (in discursive terms, through 'intertextuality') (Fairclough 1992: Ch. 4) of AIDS as a 'tropical disease', with further implications for funding and organizational arrangements. Fourth, as referred to above, another effect was the relative disregard by key agencies of many of the key clinical manifestations of women (Temmerman et al. 1990) and children with AIDS, of whom large numbers were in sub-Saharan Africa (Persson 1994).

This epidemiological consideration and 'ways of thinking' have material effects. Historically, 'Africa' has been portrayed as a 'reservoir of infection'. The construction of 'African AIDS' was a continuation of existing discourses and stereotypes of 'Africa' (Treichler 1987; Cerullo and Hammond 1988; Watney 1989; Pieterse 1990; Patton 1992). The predominance of colonial constructions of 'Africa' and medical and moral constructions of the epidemic has meant that research has not been seen as appropriate for Africa. This extraordinary position was defended and justified by a major European Union funding body (P. C. J. Huber, August 1993). This available construction ('Africa' equated with infection) was further mobilized by the media, culled from medical articles. They cited alarmingly high rates among 'prostitutes', who had been classified by epidemiologists as a key 'high-risk group'. This classification was made with no reference to the very different HIV seroprevalance rates in different regions, or the social and sexual contexts of STD and HIV transmission (Bassett and Mhloyi 1991). Neither the media nor epidemiological culture queried this problematic construction, and its possible effects. In this way, 'Africa' is presented as an undifferentiated whole, itself a conceptual and political violence (Patton 1992), and with gender implications (women threatening men's health, inviting potentially punitive measures). This was the discursive construction, one of unbridled 'promiscuity' which led to the emphasis being placed quite categorically on prevention, and especially on condom use – as in Pattern 1 countries concerned with *male-to-male* transmission.

This policy choice is problematic in that it assumes an altogether false universality. Apart from the dominant assumption that meanings attached to sexuality, illness and risk are the same everywhere, there is a blindness to gender and gender relations. Gender relations are still not seen as a central analytical category, or as constituting political interests (Seidel 1988, 1996b). However, there is some discontinuity: the assumed universality and epidemiological classification did not extend to care provision. Ethical concerns and care demands were expressed, at an early stage in the epidemic, by TASO, Uganda, the first indigenous AIDS Support Organisation and, at that time, a marginalized voice. The important ethical link between care and prevention has been stressed since, but comparatively recently. These voices argue that provision should be linked to and made available in non-judgemental primary health care settings (de Cock et al. 1993; de Bruyn and van der Hoeven 1994; Evian 1994). The link that has not been made commonly in medical literature or health economics was that this 'invisibility' of women with HIV/AIDS also extended to their invisibility as carers and family and community educators.

In a historical perspective, it may be argued that the decision to focus on prevention – without appropriate research – was framed by colonial discourse. In many African states, missionaries still play an important role in providing health care, as in Zambia and Uganda. Their medico-moral discourse (Seidel 1989, 1993) has also shaped responses to the epidemic. In a number of regions, people with HIV/AIDS are seen as 'sexual sinners'. There is a tension between advocating prevention methods and 'saving souls'. The predominance of colonial constructions of 'Africa' and medical and medico-moral constructions of the epidemic and of 'sexuality' has meant that research that was not medically-led has been actively discouraged by major funding bodies. The preferred prevention campaigns were launched in settings in which basic longitudinal data were not available about social and gender relations, or about actual practices – as opposed to stated 'beliefs'. The WHO-favoured KAP questionnaires (Knowledge Attitudes Beliefs) (Schopper et al. 1993) do not elicit sensitive information about the multiple risk environments and their gendered effects, or about women's perception of risk, nor do they map access to material and symbolic goods, including information, literacy, and support and care networks. In the hegemonic medical culture, these considerations, and even the 'why' and 'how' of eliciting such knowledge, were not prioritized, or even given conceptual houseroom.

EPIDEMIOLOGICAL DISCOURSE ABOUT RISK GROUPS

Epidemiology is concerned with the study of epidemic and certain communicable diseases, and with finding means of control and future prevention. It functions, mainly statistically, in terms of 'risk groups'. In settings where women are held responsible for the health of their families, and where in a number of languages, including Yoruba, a local term for sexually transmitted diseases/infections (STDs or STIs) translated as 'women's diseases' (Kisekka 1990), epidemiological discourse and practice have contributed to the blaming of women, and constitute a renewed focus concerned with the manipulation and control of women's bodies (Bisseret-Moreau 1988).

One example of the effect of the classification of 'risk groups' has been to identify and name a certain category of women, mainly mobile and working women, not as migrant workers, a more dignified category seemingly reserved for men, as in a major World Bank study in rural Tanzania, but in a moralistic and largely Eurocentric category as 'prostitutes'. The fact that many regular 'clients' may perceive and name these women very differently – as 'girlfriends' – is not taken into account, as these are part of marginalized discourses (see Workshop on long distance truck drivers and commercial sex workers, Pietermaritzburg AIDS Training Information and Counselling Centre 1995 (Marcus et al. 1995)). Meanwhile, the risks to women as a whole, single or married, and rural or urban, because of their particular physiology, the social construction of gender and gender relations, women's structural position, and poor genital health generally, have not been adequately addressed. Indeed, in some national and health promotion programmes married women are not even regarded as being at risk, suggesting a moral agenda, with a glaringly inadequate construction of sexuality, and one which, again, impacts on women. In this epidemiological discourse, and its application in policy and practice, it is these largely migrant women, or the more visible among them, who have been regularly rounded up, and tested for STDs and HIV. They, and rarely their 'clients', have been the principal 'targets' for health education (and, in some instances, objects of social engineering). This process and methodology have been discussed in terms of animal imagery, even in a very respectable journal (Watts et al. 1995).

The contexts in which sex is exchanged vary considerably, as do the meanings attached, and the degrees of acceptance of particular behaviours. Acceptance may be pragmatic, and depend on multiple factors, including, importantly, the weight and legitimacy of moral discourses. Some sensitive studies have actively involved representatives of sex workers acting as fieldworkers. These have highlighted women's own conceptualization of risk and their strategies used in work where a relationship of trust has been built up (Schoepf 1993a; Karin et al. 1995). These are women who may often combine sex work with hawking, especially beer-selling. Others may combine sexual favours with housekeeping or domestic servicing on a seasonal basis, or for longer periods. In other settings, where divorce is more common, these may represent periods of wealth accumulation between successive marriages (Pittin 1984). Women in the cities may be offering a form of companionship to migrant male workers, in which gifts, possibly shelter, a form of protection, and money for themselves or their children's education, may be involved (Oppong 1995). Different partners will be expected to contribute specific items to a finely balanced but fragile household budget. Other women may be 'town wives' (Nelson 1987; White 1988). A number of these mobile women will be seeking to escape from the drudgery of village life, or from contexts of violence and abuse at home (Tabet 1985; Pheterson 1990).

It is these women, often the mainstay of entire families, who have been categorized as 'carriers', or 'vectors', and among them the more visible women have been 'targeted' and harassed. The epidemiological categorization is not only blaming, but overlaps with and reinforces moral discourses – 'traditional' discourse on morality, and modern 'health messages' designed by health ministries and some NGOs which include advice to '*Avoid prostitutes*'. In this way conditions for reprisals and abuse are set up. There have been sporadic reports of the forced removal of migrant women as city 'cleansing', a form of human rights' violation.

The idea of 'risk groups' is also weak in terms of explaining the epidemic. In common with most other medical explanations, the epidemiological discourse of 'risk groups' is reductionist in that it proposes a single explanation for what is a complex social phenomenon. This is becoming more widely recognized among southern health professionals in front-line states who have been exposed to the destruction of whole communities and infrastructures, and to state and gendered violence. Their awareness has also grown through working in 'empowering' ways with the 'historically dispossessed' and with advocacy groups. As a result of this challenge, the language of 'risk groups' is being replaced by 'risk behaviours', and, more significantly for development contexts, 'risk environments' (Zwi and Cabral 1991). These accommodate and encode a conceptual shift which encompasses civil strife and displacements, and have far greater explanatory adequacy (Zwi 1993; Heise et al. 1994). These shifts, and their lexical updates, also take account of the many settings of woman and of child abuse, including rape, as part of a gendered rights discourse, taken up by community groups, yet hitherto 'unspeakable' – that is, not conceptualized, or legitimated, within the dominant medico-moral 'ways of thinking'.

GENDER AND DEVELOPMENT DISCOURSE

Another challenge to the dominant medico-moral discourse comes from the 'gender and development' discourse (Kabeer 1994). The use of *gender* as a category of analysis shifts the focus away from '*women*', and the implication that they are 'the problem', to social relations. Any analysis of gender as power relations between the sexes includes the practices that position women as a subordinate group in terms of access to resources, capabilities, power and privilege (Schoepf 1993a; Kabeer 1994: 65) and focuses on the making and remaking of gender identities. It also avoids purely economic explanations of women's subordination (Rathgeber 1990) as available in more classical Marxist analyses.

This discourse has been taken up by some major development agencies concerned with health and special interest groups working on family spacing and planning (although their earlier history and involvement in eugenics in South Africa and elsewhere is deeply problematic (Klugman 1993)). With the extension of 'rights' discourses to include sexual and reproductive rights, this has resulted in a call for more gender-sensitive programmes (Levin 1990; Carovano 1991; Gordon and Kanstrup 1992; Reid 1992; Hadden et al. 1995; KIT et al. 1995). The 1995 UN Beijing Conference on Women produced a gendered emancipatory discourse and set priorities, with the potential of reversing the hierarchy of knowledge in the interests of marginalized groups (although this may also be blocked and subverted).[4]

In these respects, there has been a clear impetus from the new government and from NGO and community groups in South Africa building on its new political culture of rights. This has been extended to include different sexualities; and 'prostitution' may be decriminalized there within the next two years. Although there is still a concern to target sex workers, pregnant women, and STD clinic attenders, in keeping with epidemiological discourse and practice, there is also a heightened gender awareness of vulnerabilities (Karin et al. 1995). Mainly from the Cape, there is an important critique which argues that to focus exclusively on women – and primarily on their biological capacities – stressing, for example, mother-to-baby transmission, is to further blame or justify the blaming of women for the epidemic (Strebel 1993, 1994). This blaming is also reported from KwaZulu-Natal (Preston-Whyte 1995), even with the first cases, and seen as a dilemma for an all-women research team. There are other examples of resistance from a small women's trade union in the Cape which refused to include information about vertical transmission in designing their own literature, challenging the 'universality' of public health discourse (Seidel 1996a, 1996b).

The Cape response is a striking illustration of the gendered rights discourse that has been able to fracture the hegemonic epidemiological discourse through activism (Preston-Whyte 1995), as well as by extending 'emancipatory language practice', a concern of post-apartheid education (Janks and Ivanic 1993). However, in terms of institutional and financial investment and methodologies, which are still largely in place, it could be argued that although there is flux among those contracting for research, for some time to come resource allocation is likely to favour a more conventional epidemiological practice influenced by and probably evaluated by normative, northern models, although alternatives are available (KIT et al. 1995; Plaat 1995).

Gender and development discourse on STD/HIV care

Gender and development discourse encourages women to have greater control of their daily lives, and challenges or seeks to modify interventions which are dependent on male decisions, or prerogatives, or normative assumptions, with the male as the norm or measure. These include assumptions that underwrite individualistic health belief models (Grace 1993), which are not grounded in women's realities as well as prevention and care programmes which fail to address current imbalances of power. This 'empowerment' discourse is extremely pervasive, particularly in NGO literature and mission statements. 'Empowerment' is a complex process deriving from diverse theoretical frameworks (Baylies and Bujra 1995), although sometimes it is used as merely a feel-good slogan. It includes 'learning up and sideways' (Schrijvers 1993), and encompasses participatory health research (de Koning and Martin 1996). It is influenced by Freirian philosophy, and by the ways in which knowledge has been produced by new social movements (Escobar 1992) in both the North and the South, giving a 'voice' to disenfranchised or otherwise marginalized communities.

A key scenario in which this discursive and paradigm shift is being acted out is in STD and HIV prevention concerning the condom, but also barrier methods and the female condom – *methods that women can use under their control* (Reid 1992; Stein 1994, 1995; Hadden et al. 1995). There are a number of discourses in circulation which impinge differently on women's lives, and which are a response and resistance to male condom promotion as the key prevention strategy adopted for 'Africa'. (These are to be distinguished from a certain moral discourse that criticizes condoms from the perspective of a very different political agenda.) These discourses have different implications for gender construction. They may be summarized as follows:

Women must 'be empowered' to practice sexual decision-making, including the introduction of [male] condom use with their sexual partner(s)

compared with:

'Bring us the female condom'.
> (ANC women activists in KwaZulu-Natal quoted by Preston-Whyte 1995; emphasis added, GS)

In South Africa, as in many other states, it is pregnant women, along with sex workers, and STD clinic attenders, who are targeted for testing and for condom promotion. As pregnant women are seen by epidemiologists as 'sentinel groups' for the HIV epidemic, it is these women attending antenatal clinics who are counselled, and who are among the first in the community to be tested. Although they may refuse consent, this is rare. In most cases, their regular partner will not wear a condom as it is not seen as appropriate for intimacy – it suggests a lack of trust, it is negatively associated with disease, and, as commonly reported, and uniquely from the male perspective, it also means reduced pleasure. As part of the counselling process, if the woman is positive, she is expected to:

1 inform the father of the baby, and any other sexual partners, of her serostatus;
2 introduce condom use or other forms of non-penetrative sex into the relationship;
3 in some settings, advise the partner(s) to come for counselling and an HIV test.

This has been the practice in Baragwanath Hospital, Soweto (the largest in southern Africa), where sympathetic women nurse–counsellors are attached to the antenatal clinic, and where there is also a small peer support group, SAFO (Society for Families and Orphans). Despite this increasingly supportive environment, and although many claim to have been infected by a regular partner, between 1994 and 1995 not one woman has been able to inform their partner – for fear of being made homeless, and other forms of violence. Informal sources suggest that in mid-1996 the situation is largely unchanged.

Antenatal clinics represent a key site for the application of 'discursive technologies', that is, teaching language practice to enhance strategic skills. Some peer group prevention programmes have reported a degree of success with some categories of sex workers (Williams 1995), a number of whom have been able to impose condom use with a client, or refuse unprotected sex. In other settings, however, and emphatically among pregnant HIV positive women at Baragwanath, such strategies have failed – because they cannot take account of the dissymmetry in power relations and the contexts of male heterosexist violence.

Partner notification is known to be enormously problematic everywhere. There are sobering studies of the effects of counselling women (Worth 1990), and, very recently, of the effects of communicating test results to women (Heyward et al.1993; Temmerman et al. 1995). These studies spark off correspondence, but do not appear to influence policy, which is rarely 'open', and not for long. It is as if this knowledge produced by HIV-positive women is of no consequence. Furthermore, the purely individualist emphasis on counselling, where counselling seems to occupy the moral high ground, and the sidelining of community groups, also has its own political economy (Colebunders et al. 1995; McCoy 1995; McCoy and Coleman 1995; Seidel 1996a).

With the aim of 'envoicing' women, there are lessons to be learned from women trying to construct the experience of rape with multiple versions of control, blame and responsibility (Wood and Rennie 1984; Msaky 1992). These are contexts in which physical violence (Motsei 1993; Rispel 1994) and specifically rape are commonplace (Armstrong 1994). As reported in workshops, rape is a common initiation into early enforced sexuality. It is frequently men who name and frame women's experience. This means that the task of 'envoicing' is a slow and non-linear process. There is a disempowering effect in that some women are also blaming themselves for this 'failure' in communicating with their partners; and may be reminded of this, in a kindly, often half-joking fashion, at each visit to the antenatal clinic when condoms are distributed.

There are other ways to develop a more gendered analysis by seeking to 'change around' and rethink this single emphasis on condoms. At present, women are expected to perform the strategic communicative tasks; and may be blamed and beaten by their partners if they succeed, or blame themselves if they fail. Other strategies are influenced by work on women's reproductive choices in a continent in which at least 150,000 women each year lose their lives through pregnancy-related conditions (*African Journal of Fertility, Sexuality and Reproductive Health* 1 March 1996).

Statistics suggest that most women who have access to family spacing methods will use the injectible methods, like Depo Provera, as opposed to the pill, IUD, or male condom (Chimera-Dam 1996). In many cases, where this is an informed choice, this has the advantage of being undetectable by their partners. Important studies have shown that women are in a better position to use methods that are under their control (Hadden et al. 1995). Gender advocacy derived from women's experiences of gender relations highlights, in some settings, the sheer irrelevance of condoms to many women (Le Palec 1993). Such gender advocacy has led, in the second decade, to the introduction of barrier methods, especially spermicides, now in Phase II trials, in Cameroon and South Africa (Karin et al. 1995; Gilmour 1995). With the backing of the South African health minister, in 1995 there were trials of femidom usage in three sites (Soweto, the Cape, and in rural KwaZulu-Natal). Early indications are encouraging. In this way, gender and development discourse, activism, and lobbying for woman-centred technologies under women's control have brought about a radical decentring (in the case of the female condom, a decentring from the male and specifically from the male organ constructed as the central reference). This is part of a broader strategy that aims at promoting health for women by advancing gender rights (Cook 1993; Heise and Elias 1995; Peters and Wolpe 1995).

CULTURALIST DISCOURSE

Apart from the discourses already identified, there is a culturalist discourse in circulation. This, too, has particular effects and outcomes. It derives from a number of epistemological strands. In the early stages of the epidemic, which occurred after the post-colonial demise of anthropology in the 1960, anthropologists were being recruited by departments of health, within medical protocols, and encouraged to recycle what were outdated and dubious ethnographies of sexual behaviours and practices (Standing and Kisekka 1989). Health professionals are organizing interventions with very little up-to-date knowledge of people's health-seeking behaviours, or their take-up and assessment of different therapies. Anthropologists were given encouragement, not to study these, but to look for culturally-bound 'exotic' practices, like scarifications, blood-letting, monkey-eating, wife-sharing, and wife inheritance (the levirate) which involved risk factors (Packard and Epstein 1991). This research focus, an application of the 'Othering' of 'Africa', of 'Africans', and of 'African AIDS', operated to the exclusion, or backgrounding, of development explanations for HIV spread, such as the colonial migrant labour system that uprooted and destroyed family and community structures. This 'thinking' also ruled gender constructions 'out of order' (Seidel 1993b) and some of their main material effects, like male inheritance laws in many regions. Key biomedical concerns like the role of contaminated blood supplies, or historically untreated STDs, now recognized as a major public health problem, were also sidelined (Bassett and Mhloyi 1991).

An important consideration is that patients' perception of the disease may continue to be at odds with that of the Western-trained professional. Consulting 'traditional healers' and seeking non-biomedical explanations will usually be construed by doctors and some nurses as compromising conventional medical practice (Crawford 1994; Mbali 1995). Traditional healers are now playing a more significant role in condom distribution and are treating HIV symptomatic diseases and some conventional STDs, as in Zimbabwe and Botswana, and, increasingly, in KwaZulu-Natal, South Africa (Green et al. 1995).

Anthropology is called upon to explain how a particular pathology has emerged in one group rather than another, and to account for the unwillingness to adopt prevention measures or other treatments which have proved effective elsewhere. This 'else-where' refers essentially to a different culture whose distinctive characteristics for adapting to medical advice have been helpful in avoiding, or in limiting, the extent of the illness in question. This leads to a dichotomy of societies, and hence of cultures – those which adapt, and those which resist the changes dictated by a health-promoting rationality. In both cases, this has given rise to a tendency to account for even minor conceptual and attitudinal differences towards a health problem by referring to cultural traits, which, in most cases, are presented as immutable. Indeed, even sensitive studies concerned with women's 'inability' to inform partners has been referred to in general terms as a 'cultural obstacle' (Scott and Mercer 1994). The problem of this type of interpretation lies initially in the ignorance of the individual initiatives (especially of the sick and their close relatives) and of the social and economic contexts (the family structures, the professional situations, and the access to precise information on AIDS) which could shape these behaviours.

Furthermore, there is a problem with trying to account for the relative failures of health interventions on the grounds that they have encountered a 'cultural problem'. A form of cultural relativism is becoming more apparent. This is further sustained by a tendency towards ethnocentrism displayed by some researchers who are convinced that, if an argument is made out for culturally-based resistance, the problem has no solution. They argue that the reason is to be found in conceptions and health practices different from those developed in the industrialized countries. Conversely, an intellectual position that constantly harks back to 'African values' ignores people's capacity to change and underestimates the factors which do not explicitly derive from cultural tradition. In both cases, analysing behaviour in purely cultural terms ignores the social and individual resources and the practices actually observed. This kind of analysis lends credence to the process of stigmatization and Othering, where the Other is totally identified with their culture.

EFFECTS OF THE CULTURALIST DISCOURSE IN CÔTE D'IVOIRE

The parameters and the limitations of a purely culturalist interpretation of HIV/AIDS are shown by our work (LV) in Côte d'Ivoire on sexuality, disclosure of serostatus, and the place of traditional medicine.

In terms of sexuality, the analyses focusing on the cultural basis of risky sexual practices help to promote a vision of Africa as a breeding ground for AIDS, and of Africans themselves as an obstacle to limiting HIV spread. The discourses in circulation about the refusal to use condoms, the absence of male circumcision in certain regions, or the practice of the levirate, are examples of a culturalist approach to AIDS which sets up culture as the only explanatory factor in the current situation of the continent having to face up to AIDS. Within this culturalist framework, the refusal, or, at least, the reticence with regard to condom use, is justified by two types of argument. First, it is a form of contraception, and African populations in general are said to be opposed to all forms of birth control. Second, condom use is said to go against certain cultural representations of fluids and exchanges of body fluids in as much as the nourishing sperm cannot be deposited in the vagina. These two responses are part of a series of cultural banalities that mask the fact that the difficulty in accepting condom use – which is by no means general throughout the continent – cannot be explained by cultural traits. It does not address, for example, the central question of negotiating sex (Ulin 1992), and the power relations between women and men. Such considerations are both more universal and more particularistic, and cannot be reduced to problems of local culture (in terms of a region, or an ethnicity), or, indeed, to 'African' culture.

The absence of male circumcision (and the absence of monogamy or of matrilineal descent) have been proposed by the Caldwells (1993) as factors contributing to HIV spread. They draw on an explanation derived from the biomedical literature in the early 1970s, and which enjoys a large measure of consensus. The Caldwells have superimposed an 'AIDS belt' on maps to illustrate the use of these cultural practices in Africa. The designation of these zones with their notion of cultures at risk is both problematic and dangerous. From anthropological and epidemiological perspectives, what is set out here as the norm can be contradicted by a whole range of exceptions. In Côte d'Ivoire, there is no evidence whatsoever that the practice of circumcision has contributed to limiting HIV spread. No doubt the presence of certain medical co-factors, like STDs can be adduced. But in this case, what is the point of using maps if not to highlight the relation between HIV spread and the geographical representation of cultures? In a more recent update, Caldwell (1995) recognizes the exceptional situation of the Abidjan region. In our view, this is an additional reason for avoiding any geographical representation of disease based on a notion of a 'belt' which, by definition (and visual representation) sets itself up as all-inclusive; and in so doing draws attention to 'risk cultures'. Furthermore, by presenting cultural practices in their 'positive' or 'negative' lights, as if somehow fixed or immobile, the researcher is not able to reflect on their dynamics.

The levirate – a practice by which a widow must marry her brother-in-law – is often presented as a 'cultural fact'. This is being interpreted in a number of different ways in the context of AIDS, as 'cultural specificities', and hence as obstacles. Many anthropologists offer quite different explanations. In the event, if a woman is given into the care of, and even married to, her brother-in-law without any sexual consummation (which is generally the case if the widow is elderly), the aim of the levirate is still achieved (to live within the family line to which the children belong). And in this way the possible infection of another person through sexual transmission is avoided. If it is a young widow, the problem lies not so much in the levirate but in the risk of transmitting the virus, and hence the need for a form of protected sex. This is the function of IEC (Information Education Communication) campaigns. In general, if attention is focused on the risk of transmission to partners, and on educating family and carers in prevention and care, then the stigmatizing effect of the culturalist discourse on sexuality, male circumcision and the levirate may be avoided.

Metaphors in doctor–patient communication

A second major effect of the culturalist discourse is found in the ways in which metaphors work. HIV patients living in Abidjan were followed up over a period of four years while they were undergoing simultaneous treatment for tuberculosis, a common co-factor. When hospital doctors explain HIV serostatus to patients, they do so by means of a metaphor. They say that the HIV positive patient has 'bad blood', or 'weak blood', or 'microbes in the blood'; and they do this to avoid a panic reaction. Patients questioned about this experience said they preferred a precise explanation of their serostatus to metaphorical language. The problem is that this metaphor, and the deliberate avoidance of phrases like the 'HIV virus', fails to convey that they are HIV positive. There is a further paradox and 'mismatch' in that the blood metaphor, apart from lacking precision, sets up a deep-seated fear and panic reaction, precisely what doctors were seeking to avoid in eschewing a direct explanation. Patients completing their anti-TB treatment look and feel as if they are cured of all their health problems. They do not associate blood with HIV, and using a blood metaphor to give HIV test results does not convey the facts, so that after leaving the clinic patients feel they can abandon preventive measures.

Metaphor as a means of accessing cultural representations in this context is unhelpful. Similarly, the temptation to encourage 'shared confidentiality' (the sharing of sensitive information by health professionals and named family carers, as in the model developed by the Chikinkata, in rural Zambia) presupposes that the family not only has the capacity to accept the illness, but also that its members will offer support and be active on the patient's behalf. In some settings, a supportive response from close family may exist and may be encouraged through community-based and peer-led education, as in rural KwaZulu-Natal, South Africa (McCoy 1995; McCoy and Coleman 1995; Nxumalo 1996; Seidel 1996a). However, to assume that this is the general case suggests an a priori cultural bias based on stereotypes. A prime example is the stereotype of the hard-pressed but infinitely inexhaustible support of the extended family throughout 'Africa', despite its variety of forms and changing patterns, and the evidence to the contrary. Furthermore, systematic family solidarity which can be observed for certain diseases will not necessarily be mobilized when the group is confronted with a case of AIDS.

The use of metaphor to convey information about disease and illness and to inform family members takes on a different dimension when applied to a seropositive woman. The risks involved in conveying serostatus through the blood metaphor are much greater when the recipient is a woman. When an unmarried woman is told that 'her blood is bad', and that she should not have a child, she will deduce this information to mean that there is no possibility of her finding a man who will agree to marry her knowing that they would not have children together. Furthermore, in a number of African contexts, including in Côte d'Ivoire, there is a lack of clarity in the information imparted about the rates of mother-to-child transmission (Desclaux 1994). The potential baby/child is talked about as being systematically infected if the mother is seropositive, and irrespective of the dates when she was first infected, or reinfected, or of her viral load, all of which are significant. Transmission rates for perinatal transmission in Africa vary between 30 and 40 per cent. The uncertainties this information generates, far from helping a woman to 'live positively' with the virus, only serve to heighten her anxiety.

These women's experiences suggest the dangers of health professionals resorting to metaphors as if they had a fixed, indisputable meaning shared by all, and irrespective of gender. In institutionalized settings women patients are not able to engage the doctor as an active subject, or challenge them through advocacy or other representative channels. Culturalist assumptions deflect practitioners from gaining a good knowledge of the family, social contexts and support mechanisms available to HIV positive women and women with AIDS. This is because these discourses position women as mothers and carers for men – a further instrumentalization of women (see Carovano 1991; Seidel and Ntuli 1996).

Culturalist discourse and assumptions about traditional healers

The third aspect of culturalist discourse in Côte d'Ivoire relates to 'traditional healers'. Modern 'Western' medicine is usually set up in opposition to traditional healing. Furthermore, the latter is seen as an undifferentiated cultural trait. Our Abidjan study shows that this 'way of thinking' limits an understanding of patients' pragmatic health-seeking behaviours. According to our observations, seropositive patients seeking treatment as well as an explanation for their illness have recourse to different representations of 'traditional' medicine. They move frequently from one healer to another. Unsuccessful treatments by healers are common. More to the point, they are recognized and interpreted by the patient. The patients do not enthuse about traditional medicine as such, but emphasize the skills of one healer compared with another, and the fact that they offer different approaches to modern medicine. In other words, they displace the simplistic, static and conventional dichotomy of modern versus traditional medicine, and focus instead on comparisons between treatments that have been clearly identified. Self-medication using plants will be preferred to a healer whose treatments are very expensive. There is also a preference for the small-scale health structure as opposed to care provision dispensed in large hospitals. Patients compare, test and evaluate these different treatments in relation to their needs – treatment, or psychological support, or explanations about the cause or likely progression of the illness. In this way, the patients' health-seeking behaviours, which at this stage are chosen independently and outside of the category of 'modern' or 'traditional', illustrate the inadequacy of any culturalist interpretation.

It follows that cultural interpretations of illness (its manifestations, treatment and prevention) should be regarded with caution. There is danger in any explanations of behaviour which, under the guise of 'African specificities', are prevented from mapping the changing and innovatory responses both of people living with HIV/AIDS, and of doctors and nurses. The range of these responses can only be fully taken into account in a broad dialogue to which anthropology can contribute.

CONCLUSION

What policy debates are being engaged around these discourses and what are their implications? The effect of the overlapping arguments and especially the culturalist discourse which constructs 'Africa' as incapable of change – including adapting to condom use – and which 'explains' this in terms of certain immutable 'cultural traits', and 'cultural facts', would seem to have had a negative impact on international funding. This culturalist discourse also leads to various doomsday scenarios which are being associated with 'Africa' as an undifferentiated whole. Such doomsday scenarios are not attached to other continents. This is compounded by effects of the neo-liberal discourse and its individualistic and medico-moral health promotion frameworks (Grace 1993) whereby someone who gets ill or infected, including through HIV, has only themselves to blame.

Now that it is clear that there is no 'magic bullet', and that major medical funding is also hard to come by, there is a small policy window open to social scientists, at least in southern Africa, where there is growing recognition of the usefulness of their contribution and of refined qualitative methodologies to analyse the social dimensions of HIV spread. However, this may be happening through default. Furthermore, social sciences have developed very unevenly throughout the continent, suggesting that further capacity-building is crucial. This calls for sensitive North–South as well as South–South cooperation and exchange. The latter is not likely to be seen as a funding priority.

Policy discussions around HIV in Africa, particularly in international gatherings and in most clinical articles papers, with few exceptions (e.g. Cliff and Smallman 1991), tend to assume that HIV spread is somehow occurring in a political vacuum and as if the purely medically-defined priorities – identified as the early treatment and prevention of STDs – could be uniformly and immediately addressed, without competing priorities. In South Africa, where the epidemic is still in its ascendant phase and is seen primarily to be affecting young women, HIV spread is taking place, as in many other settings on the continent, in situations of civil unrest and high levels of violence. Outside the AIDS service organizations, AIDS is seen as a secondary problem compared with violence in the townships, which is now targeted at whole families and which in turn leads to homelessness, another major risk factor (Evian 1995). These constraints are particularly well understood by community workers, but less so by many urban-based health professionals who have been largely shielded from violence. These professionals are closer to the policy community than are grass roots health workers. One woman community health worker put it like this: 'We could take a condom and use it to cover our whole house – but would that protect us?'

These are some of the constraints of HIV and STD policy-making and implementation in a country in transition, where policy is said to be 'people-led', and where the contribution of NACOSA (National AIDS Convention of South Africa) has been impressive. However, inevitably, it is also largely dependent on external funding; in the post-apartheid period, the former international sources of NGO sponsorship now go directly to government, thereby effectively limiting NGO participation. Research that uses more dialogic methodology (Bakhtin 1981) to elicit and engage with the experiences, needs and priorities of the most vulnerable, liaising where possible with their associations, and subsequently confronting these experiences with medical knowledge, discourse and medical practice, and with culturalist discourses, is of paramount importance. Findings may be used to lobby decision-makers and stake holders (Heise et al. 1994), although, realistically, policy windows do not remain open for long. This is part of a politico-discursive practice. However, such work and initiatives are rare. Furthermore, knowledge gained in this way – by studying 'sideways' (Schrijvers 1993) or by creating 'productions of sense' from minority discourses (Guillaumin 1978) – have to fight for recognition, against an epistemological violence. Could it be that the increased privatization of research and consortia 'bids' within neo-liberal frameworks increasingly dominated and cost-driven by the World Bank, and the limited funding available for largely qualitative work within anthropological rather than managerial time frames, breed more compliant researchers who are insufficiently challenging dominant discourses?

ACKNOWLEDGEMENTS

Gill Seidel would like to thank TASO, Uganda, especially Noerine Kaleeba; colleagues at the Universities of Ile-Ife and Lagos in Nigeria. In South Africa, in 1994: the British Council and institutional hosts, the Centre for Health Policy, University of the Witwatersrand, Johannesburg, community groups, Alan and Claire Fleming (Baragwanath Hospital and SAFO, Soweto), Clive Evian (Forbes International), and colleagues in Social Psychology, University of Cape Town; and in 1995: the Centre for Epidemiological Research, Durban, the regional NACOSA, Diakonia, and colleagues at Hlabisa Hospital, at Amatikulu Primary Health Care Training Centre and at the University of Natal. She would also like to thank the Nuffield Foundation, which supported this work.

Laurent Vidal would like to thank Dr Malick Coulibaly, Director of the Programme National de Lutte contre le SIDA (PNLS) (Côte d'Ivoire) and Doulhourou Coulibaly of the PNLS Tuberculosis Department. As former Chief Medical Officers of the Anti-Tuberculosis Centre of Abidjan, they supported this research on people infected with HIV from 1990–4. Thanks also to Dr Adama Coulibaly of the Department of Epidemiology at the Institut National de Santé et Développment in Paris for the invitation to participate in the UNESCO Symposium on Illness, Culture, Communication and Environment, Bamako, March 1995.

NOTES

1 The work on culturalist discourse in Côte d'Ivoire draws on an article by
   L. Vidal, presented at the Symposium 'Illnesses, culture, communication, and environment', UNESCO, Bamako, March 1995. (The French
   text was translated by GS.)
2 This includes important critiques of the Cartesian universal subject, the
   subject of Enlightenment discourse (Capitan 1988, 1993). This 'universalism' has profoundly shaped Western thought and categories, including
   public health discourse. The approach to discourse developed here
   embraces largely French work in discourse, linguistics, semiotics, sociology, anthropology, philosophy, social policy, social theory; while
   feminist epistemology offers a critique of this knowledge production.
   Feminist theoretical work concerned with relations of domination is
   exemplified in the French journal *Questions féministes* from 1978 (translated in part in *Feminist Issues*, Berkeley: University of California); also
   in other works of Guillaumin (for example, 1972, 1992), Mathieu (1991),
   Michard-Marchal and Ribéry (1982) and Michard (1997). For work
   produced by members of the CNRS team set up by M. Tournier and G.
   Seidel to investigate discourses of the Right, see Seidel 1984, 1988.
3 The approach to discourse adopted here is a more historicized and political project than both 'critical linguistics', and psychological discursive
   work in the UK. It does, however, share post-colonial concerns with
   newer work from feminism and psychology in as much as minority
   discourse places oppression at the centre of its concerns. This approach
   is distinguished from applied language studies in that it has a more
   heightened   concern   with   social   and   critical   theory   than   the
   linguistically-based work derived importantly from Hallidayan linguistics (Fairclough 1989, 1992), although there are affinities in terms of
   'emancipatory discursive practices'. Analyses of social movements, as
   exemplified in Laclau (1996) and Escobar (1992), and how they bring
   about 'new productions of sense', have also been important points of
   reference, although gender is not a central category in that work. The
   international journals that best represent this work and some of these
   key influences are *Discourse and Society* (Sage) edited by T. van Dijk,
   University of Amsterdam (see Van Dijk 1990) and *Feminist Issues*
   (Berkeley: University of California).
4 In government and international fora, which include NGOs, a determined post-Beijing challenge continues to be organized to reproductive
   rights and to sexually-defined issues. This challenge is led by the
   Vatican, as exemplified in the UN Habitat II Conference (Istanbul, June
   1996) (*Open File* July 1996: 1).

REFERENCES

Armstrong, S. (1994) 'Rape, an invisible part of apartheid's legacy', in C.
   Sweetman (ed.) *Population and Reproductive Rights*, London: Zed Press.
Bakhtin, M. (1981) *The Dialogic Imagination*, Austin: University of Texas
   Press.

Bassett, M. T. and Mhloyi, M. (1991) 'Women and AIDS in Zimbabwe: the making of an epidemic', *International Journal of Health Services* 21 (1): 143–56.

Baylies, C. and Bujra, J. (1995) 'Discourses of power and empowerment in the fight against HIV/AIDS in Africa', in P. Aggleton and G. Hart (eds) *AIDS, Sexuality and Risk*, London: Taylor and Francis.

Berer, M. and Ray, S. (eds) (1993) *Women and HIV/AIDS. An International Resource Book*, London: Pandora.

Bisseret-Moreau, N. (1988) 'The discourse of demographic "reproduction"', in G. Seidel (ed.) *The Nature of the Right. A Feminist Analysis of Order Patterns*, Amsterdam: Benjamins (Critical Theory Series).

Bloch, M. (ed.) (1975) *Political Language and Oratory in Traditional Society*, London: Academic Press.

Caldwell, J. C. (1995) 'Lack of male circumcision and AIDS in sub-Saharan Africa – resolving the conflict', *Health Transition Review* 5 (1): 113–17.

Caldwell, J. and Caldwell, P. (1993) 'The nature and limits of the sub-Saharan epidemic', *Population and Development* 18 (4): 817–48.

Capitan, C. (1988) 'Status of women in French revolutionary/liberal ideology', in G. Seidel (ed.) *The Nature of the Right,* Amsterdam: Benjamins (Critical Theory Series).

—— (1993) *La Nature à l'Ordre du Jour 1789–1793*, Paris: Kimé.

Carael, M. (1990) 'Women's vulnerability to STD/HIV in sub-Saharan Africa: an increasing evidence', paper presented to the IUSSP seminar on Women and Demographic Change in sub-Saharan Africa, Dakar, March.

Carovano, K. (1991) 'More than mothers and whores: redefining the AIDS prevention needs for women', *International Journal of Health Services* 21 (1): 131–42.

Cerullo, M. and Hammond, E. (1988) 'AIDS and Africa: the western imagination and the dark continent', *Radical America* 21 (2/3): 17–23.

Chimera-Dam, J. (1996) 'Contraception prevention in rural South Africa', *International Family Planning Perspectives* 21 (1): 4–9.

Cliff, S. A. and Smallman, M. R. (1991) 'Civil war and the spread of AIDS in Central Africa', *Epidemiological Infections* 107.

Colebunders, R. et al. (1995) 'Improving the quality of care for persons with HIV infection in sub-Saharan Africa', *Tropical and Geographical Medicine* 457 (2): 78–81.

Collignon, R., Gruénais, M-E., Vidal, L. (eds) (1994) 'L'Annonce de la séropositivité', *Psychopathologie Africaine* (Paris) 26 (2).

Cook, J. (1993) 'International human rights and reproductive rights', *Studies in Family Planning* 24 (2): 73–86.

Crawford, A. (1994) 'Black patients/White doctors', paper presented to the First World Congress of African Linguistics, Kwasuleni, Swaziland.

de Bruyn, M. and van der Hoeven, F. (1994) 'Primary health care and AIDS: African experience', *AIDS Bulletin* (South Africa) 3 (1): 1–4.

de Cock, K., Lucas, S. B., Agness, J., Kadio, A. and Gayle, H. D. (1993)

'Clinical research, prophylaxis, therapy and care for HIV disease in Africa', *American Journal of Public Health* 83 (10): 1385–9.

de Koning, K. and Martin, M. (eds) (1996) *Participatory Research in Health*, London: Zed Press.

Denenberg, R. (1990) 'Unique aspects of HIV infection in women and symptoms', in C. Chris, M. Pearl and ACT UP/New York Women and Book Group (eds) *Women, AIDS and Activism*, Boston: South End Press.

Desclaux, A. (1994) 'Silence as a form of public health policy? Breastfeeding and HIV transmission', *Sociétés d'Afrique et SIDA* (Bordeaux) 6 (octobre): 2–4.

Escobar, A. (1992) 'Anthropology and the study of social movements', *Critique of Anthropology* 12 (4): 395–432.

Evian, C. R. (1994) 'Addressing AIDS in a primary health care way', *AIDS Bulletin* (South Africa) 3 (1): 1–4.

—— (1995) 'The socio-economic determinants of the AIDS epidemic in South Africa – a cycle of poverty', *South African Journal of Medicine* (editorial) 38 (9): 635–6.

Fairclough, N. (1989) *Language and Power*, London: Longman.

—— (1992) *Discourse and Social Change*, Cambridge: Polity Press.

—— (ed.) (1993) *Critical Language Awareness*, London: Longman.

Frankenberg, F. (1989) 'One epidemic or three?' in P. Aggleton, G. Hart and P. Davies (eds) *AIDS – Social Representations, Social Practices*, London: Falmer Press.

Gilmour, E. (1995) 'Nonoxyl 9 and women's struggle against HIV infection', *AIDS Analysis Africa* (SA edition), December–January 1995/6: 1.

Gordon, G. and Kanstrup, C. (1992) 'Sexuality – the missing link in women's health', *IDS Bulletin* (International Development Studies, University of Sussex) 23 (1): 29–37.

Grace, V. M. (1993) 'The marketing of empowerment and the construction of the health consumer', *Health Promotion International* 8 (12): 147–57.

Green, E. C. et al. (1995) 'The experience of an AIDS-prevention program focused on South African traditional healers', *Social Science and Medicine* 40 (4): 503–15.

Grillo, R. (ed.) (1989) *Social Anthropology and the Politics of Language*, London: Routledge.

Gruénais, M-E. and Vidal, L. (1994) 'Médecins, malades et structures sanitaires: Témoignages de practiciens à Abidjan et Brazzaville', *Psychopathologie Africaine* XXVI (2): 247–63.

Guillaumin, C. (1972) *L'idéologie raciste. Genèse et langage actuel*, Paris/Hague: Mouton.

—— (1992) *Sexe, Race, et Pratique du Pouvoir, L'Idée de Nature*, Paris: Côté-femmes editions.

Hadden, B. et al. (1995) 'Women's health-seeking and contraceptive behaviour and its implications for STD/HIV prevention' (Abstract WeD 895), paper presented to 9th International Conference on AIDS in Africa, Kampala, Uganda.

Hamblin, J. and Reid, E. (1993) *Les femmes, l'epidémie d'infections par le*

VIH et les droits de la personne: un impératif tragique, Programme VIH et développement, New York: PNUD.

Heise, L. L. and Elias, C. (1995) 'Transforming AIDS to meet women's needs: a focus on developing countries', *Social Science and Medicine* 40 (7): 931–43.

Heise, L. L. et al. (1994) 'Violence against women: a neglected public health issue in less developed countries', *Social Science and Medicine* 29 (9): 1165–79.

Heyward, W. L. et al. (1993) 'Impact of HIV counselling and testing among child-bearing women in Kinshasa Zaïre', *AIDS* 7 (12): 1633–7.

Janks, H. and Ivanic, R. (1993) 'Critical language awareness', in N. Fairclough (ed.) *Critical Language Awareness*, London: Longman.

Kabeer, N. (1994) *Reversed Realities – Gender Hierarchies in Development Thought*, London: Verso.

Karin, Q. A., Karin, S.S.A., Soldan, K. and Zandi, M. (1995) 'Reducing the risk of HIV infection among South African sex workers: socio-economic and gender barriers', *American Journal of Public Health* 85 (11): 1521–1525.

Kisekka, M. N. (1990) 'AIDS in Uganda as a gender issue', *Women's Health In Africa, Women and Therapy* 10 (3): 35–54.

KIT (Royal Tropical Institute), WHO and SAFAIDS (1995) *Facing the Challenges of STDs, HIV/AIDS: A Gender-based Response*, Amsterdam: KIT.

Klugman, B. (1993) 'Balancing means and ends: population policy in South Africa', *Reproductive Health Matters* 1 (May): 44–57.

Laclau, E. (1996) *Emancipation(s)*, London: Verso.

Levin, C. (1990) 'Women and HIV/AIDS research: the barriers to equity', *Evaluation Review* 14: 447–63.

Marcus, T., Oellermann, K. and Levin, N. (1995) *AIDS Education and Prevention – a Feasibility Study for a Pilot Intervention with Commercial Sex Workers and Long Distance Truck Drivers in the Natal Midlands*, Pietermaritzberg: University of Natal.

Mathieu, N-C. (1974) 'Notes towards a sociological definition of sex categories', *The Human Context* 6 (2) (French edition 1971).

—— (ed.) (1985) *L'Araisonnement des femmes. Essais en anthropologie des sexes*, Paris: Editions de l'Ecole des Hautes Etudes en Sciences Sociales, Collection Les Cahiers de l'Homme.

—— (1991) *L'anatomie politique, Catégorisations et idéologies du sexe*, Paris: Côté-Femmes, Collection recherches.

Mbali, C. (1995) 'Multi-lingual medical communication – the challenges for curricular development', Durban: Natal Medical School (unpublished paper).

McCoy, D. (1995) 'Appropriate HIV testing and counselling – making the most of limited resources', *AIDS Scan* (editorial) 7 (4): 1–2.

McCoy, D. and Coleman, R. (1995) 'Responding to the HIV epidemic in a rural district health service in KwaZulu-Natal (Hlabisa Health Ward)', *Epidemiological Comments* 22 (7): 144–7.

Merson, M. (1990) 'Report on the Meeting on research priorities relating to women and HIV/AIDS', Geneva: WHO, Global Programme on AIDS, 3 (November): 19–20.

Michard, C. (1997) *Le Sexe et le Genre en Français Contemporain*, Paris: Editions L'Harmattan.

Michard-Marchal, C. and Ribéry, C. (1982) *Sexisme et Sciences humaines*, Lille: Presses Universitaires de Lille.

Motsei, M. (1993) 'Detection of women battering in health care settings: the case of Alexandra Health Centre', Johannesburg: University of the Witswatersrand (Women's Health Project and Centre for Health Policy).

Msaky, H. I. (1992) 'Women, AIDS and sexual violence in Africa', *Vena Journal* 4 (2).

Nelson, N. (1987) ' "Selling her kiosk": Kikuyu notions of sexuality and sex for sale in Mathare Valley, Kenya', in P. Caplan (ed.) *The Cultural Construction of Sexuality*, London: Tavistock.

Nxumalo, Z. (1996) 'Peer group education to empower against HIV infection in KwaZulu-Natal, Policy Report' (provisional title), M.Sc. thesis, London School of Hygiene and Tropical Medicine.

Oppong, C. (1995) 'A high price to pay: for education, subsistence or a place in the job market', *Health Transition Review* 5 (supplement): 35–56.

Packard, R. P. and Epstein, P. (1991) 'Epidemiologists and the structure of medical research on AIDS in Africa' (Boston University Africa Studies Center, Working Papers No 137, 1989), *Social Science and Medicine* 29: 265–76.

Palec, A. le (1996) 'Le SIDA, une maladie des femmes', paper presented to the International Conference on Social Sciences and AIDS in Africa, Senegal, 4–8 November.

Palec, A. le and Diarra, T. (1995) 'Révélations du SIDA à Bamako. Le "traitement" de l'information', in J-P. Dozon and L.Vidal (eds) *Les sciences sociales face au SIDA. Cas africains autour de l'exemple ivoirien*, Abidjan: ORSTOM Petit-Bassam.

Parkin, D. J. (1984) 'Political language', *Annual Review of Anthropology* 13: 345–65.

Patton, C. (1992) 'From nation to family; containing "African AIDS" ', in A. Parker et al. (eds) *Nationalisms and Sexualities*, London: Routledge.

Persson, E. (1994) 'The threat of AIDS to the health of women', *International Journal of Gynaecology and Obstetrics* 46: 189–93.

Peters, J. and Wolper, A. (eds) (1995) *Women's Rights, Human Rights*, London: Routledge.

Pheterson, G. (1990) 'The category of "prostitute" in scientific enquiry', *Journal of Sex Research* 27 (3): 397–407.

Pieterse, J. N. (1990) *White on Black. Images of Africa and Blacks in Western Popular Culture*, New Haven/London: Yale University Press.

Pittin, R. (1984) 'Marriage and alternative strategies: career patterns of Hausa women in Katsina City', Ph.D. thesis, SOAS, London University.

Plaat, M. V. (1995) 'Beyond technique: issues in evaluating for empowerment', *Evaluation* 1 (1).

Preston-Whyte, E. (1995) '"Bring us the female condom": HIV intervention, gender and political empowerment in two South African communities', *Health Transition Review* 5 (supplement): 209–22.

Ranger, T. and Stack, P. (eds) (1992) *Epidemics and Ideas*, Cambridge: Cambridge University Press.

Rathgeber, E. M. (1990) 'WID, WAD, GAD: trends in research and practice', *Journal of Developing Areas* 24: 489–502.

Reid, E. (1992) 'Gender, knowledge and responsibility', in J. M. Mann et al. (eds) *AIDS in the World*, Cambridge MA: Harvard University Press.

—— (1995) 'Placing women at the centre of the analysis: the case of HIV/AIDS', *Pacific Health Dialogue* 2 (1): 69–72.

Rispel, L. (1994) 'Community strategies to overcome violence against women in the greater Johannesburg area', Draft, Centre for Health Policy, University of the Witwatersrand.

Schoepf, B. G. (1993a) 'AIDS action-research with women in Kinshasa, Zaire', *Social Science and Medicine* 37 (11): 140–3.

—— (1993b) 'Women at risk: case studies from Zaire', in M. Berer and S. Ray (eds) *Women and HIV/AIDS*, London: Pandora.

Schopper, D., Doussantousse, S. and Orav, J. (1993) 'Sexual behaviours relevant to HIV transmission in a rural African population. How much can a KAP survey tell us?' *Social Science and Medicine* 37 (3): 401–12.

Schrijvers, J. (1993) *The Violence of 'Development': A Choice for Intellectuals*, Amsterdam: International Books.

Scott, S. J. and Mercer, M. A. (1994) 'Understanding cultural obstacles to HIV/AIDS prevention in Africa', *AIDS Education and Prevention* 6 (1): 81–9.

Seidel, G. (ed.) (1984) 'Le discours d'exclusion, les mises à distance, le non-droit, Introduction au numéro spécial', *L'Autre, L'Etranger, présence et exclusion dans le discours, MOTS* 8: 5–16.

—— (1987) 'The white discursive order. The British New Right's discourse on cultural racism', in M. Diáz-Diocaret, T. van Dijk and I. Zavala (eds) *Literature, Discourse, Psychiatry*, Amsterdam: Benjamins.

—— (ed.) (1988) *The Nature of the Right. A Feminist Analysis of Order Patterns*, Amsterdam: Benjamins (Critical Theory Series).

—— (1989) ' "Thank God I said NO to AIDS": on the changing discourse of AIDS in Uganda', *Discourse and Society* 1: 61–84.

—— (1993a) 'The competing discourses of HIV/AIDS in sub-Saharan Africa: discourses of rights/empowerment vs discourses of control and exclusion', *Social Science and Medicine* 36 (3): 175–94.

—— (1993b) 'Women at risk: gender and AIDS in Africa', *Disasters* 17 (2): 133–42.

—— (1994) 'The marginalisation of the critical social sciences in AIDS interventions in Africa', unpublished seminar, Department of Social Psychology, University of Cape Town.

—— (1996a) 'Confidentiality and HIV status in KwaZulu-Natal, South Africa: implications, resistances and challenges', *Health Policy and Planning* 11 (4): 418–27.

—— (1996b) 'Le deuxième sexe de la prévention, *Journal du SIDA*, numéro spécial Afrique, juin/juillet: 32–5.

—— (1996c) 'Représentations des femmes dans le discours sur le

VIH/SIDA en Afrique sub-Saharienne', C. Capitan and C. Viollet (eds) *MOTS* (Numéro spécial, Sexes et Textes) 49 (décembre): 48–70.

Seidel, G. and Ntuli, N. (1996) 'HIV, confidentiality, gender and support in KwaZulu-Natal' (correspondence), *Lancet* 347: 469.

Sontag, S. (1979) *Illness as a Metaphor*, Harmondsworth: Penguin.

Standing, H. and Kisekka, N. (1989) *Sexual Behaviour in Sub-Saharan Africa: A Review and Annotated Bibliography*, London: Overseas Development Administration.

Stein, Z. (1994) 'Methods women can use', Communication to the Tenth International Conference on AIDS, Yokohama, Japan.

—— (1995) *American Journal of Public Health* (editorial) 85: 1485–6.

Strebel, A. (1993) 'Good intentions, contradictory outcomes?' *CHASA Journal of Comparative Health* 4 (1): 22–5.

—— (1994) 'The discourses on women and AIDS in South Africa', Ph.D. thesis, Dept of Social Psychology, University of the Western Cape.

Tabet, P. (1985) 'Fertilité naturelle, reproduction forcée', in N-C. Mathieu (ed.) *L'Araisonnement des femmes. Essais en anthropologie des sexes*, Paris: Editions de l'Ecole des Hautes Etudes en Sciences Sociales, Collection les Cahiers de l'Homme.

Temmerman, M., Ndinyaachola, J., Ambari, J. and Piot, P. (1990) 'Infection with HIV as a risk factor for adverse obstetrical outcome', *AIDS* 4: 1087–93.

—— (1995) 'The right not to know HIV test results', *Lancet* 345: 969–70.

Treichler, P. (1987) 'AIDS, homophobia and bio-medical discourse: an epidemic of signification', *Cultural Studies* 1: 3.

Ulin, P. (1992) 'African women and AIDS: negotiating behavioural change', *Social Science and Medicine* 34 (1): 63–73.

Van Dijk, T. E. (1990) 'Discourse and society: a new journal for a new research focus', *Discourse and Society* (editorial) 1 (1): 5–16.

Vidal, L. (1995) 'Enjeux d'une anthropologie de la connaissance du SIDA. Expériences des séropositifs des Centres Anti-Tuberculeux d'Abidjan', in J-P. Dozon and L. Vidal (eds) *Les sciences sociales face au SIDA*, Abidjan: Centre ORSTOM de Petit Bassam.

—— (1994) 'Le temps de l'annonce. Séropositivités vécues à Abidjan', *Psychopathologie Africaine* XXVI (2): 265–82.

Watney, S. (1988) 'AIDS, "moral panic theory" and homophobia', in P. Aggleton and H. Homans (eds) *Social aspects of AIDS*, Lewes: Falmer Press.

—— (1989) 'Missionary position, "Africa" and race', *Feminist Journal of Cultural Studies* 1: 83–100.

Watts, C., Foster, G. and Zwi, A. (1995) 'Using capture–recapture in promoting public health', *Health Policy and Planning* 10 (2): 198–203.

White, L. (1988) 'Domestic labour in a colonial city: prostitution in Nairobi 1900–1952, in S. B. Stichter and J. L. Parpart (eds) *Patriarchy and Class. African Women in the Home and Workplace*, Westview: Boulder.

Williams, E. E. (1995) 'Sexually transmitted diseases and condom interventions among prostitutes and their clients in Cross River State', *Health Transition Review* 5 (supplement): 223–8.

Wodak, R. (ed.) (1988) *Language and Power*, Amsterdam: Benjamins.

Wood, L. A. and Rennie, H. (1984) 'Formulating rape', *Discourse and Society* 5 (1): 125–48.

Worth, D. (1990) 'Sexual decision-making and AIDS: why condom promotion among vulnerable women is likely to fail', *Studies in Family Planning* 20: 297–307.

Zwi, A. D. (1993) 'Reassessing priorities: identifying the determinants of HIV transmission', *Social Science and Medicine* (editorial) 36 (5): iii–viii.

Zwi, A.D. and Cabral, A. J. (1991) 'Identifying "high risk situations" for preventing AIDS', *British Medical Journal* 303: 1527–9.

Chapter 4

Patients' bodies and discourses of power

Helle Ploug Hansen

Anthropology today has moved away from studying 'a people' as a bounded culture, and anthropologists no longer find it appropriate to speak about 'migrants', 'Italians' or other social categories as bearers of a culture. Culture is not something already given, but rather something that is continuously generated and negotiated in the society (Liep and Olwig 1994: 12). This new perspective on culture implies among other things that anthropology has reconceptualized its *field of research*. Fieldwork is no longer conducted in ethnographic islands studying a local population, and the previous images of cultures as systems of meaning or as texts are obsolete (Hastrup and Hervik 1994: 2). The ethnographer is no longer considered an objective and neutral person distantiated from the field of research. Rather, fieldwork can be understood as an intersubjective experience in which the ethnographer invests herself and becomes a part of the field of research. In my chapter, this perspective of culture and fieldwork form the background of a study of policy in a hospital setting.

POLICY IN A HOSPITAL SETTING

Anthropologists are seeking new strategic goals for their scientific life with a shift of interest from structure to practice, or from pattern to process (Hastrup and Hervik 1994: 3). In this chapter, policy is viewed as a strategic goal of science and understood as a site where nurses, doctors and patients compete about the symbolic capital which is recognized within this particular field (Bourdieu 1990: 68). Following Bourdieu, a *field* can be understood as a group of people (here nurses and doctors). Through symbolic and social solidarity they use values, symbols and forms of behaviour as signs of their fellowship, and establish common goals for what is worth striving for. Within the field, nurses and doctors continuously seek control over the knowledge and the qualities (the symbolic capital) that give access to their specific fields (ibid.: 66–7).

In the communication among nurses, doctors and patients on the oncology ward, different discourses of power are at stake. Following a Foucauldian approach, I see power in the context of the medical encounter not as a unitary entity, nor as something that is only repressive, but rather as something that is constitutive and enabling, producing subjectivity and knowledge (Foucault 1980: 59; Lupton 1994: 111). Power can thus be viewed as a strategic relation which is invisible and diffuse. It is everywhere enforced as much by authority figures as by unconscious self-surveillance (Lupton 1994: 112).

I argue that these discourses of power can be understood as means to get access to symbolic capital and that a study of policy is, among other things, inseparable from issues of power. In relation to the field of nurses and doctors, symbolic capital is connected to the high status of the written hospital policy document and the nurses' policy document. The empirical data I present were gathered through one year of ethnographic fieldwork studying a highly specialized medical oncology department at a university hospital in Copenhagen, Denmark.[1] The oncology department included two floors with room for sixty patients, an out-patient clinic and a radiotherapy department. Participant-observation of nurse–doctor communication and nurse–doctor–patient communication, ethno- graphic interviews with patients and health personnel and different kinds of written hospital policy documents formed my field of research. The biologist and anthropologist Gregory Bateson's theory of communication was the meta-theoretical framework within which data was constructed and analysed. Following Bateson, communication includes verbal and non-verbal communi- cation (gestures, mimicry, behaviour, acts, etc.) as well as silence and passivity. Through communication human beings create meaning. Some of the presented data will be analysed following the theories of anthropologists Lock and Scheper-Hughes (1990: 50), who divide the human body into three bodies at three separate but over- lapping conceptual and analytical levels. The first level is the individual body, understood in a phenomenological sense of the lived experience of the body-self. The second level is the social body, referring to the representational uses of the body as a natural symbol with which to think about nature, society, and culture. At the third level is the body-politic, in which the state controls, regulates and surveys the conduct of bodies on the individual and group level in order to maintain social stability (Lock and Scheper-Hughes 1990: 50; Lupton 1994: 21–2).

THE HOSPITAL AS A NEGOTIATED ORDER

In 1963 the sociologists Strauss, Schatzman, Ehrlich, Bucher and Sabshin made a pioneering attempt to conceptualize the hospital as a continuing process of organizing and negotiating meaning (Strauss et al. 1963: 147–70). They analysed the hospital as a *negotiated order* showing how the policy of the hospital, to return patients to the outside world in better shape, was the symbolic cement that held the organization together (ibid.: 154). This vaguely articulated goal was adhered to by all the health care professionals, but masked disagreement and discrepancies on how to achieve this goal. Their analysis was action-oriented and located culture in the surface of everyday activities (Wright 1994: 20). Strauss et al. emphasized the importance of regarding negotiations in the hospital as processes of give-and-take, diplomacy, and bargaining, focusing on the grounds for negotiation and the relationship of rules to negotiation (Strauss et al. 1963: 148–9).

My ethnographic data also revealed that the hospital policy was adhered to by all health care professionals, as well as some of the patients. But I suggest that the aim of negotiation between nurses and doctors is not so much a question about give-and-take or about diplomacy. As I shall show, the ongoing processes of negotiation by means of discourses of power are more about getting access to the symbolic capital which is recognized within the field.

THE HOSPITAL POLICY DOCUMENT

When I started my fieldwork study, I joined the newly employed health care professionals for a common introductory lecture to the hospital given by the director of the hospital in the lecture room. He read parts of the hospital policy document aloud, and encouraged us to make these goals our own. During my fieldwork in the oncology department I recognized that some parts of the hospital policy document played a particularly active part in the ongoing communication between nurses themselves, nurse aides and nurses, and between nurses and doctors.

The policy document had one overall aim: to give patients every possible investigation, treatment, care and service in all phases of life within the given resources. It was divided into four goals: (1) patient-related, (2) education and science related, (3) cooperation-related, and (4) information-related. Each of these goals was divided into four to six sentences. I shall only mention a few sentences of importance for my later analysis.

The patient-related goals attached special importance to equal communication and cooperation between patients and health care professionals with respect for the patients' integrity. The cooperation-related goals attached special importance to communication and dialogue between health care professionals. The information-related goals attached special importance to high levels of information about investigation, treatment, care and service to patients and relatives, and joint responsibility to patients.

These goals were also recorded in the oncology nurses' policy document which was handed out to all newly appointed nurses or nurse aides in the oncology department. On Danish television and in the newspapers, patients, relatives and health professionals frequently debate the need for better communication and high levels of information within the hospital setting. My argument is that this specific hospital policy document does not differ from the goals and ideals that are encompassed in the wider context of medical policy in Denmark in the 1990s.

THE CLINICAL PRAXIS

The next part of this chapter focuses on the process of policy in the clinical praxis of the oncology department in relation to how nurses and doctors administered the goals of equal cooperation between patients and health care professionals, communication between health care professionals, and high levels of information and joint responsibility.

The daily communication among nurses, and between nurses and doctors, often contained issues about the importance of high levels of information to the patients and their relatives, and the necessity for good communication and equal cooperation. During my participant-observation, dialogues with the nurses often contained sentences such as: 'If we are short of time we give priority to communicating well with the patients instead of for instance washing their backs or their feet. To listen to the patients and give understandable information is extremely important.' The nurses and doctors often said: 'We always encourage the patients to ask questions and to cooperate with us. A high level of information is a very important component in the treatment and care of cancer patients.' When I asked them if they could give me some examples of the information given, they often seemed a bit surprised and answers such as the following were common: 'Well, you know, information about treatment, diagnosis, investigation, side-effects of chemotherapy and so on.' The hospital policy document, the nurses' policy document, and the ongoing communication in the oncology ward demonstrated that nurses and doctors nearly always talked about information and communication as *form* without a *content*, or if they mentioned a content it was in a rather generalized non-specific way. From this point of view high levels of information, equal cooperation, etc., became a rather simple and unproblematic concept.

Following the Batesons' theory of communication, I suggest that the absence of a content can be understood as a feature of *non-communication*, which means that under certain circumstances some things are not communicated to someone (Bateson and Bateson 1990: 87–9). Within this perspective, communication about the content is unwanted, not because of fear but because communication would challenge the idea that it is unproblematic to receive informed consent about a new experimental treatment, or to break bad news to cancer patients about diagnoses, prognoses, hope, life and death. In relation to talking about the process of information and communication, both nurses and doctors have established common goals for what is worth striving for (the symbolic capital). They form one group of people (a field). This shows that Bourdieu's concepts of *field* and *capital* are dynamic and changeable. They are always defined and judged in social relationships (Bourdieu 1990: 14–15).

My participant-observation in the oncology department also revealed that the simplicity and the common goals encapsulated in the hospital policy document, the nurses' policy document and the ongoing nurse–doctor communication were absent in nurses' and doctors' communication with patients. Only in situations where treatment or caring actions were under attack, could the hospital policy be used as a justificatory rationale in the same way as Strauss and colleagues showed from their hospital study (Strauss et al. 1963: 154). Communication among nurses, patients and doctors showed that competition about the symbolic capital which was recognized within their particular field was at stake all the time. Communication was riddled with complexity and blurred the simplicity of the official written policy. Through different discourses of power, the hospital policy document and the nurses' policy document were articulated.

To grasp this complexity, participant-observation could not have been done in one site only. The ethnographer needs to include different sites or levels in the policy process (Wright and Shore 1994: 6). One site of the policy process was the hospital policy document and the nurses' policy document. Another site of the policy process was the ongoing nurse–doctor communication and the ongoing patient–nurse–doctor communication in the oncology department. Until now, I have focused on the policy documents and nurse–doctor communication. The next part of this chapter focuses on patient–nurse–doctor communication. I suggest that the *daily round* can be viewed as prototypical of this communication in relation to the administration of the hospital policy document, the nurses' policy document and nurse–doctor communication.

THE DAILY ROUND AND ITS INTERPRETATION

The aim of the round is to inform patients about investigations (perhaps make investigations on the patient's body), treatment, diagnosis and prognosis, care and service, and to answer questions from the patients. In the oncology department the round was divided into three parts. During the first part, the doctor and the nurse sat in the nurses' quarters preparing the round. The doctor read the records of each patient, while the nurse was sitting silently beside him only verbally interrupting him when there was something he did not know about, or if he asked her about something.[2] When this part had come to an end, the doctor and the nurse began the second part – *the round itself*.

The nurse pushed a little 'round wagon' on wheels in front of her, and the doctor walked beside her. In the sick rooms, the doctor asked questions, carried out tests, told patients about the results of earlier investigations and treatment, gave orders to the nurse about new tests, treatments, etc., and asked the patient if they had any questions. The nurse often stood behind the doctor at the foot of the bed. After the round, the doctor and the nurse began the third part, again in the nurses' quarters. The doctor dictated prescriptions into his dictaphone. The communication between the doctor and the nurse followed the same routine as in the first part of the round with the nurse sitting mainly silent.

In the beginning of my participant-observation of the daily rounds I found myself caught in a kind of political economy approach, informed by Marxist critiques of the nature of the capitalist economic system. This was the dominant intellectual approach in the 1970s when I received my education as a nurse (I started my anthropological career in the late 1980s). Within the political economy approach, I took over the nurses' perceptions of the daily round and interpreted the round as a routine, where the doctors made the important decisions about the patients, and where the nurses spent a lot of time waiting for the doctors. Day after day I sat in the nurses' quarters waiting together with the nurses for the doctors. In these waiting situations, the nurses often told me about how difficult it was to cooperate with the doctors about a precise moment of time to go on the round.

From this site the round became predictable. The doctor was embodied with power and control to administer time and the hospital policy document. The nurse was the passive helper in the background and the patient was a more or less helpless victim of the Danish health care system. I interpreted the doctor–patient relationship from a macro-social perspective as the equivalent of the capitalist–worker relationship, in which the former exploits the latter, and where the nurse becomes the advocate of the patient (Lupton 1994: 10).

After a few months, I changed my site of participant-observation. Instead of accompanying the nurses while waiting for the doctors, I followed the doctors in their daily work which was not only bound to the oncology department, but also included the out-patient clinic and the radiotherapy department. By doing so, it became clear that although the doctors were the ones who spoke during the rounds, it did not necessarily mean that the doctors also possessed the *power*. In our society, we have a tendency to presume that those who speak in public also are the ones who make the decisions (Knudsen 1990: 61).

The waiting, the passivity, and the silence of the nurses were not without meaning. Even though the nurses often stood in the background during the round itself, this was not sufficient to conclude that the doctor alone made decisions about the patient. Leaving my former political economic approach behind, I became aware of the nurses' non-verbal communication. If, for instance, a nurse did not agree with the doctor she could do several things. During the first part of the round, she could simply open the patient's record at the pages to which she wanted the doctor to pay attention, or she could point with her finger (rather obtrusively) to specific sentences in the record. During the round itself, she sometimes placed herself in front of the door so that the doctor could not leave the sick room before she was satisfied with the information given to the patient, or she sought eye-contact with the doctor, or said to the patient: 'You had something to ask the doctor, hadn't you?'

During the final part of the round, the nurse sat listening to the doctor's dictating. If she discovered that he had forgotten something, or if she did not agree with him, she interrupted his dictating by saying, for example: 'We usually do it in another way'. Especially if a new doctor went on the round, the following negotiation between the nurse and the doctor was predictable. The doctor would listen to the nurse's arguments and, after sitting silently for a moment, he would nod his head and agree with the nurse. If the nurse and the doctor could not come to an agreement, the nurse often sought her head nurse for support and increased power. As Strauss and colleagues showed, negotiations and agreements do not occur by chance. There is a patterned variability of negotiation, including, for instance, how agreements are made and who contracts with whom (Strauss et al. 1963: 162). I shall provide an example of this negotiation later in the chapter in relation to Case 3.

I would argue that both the doctors' verbal communication and the nurses' non-verbal communication can be understood as important parts of the discourses of power that control the social space, where the round is inscribed. These discourses of power take an active part in the administration of the hospital policy document and the nurses' policy document. What follows are three ethnographic examples to show how the hospital policy is articulated within the daily round.

Case 1: An uneasy feeling

This morning I have had a short dialogue with the doctor about 'a high level of information to the patients'. He has stressed that it is very important that patients understand the information given, and that they are allowed time to ask questions. The first part of the round is finished and we are on our way to the patients. The doctor walks into the sick room, holds the door for the nurse and me and closes it. The patient, a woman in her forties, is lying in bed. Her husband is standing beside her, holding her hand. The doctor goes to the patient's bed in a determined way. He looks for a short moment in the patient's record (which he already has studied during the first part of the round) and says: 'How are you today?'

The woman looks at him saying while shivering all the time: 'I'm freezing and it's difficult for me to breath.'

DOCTOR   Yes, it's an uneasy feeling. But it is not dangerous. It's because of your lungs. (*The doctor smiles and takes the hand of the woman. The nurse also smiles and moves closer to the bed.*)

PATIENT   Why do I have a fever now. I thought that I was going home soon?

DOCTOR   It's your disease. It has reached the lungs, but we think we have a new kind of medicine that can kill it. It is only a small part of your lungs that is being attacked.

PATIENT   I don't understand. I'm not feeling well. And what about my brain. Are there any metastasis? I want to get an answer on my CT-scan.

DOCTOR   The result has not arrived yet. And as I said, don't worry about your fever. We will find some medicine that can help you. Do you have more to ask me about?' (*Simultaneously he closes the record, and turns his back on the woman.*)

The woman shakes her head. The nurse seeks eye contact with the patient and says: 'I'll come back and talk things over with you when we have finished the round.'

PATIENT   (*in a determined way*) No, you don't have to. I'll talk with my husband.

The nurse smiles and claps the hand of the woman: 'Of course I'm coming. We are here to take care of you. We are here for your sake.'

The woman looks as if she is going to say something, but she only looks at her husband and mumbles: 'I just want to know what is going on in my body. I need information from the doctor.'

Case 2: The big toe and the stomach

A sixty-year-old woman is sitting, smiling, in a chair beside her bed when the doctor, nurse and I enter her room.

PATIENT Good morning doctor.

DOCTOR Good morning. How are you today?

PATIENT My stomach is so big (*she lifts her quilt, so the doctor can see her huge stomach*).

DOCTOR Yes, unfortunately your disease has come back. I have arranged a treatment tomorrow, we shall remove the liquid in your stomach. Don't worry. We will give you a local anaesthetic. We use . . .

PATIENT (*interrupting him*) No, it's not from the disease I got this big stomach. You see – more than a week ago I went to do some gardening and I sprained my left big toe, and two days after my stomach started to grow.

DOCTOR (*smiling*) No, no, it is *not* because of the sprain on your big toe. As I told you it's because of your disease.

The woman and the doctor were arguing for five minutes about the cause of the swollen stomach. At last the woman turned to the nurse, saying: 'Do you believe the doctor? Why do you always want to explain everything in my body in biomedical terms?'

The nurse seemed a bit confused before she answered: 'Well, I think it is the disease that has caused the big stomach, but it's more important that you get rid of it in a hurry. Isn't it?'

The woman nodded her head. The doctor smiled to the woman and to the nurse and they left the room. Back in the nurses' quarter the doctor laughed and said: 'This woman is crazy. She wouldn't understand that the disease has come again. She didn't listen to my information.'

The nurse answered him: 'I think you should have listened more to her explanation. I'll go and talk with her later.'

Case 3: The body at war

A ninety-year-old man is at the hospital for the first time in his life. He has an incurable cancer in the bladder with metastasis everywhere in the body. He has just arrived and the doctor is going to tell him about an experimental chemotherapeutic treatment. He needs to get an informed consent form from the patient before the treatment can be started. During the first part of the round the nurse had showed her disagreement with the doctor. She had listened to the doctor's argument, then she said: 'This man is too old for treatment. It would not do him any good. Lots of side effects and you know it. Let him die. And this is a new treatment, we don't know anything about it yet. Give him some painkillers and good nursing care.' For a while they were arguing, but at last the doctor said: 'I'll suggest this treatment for him. I think it will do him good.'

The nurse did not say any more and they went to the sick room. Here the doctor did the talking. The nurse stood silently in the background, close to the door, as if she did not want to be seen. The doctor said to the patient and his wife: 'Good morning. How are you today?'

The patient very slowly lifted his head from the pillow and started: 'Well . . .'

The doctor interrupted: 'We can offer you a treatment. It will give you a good time together with your wife, because it will knock down your cancer for a while.'

The wife stood beside the bed holding her husband's hand. She looked at the doctor and said: 'I really don't know if we are interested in treatment . . . , side effects and so on. And what about the immune system? It will protect his body, won't it? What will happen if the medicine not only kills the cancer cells, but also the normal cells . . . ? But if you say this will be the best for my husband, we agree.'

The doctor answered in this way: 'Well, it's right. The chemo can't distinguish between cancer cells and other cells. But we will carefully follow the immune system of your husband, don't worry [said in a joking fashion] and we will fight – and there are side effects, but not all patients get them, and we have medicine for those too.' The nurse did not wait until the doctor finished talking. She left the sick room and went directly to the office of the head nurse to tell her this story. The head nurse followed her back to the nurses' quarter where the doctor was already dictating his decisions. The head nurse interrupted him asking why such an old, dying patient should receive treatment. The doctor repeated what he had said earlier to the nurse and, before he continued his dictating, he said: 'I have informed both the patient and his wife about the treatment and the side-effects. It is their decision to say Yes or No.' The nurse and the head nurse shook their heads and left the doctor alone.

The plan of the doctor was that the old man should start treatment the next day, but the nurses delayed the execution of the treatment for two days with the excuse that there were no free beds in the chemotherapy unit. By this time, the old man was too sick to receive the treatment, and instead he was given terminal nursing care.

DISCOURSES OF POWER

These three cases show that nurses, doctors and patients communicate within different discourses of power. These discourses demonstrate conflicts of interest between patients, nurses and doctors. I argue that these conflicts of interest are expressed over a struggle for power over the sick body. This struggle may be explicit or implicit, and involves negotiation and manoeuvre at every step in the encounter.

I argue that the hospital policy is the underlying principle for the actions of the nurses and the doctors. It is an abstract justificatory rationale only verbally expressed when actions are under attack, as in Case 3 where the doctor says: 'I have informed both the patient and his wife about the treatment and the side-effects. It is their decision to say Yes or No', or in Case 2 where the doctor says: 'She didn't listen to my information', and the nurse answers: 'I'll go and talk with her later'.

I also argue that these discourses have a common concern: the patients' sick bodies. However, it seems as if patients, nurses and doctors are not communicating about the same body. The next part of my chapter focuses on their communication about the sick body.

A discourse of experience

The patients communicate in what may be called a *discourse of experience* centred around his or her lived and experienced body-self. Following Lock and Scheper-Hughes' analytical distinction of the three bodies, this discourse of experience may be understood within the level of the first of the three bodies: the individual body (Lock and Scheper-Hughes 1990: 50). The patient seeks information about and power over that part of his or her sick body which is invisible for him or her, for instance, saying: 'I just want to know what is going on in my body' (Case 1).

One way for the patient to reach an understanding of the lived body is to speak within a medical discourse, saying, for instance: 'Are there any metastasis? I want to get an answer on my CT-scanning' (Case 1). Another way is to try to get the doctor and nurse interested in their experienced view of the body functions by saying, as in Case 2, for instance: 'I sprained my left big toe, and two days after my stomach started to grow.'

A discourse of caring

The nurses communicate in what may be called a *discourse of caring*. In terms of Lock and Scheper-Hughes' analytical distinction, the discourse of caring can be understood within the level of the third of the three bodies – the body politic. Within the discourse of caring, I argue that the body politic has as its point of reference the patient's individual body, his or her feelings and illness experiences (the first body), and the representational uses of the body as a natural symbol in conceptualizing nature, society and culture (the second level social body) (Lock and Scheper-Hughes 1990: 50–1). The nurse seeks information about, and power over, that part of the patient's individual body which is connected to the patient's feelings and illness experiences (the first body). For instance, she tries to encourage the patients to talk about their feelings by saying: 'I'll come back and talk things over with you when we have finished the round', and later, 'Of course I'm coming. We are here to take care of you. We are here for your sake' (Case 1).

Following Lock and Scheper-Hughes, the body politic refers to the regulation and control of bodies (individual and collective) in sickness, reproduction, work, etc.: 'the stability of the body politic rests on its ability to regulate populations (the social body) and to discipline individual bodies' (Lock and Scheper-Hughes 1990: 51).

The symbolic, representational uses of the body in conceptualizing nature, society and culture (the social body) are inherent in the nurse's statements: 'This man is too old for treatment. . . . Give him some painkillers and good nursing care' (Case 3). Here the cultural construction of, and about, the body (too old for treatment) is useful in sustaining a particular view of society and social relations (Lock and Scheper-Hughes 1990: 61).

A medical discourse

The doctors are communicating within what may be called a *medical discourse* centred around that part of the sick body that is visible to his professional and technological gaze, but invisible for the patient. Following Lock and Scheper-Hughes, I argue that the medical discourse may also be understood within the level of the body politic. The doctors concentrate their responsibilities first and foremost around the physical body, as an object to be examined, treated and tested, for instance, saying: 'It's your disease. It has reached the lungs, but we think we have a new kind of medicine that can help you. It is only a small part of your lungs that is attacked' (Case 1), or 'But we shall carefully follow the immune system of your husband, don't worry [said in a joking fashion] and we will fight – and there are side effects, but it's not all patients that get them, and we have medicine for those too' (Case 3). These statements show the symbolic, representational uses of the body in conceptualizing nature, society and culture (the social body).

The understanding of the *body at war* is similar to the ethnographic data presented in the book *Flexible Bodies* by the anthropologist Emily Martin (1994). She describes how it was a widespread idea across social categories of class, sexuality, gender and age to understand the immune system as something inside our bodies that protects us from disease (ibid.: 65). The doctors' use of the metaphors 'to fight' and 'to kill' may be understood as a body politic, not only regulating and controlling individual patients in the hospital, but also as a powerful part of the media coverage of the immune system (ibid.: 62).[3]

The doctor, in communicating with patients, may ask questions within a discourse of experience, for instance: 'How are you today?' (Case 1), but he shifts to the medical discourse when he answers: 'Yes, it is an uneasy feeling. But it is not dangerous. It is because of your lungs' (Case 1), or he does not answer at all – for instance, when he asks, 'Do you have any questions?' (Case 1), and immediately turns his back on the patient and closes the record. I would argue that questions like these are an important part of the power relations in patient–doctor communication. These questions are not value-free, but are part of the struggle for symbolic capital. Following the anthropologist Armstrong (1982: 110), when the doctor's hand is applied to the patient's abdomen and he asks a question such as 'How do you feel?', or when the stethoscope is placed gently on the patient's chest, these actions may be looked at as the stuff of power.

CONCLUSION

In this chapter, policy within a hospital setting has been my field of research. Focusing on policy as the strategic goal of science implies that it is not sufficient to look only at micro-social processes such as patient–nurse–doctor relationships in the oncology department, or only to look at macro-social processes – for instance, the written hospital policy document, the nurses' policy document, questions of economics, and the wider context of medical policy. What is needed is a research strategy through which the anthropologist is able to analyse connections between micro and macro processes (Wright and Shore 1994). I have tried here to connect the written hospital policy document, the nurses' policy document with the nurse–doctor and the nurse–patient–doctor relationships in the clinical praxis. Using the daily round, I have examined some of the ways patients, nurses and doctors compete about the symbolic capital which is recognized within their particular field. Because the goals of hospital policy – for instance, equal cooperation and communication among patients, nurses and doctors, and high levels of information – are not material objects or things that can be acquired once and for all, patients, nurses and doctors continuously have to strive for them, along with other things, through different discourses of power.

I have focused on these different discourses of power, showing that they have the patient's body as a common rotation axis. In seeking control over symbolic capital, patients, nurses and doctors are communicating about different bodies in the discourse of experience, the discourse of caring, and the discourse of medicine. The patient's body is not one entity, but a social and cultural construction vulnerable to ideological shifts, discursive processes and power struggles. Following the anthropologists Lock and Scheper-Hughes, the patient's body was divided into three bodies at three conceptual and analytical levels. Especially the third body, the body politic, became of particular interest in the process of showing how the hospital policy document and the nurses' policy document were articulated within different discourses of power. The body politic, to maintain social stability, exerts control and regulates bodies, not only at the level of the individual patient, but also at group levels. It is important to point out that the power and control involved in the body politic is not simply about doctors' (and nurses') supreme surveillance over the patient's body. As Silverman has pointed out (1987: 225–6), patients are not pounded into submission. Today, they are rather incited to speak and encouraged to take responsibility for their own behaviour. Within such a framework, the power relations become more diffuse, subtle and invisible. What I have tried to show is that policy can be understood as a field where nurses, doctors and patients compete about the symbolic capital which is recognized within this particular field. The different discourses of power as a means to get access to the hospital policy may be understood as taking part in performing the art of government.

NOTES

1 The fieldwork was part of a Ph.D. project financed by the Danish Cancer Society and the Danish Medical Research Council from January 1990 to April 1993.
2 In the oncology department, all nurses except one were female, most of the doctors were male. The nurses mentioned in this chapter are all female and the doctors male.
3 Emily Martin shows that 'flexibility' has become a new valued way of understanding the immune system, and that just as immunological flexibility is coming to define biological superiority, personal flexibility is coming to define economic superiority (Martin 1994).

REFERENCES

Armstrong, D. (1982) 'The doctor–patient relationship: 1930–80', in P. Wright and A. Treacher (eds) *The Problem of Medical Knowledge: Examining the Social Construction of Medicine*, Edinburgh: Edinburgh University Press.
Bateson, Mary and Bateson, Gregory (1990) *Hvor Engle ej tør Træde*, Copenhagen: Rosinante. (In English: *Angels Fear – Towards an Epistemology of the Sacred* (1987).)
Bourdieu, Pierre (1990) *The Logic of Practice*, Cambridge: Polity Press.
Foucault, Michel (1975) *The Birth of the Clinic: An Archaeology of Medical Perception*, New York: Vintage Books.
—— (1980) 'Body/Power', in *Power/Knowledge. Selected Interviews and Other Writings 1972–1977*, New York: Pantheon Books.
Hastrup, Kirsten and Hervik, Peter (1994) 'Introduction', in K. Hastrup and P. Hervik (eds) *Social Experience and Anthropological Knowledge*, London: Routledge.
Knudsen, Anne (1990) 'Tavshed er magtens Tegn. Prestige, ære og magt i de mediterrane samfund', in L. Andersen, L. Wedell Pape and M. Rostgaard (eds) *Livsmagt. Nye perspektiver på kultur, magt og køn*, Aarhus: Aarhus Universitetsforlag.
Liep, John and Fog Olwig, Karen (1994) 'Kulturel Kompleksitet', in John Liep and Karen Fog Olwig (eds) *Komplekse liv. Kulturel Mangfoldighed i Danmark*, Copenhagen: Akademisk Forlag.
Lock, Margaret and Scheper-Hughes, Nancy (1990) 'A critical-interpretative approach in medical anthropology: rituals and routines of discipline and dissent', in T. M. Johnson and C. F. Sargent (eds) *Medical Anthropology*, 47–73, London: Praeger Publications.
Lupton, Deborah (1994) *Medicine as Culture. Illness, Disease and the Body in Western Societies*, London: Sage Publications.
Martin, Emily (1994) *Flexible Bodies. Tracking Immunity in American*

Culture. From the Days of Polio to the Age of AIDS, Boston: Beacon Press.

Silverman, D. (1987) *Communication and Medical Practice: Social Relations in the Clinic*, London: Sage Publications.

Strauss, A., Schatzman, I., Ehrlich, D., Bucher, R. and Sabshin, M. (1963) 'The hospital and its negotiated order', in E. Freidson (ed.) *The Hospital in Modern Society*, London: Free Press of Glencoe, Collier-Macmillan Limited.

Wright, Susan (1994) 'Culture in anthropology and organisational studies', in Susan Wright (ed.) *Anthropology of Organizations*, London: Routledge .

Wright, Susan and Shore, Cris (1994) 'Introduction: Why an anthropology of policy?', paper given at Biannual Conference of European Association of Social Anthropologists, Oslo University, 25 June.

Part II

Policy as cultural agent

Chapter 5
Free to make the right choice?
Gender equality policy in post-welfare Sweden

Annika Rabo

In Sweden sexual equality has become one of the most important goals of public life. It is an area of Swedish political culture where we find total consensus in public statements. Swedish women and men should enjoy the same rights and obligations, with equal employment opportunities so that they can be economically independent. They should have opportunities to care for children and their home, and opportunities to participate in the political life of society. *Jämställdhet* (equality between the sexes)[1] is part of the larger concept of *jämlikhet* (equality). The concepts of gender equality and class equality are not uncontested among Swedes, but they have been ingrained as both uniquely and typically Swedish in the post-war period. Debates about *jämställdhet* and *jämlikhet* have been fierce, but conducted within a very Swedish context. Only a 'real' Swede can voice an opinion against *Swedish* equality.

All Swedish public institutions, including schools and universities, are legally obliged to follow the *jämställdhets*-policy of the state. The educational system in Sweden has, until very recently, been exceedingly centralized where policy-makers and schoolteachers saw the mandatory school as an important vehicle for social and economic change. Increased equal educational opportunities for 'disadvantaged' individuals like working-class youth and women, were considered an instrument towards a better society, and a sign of such a good, progressive and *Swedish* society.

Today Sweden, like similar countries, is moving away from polices of generalized welfare distribution. Sweden, it is said, can no longer afford a huge public sector (employing mainly women). Concomitantly, a number of official reports have been produced which analyse *jämställdhet* and education. There is a widespread belief that women constitute an untapped resource, particularly in higher education, yet that women tend to make 'wrong' educational choices.

This chapter analyses how issues of higher education, *jämställdhet* and gender intersect today with a change of policy from centralized regulation to principles of 'free choice'. There are great political controversies in this intersection. The state has overall control over educational policies and stands as a guarantee for a policy of sexual equality. Yet the same state controls the dismantling of the welfare state. These controversies can be under-stood as a reworking of the meanings of gender and educational equality in Sweden today. They also suggest how the future of Swedish society is being debated. Traditional Swedish welfare policy has underlined the similarity (*likhet*) of citizens and used policy as an instrument to create sameness and equality.[2] The success of Swedish welfare policies depended to a great extent on a belief in the uniquely Swedish character of this model. The ideal of 'free choice', on the other hand, opposes the egalitarian goals of earlier definitions of Swedishness. Welfare and education policies in Sweden have been amply analysed by political scientists, sociologists and educationalists, usually from an instrumentalist point of view, which evaluates policy from the stated goals of policy-makers. An anthropology of policy differs in that policy is simultaneously anal-ysed as working through symbols and social action. Policy both 'says' and 'does' in ways which defy simple evaluations.

This chapter presents a brief background to the now classic Swedish welfare policies and the current dismantling of the welfare state. The second section examines equality between the sexes as official policy. The third section explores higher education as a field where public spending is still high and where hopes for the future are crystallized. Recent state-commissioned reports on sexual equality in higher education are utilized to highlight problems and contradictions in official policy-making and policy-interpretation. The intersection between gender and higher education is one of many sites for analysing the ways that policy-makers try to 'orga-nize and control' citizens in a complex post-industrial state with lingering welfare expectations. This particular Swedish case study highlights the fact that in contemporary European states ideas about cultural difference and similarity – within and across nations – are linked to political struggles in complex ways.

WELFARE STATE WITH A HUMAN FACE

Until the end of the 1980s, many Swedes without much reflection felt that 'the welfare state' was a Swedish invention and prerogative. 'Welfare' and 'state' were nowhere better or more 'natural' than in our blessed little corner of the world. Many Swedes were very clearly opposed to the dominant Social Democratic rule and hegemony in public institutions. Many felt that taxes were too high, and welfare distribution too extensive. But underneath this grumbling, welfare was somehow felt to be uniquely Swedish. We might grudgingly concede that others had a welfare state too (mainly Norway and Denmark), but we were the originators and the inspirators. The transformation of Sweden from an agrarian to an industrial and urban society was quick and dramatic. Most Swedes were very poor a hundred years ago. About one quarter of the population migrated to the United States between 1860 and 1930, with a peak around 1890. Between 1955 and 1995 Sweden instead received huge numbers of migrants, with a peak in 1970.[3] Industry needed labour. Today, 10 per cent of the workforce are unemployed and another 6 per cent are 'employed' in continuing education of various kinds. Among migrants without Swedish citizenship unemployment reaches 25 per cent.

Much has been written about Sweden's rapid economic and political transformation in the post-war period, which coincides with strong Social Democratic governments. Swedish social scientists have debated the social engineering aspects of Swedish welfare where the state intervened into most aspects of society. It is said that Swedes found it difficult to differentiate between 'state' and 'society' when the welfare model was politically strong and economically viable. Applied social science in Sweden, many contend, was a product of the welfare state, where the scientists became, in reality, engineers in the construction of a model society. The salient features of this classical Swedish model included an active labour market and manpower policy designed to keep unemployment low, comprehensive social security policies and a large public service production sector. It included regulations and public subsidies in agriculture and housing, and finally 'a system of extensive resource extraction – i.e. taxation – to finance this public household' (Olsson 1990: 26). This model depended on a strong political consensus, the establishment of welfare bureaucracies and economic growth. Key political shibboleths were 'equality, security and solidarity'. The concept of *folkhemmet* (the 'folk' home) conveyed the ideals of the good society in which all people could live in dignity (Rosendahl 1985).[4]

Today, Swedes are 'European', and we tell ourselves that we have to 'converge' with the rest of Europe, that is, become like 'them' and stop considering ourselves as special and unique. Alternatively, we tell ourselves, or are told, that Sweden can make a positive contribution to European Union social policies. Domestically, there is much talk of crisis and of the dismantling of the comprehensive welfare system. Some scholars claim that so far the Swedish welfare model has survived quite well (e.g. Olsson 1990: 35). The stated ambition among all political parties over the last decade, however, has been to stress 'efficiency' and decentralization and to allow more 'private initiatives' in social services.

There have been few gender analyses of the political ideology of the welfare model. Swedish social scientists at times carved out niches for research that followed gender divisions. Female sociologists studied child care and the life of women (in Swedish called 'the little life'). Male sociologists studied 'class' or 'politics'. Very few scholars (or politicians and bureaucrats) even thought of the welfare model in gender terms. Yvonne Hirdman (1989) – one of the first to study power and gender hierarchy in connection with the building of the Swedish folk home – shows how politicians and scientists from the 1930s cooperated to 'put life in order' (*lägga livet tillrätta*), i.e. to order the private home life of women (and men) to produce equal and modern individuals. Hirdman claims that the Social Democratic family ideal was in essence bourgeois. The home was glorified as a safe haven away from the bustle and tension of public life.[5] In the home, the important work of educating the new (and better) generation was bestowed on women. The home should be clean, practical and beautiful. Houses should be planned with a view of rational utilization. Families and family life must be planned. Hence, women in Sweden, especially working-class women, were the targets of various campaigns ordering this 'little', but important, life. Early folk-home engineers did not plan that (married) women and men should do the same tasks. Women who had been active in production, mainly in agriculture, became housewives in the industrial society .

Hirdman paints a rather sinister picture of the ideals of the Social Democratic heyday. Many bourgeois critics have drawn a similar picture over the last decade, claiming that through the ideology of *folkhemmet*, all initiative is taken away from the individual, who is rendered helpless and passive by too much 'spoon feeding' from the state. Hence, the current 'crisis' is a result of people 'wanting too much' and 'giving too little'. Swedes have been spoiled by welfare policies. This is not the ideological perspective of Hirdman. She uses gender as an analytical tool to reflect on the paradox of social engineering in the folk home. The aim of the experts and the politicians was to increase human dignity and the economic welfare for each citizen. To fulfil this holy promise, the dignity of stubborn individuals, who did not know their own best interests, had to be violated. Women were deemed unreasonable and stubborn and much more than men, were spoken to, told off, and violated (Hirdman 1989: 227ff.).

In the last decade, the cracks in the Swedish welfare mirror are widening. The Social Democratic party has made a U-turn on major political tenets. The first priority of the current government is to fight inflation and reduce the budget deficit. High unemployment is accepted as an instrument for achieving this end. The public sector has had major cutbacks (as has the private) and we are told that 'we cannot afford' the welfare system that was deemed a human right a decade ago. The dismantling of the welfare state is not gender neutral, but gendered, just as was the establishment of welfare policies. Citizens are divided by some economists into 'feeders' (*närande*) and 'eaters' (*tärande*), where most public sector employees, the elderly and children are 'eaters'. The metaphors used in the public debates by (male) politicians and economists and employers all allude to the destructive appetite of the 'eaters'.[6] Most Swedish politicians still, however, adhere to ideals of sexual equality.

POLICIES OF EQUALITY BETWEEN WOMEN AND MEN

'Sweden is the world's most *jämställd* country', so says the United Nations Development Programme in a report published in 1993.

> Sweden has the highest frequency of female employment and the lowest wage-differences between women and men . . . From an international perspective of equality between the sexes, Sweden is the best country for women to live in.
>
> (Hedlund 1993: 109)

All Nordic countries score high on the scale of equality between men and women. Finland, Denmark and Sweden have the highest percentage of female members of parliament.[7] Yet some feminists claim that in the Scandinavian corporate, redistributive state, women have little political power outside parliament. 'Powerful organizations and institutions rather than voters and political parties have become the central gatekeepers' (Hernes 1984: 30). Unions and employers' associations have very few female leaders. In Sweden only about 10 per cent of the 'higher' leadership positions in the private sector are filled by women, and around 30 per cent in the public sector (Hedlund 1993: 121).[8] Swedish women receive more education than men today. But while 83 per cent have employment, only 38 per cent of those working are full-time. This high level of part-time employment is a salient feature of the Swedish female labour activity. Critics of the Swedish/Scandinavian system stress that while a large percentage of women are employed, the labour market is highly gender segregated. Of all working women, almost half are employed in teaching, health care and the social service sector. Only 9 per cent of all employed men work in these sectors. In industry and the building sector almost the opposite holds true. Yet in industries, women have the most repetitive and monotonous jobs (Hedlund 1993: 117). Since women mainly work part-time, men earn much more than women in spite of the principle of wage equality. Women dominate the public sector numerically but do not truly influence public policy in those organizations. Women in Scandinavia, according to Hernes, are both clients and employees of the welfare state, yet are not equal to men as citizens (1984: 32). Åsa Regner argues that women are hit by economic recession in different ways than men. Enormous amounts of (public) money is spent on re-educating Sweden's unemployed. Women and men get an 'equal share', in one sense, but the projects aimed at men are more expensive and men receive support to start their own business more often than women (Svenska Dagbladet, 11 April 1996).

Claims that Sweden is a haven of equality between the sexes are arguable. Some stress that Sweden's legal system provides a framework for equality between women and men. Many Swedish welfare policies were formulated earlier than in other countries and have influenced their public policies too. In Sweden (and Scandinavia in general) regional and class differences in lifestyle are less pronounced than in most other European countries because state policies and state institutions have been very influential in reducing blatant economic differences. In Sweden, both sexes agree that children should not stop women from working – an idea that has won increasing support with the development of social policies in this century. In 1920 married women were no longer defined as legal minors. In 1925 the Swedish parliament passed a law ensuring equal pay for men and women employed by the state.

In 1976 the European Community legislated against sexual discrimination. Unions and employers' associations in Sweden, however, opposed a formal law. Instead, an agreement was reached in 1977 which provided a framework for sexual equality in the labour market and was complemented through local, and more specific, agreements. Nothing much came out of this, however, and in 1980 the Swedish parliament instead passed a law making discrimination between men and women illegal.

In 1979 the office of *jämställdhetsombudsman (jämO)*, a state authority charged with safeguarding principles of equality between the sexes, was established. This ombudsman (who is a woman) is used mainly by women who feel they have been unfairly judged when applying for a job, or given unequal pay in comparison with their male counterparts. The role of *jämO* is to help applicants in industrial tribunals. Groups of employees cannot apply to *jämO*, only individuals. *JämO* has had one successful case where (with the help of European Community legislation) a female economist employed by a Swedish borough was judged to have an unfair salary compared to a male economist. A recent test case in 1996 involved a midwife who used new European Union legislation to claim unfair discrimination when compared to male hospital technicians. *JämO* conducted a job evaluation and advocated a salary increase for the midwife to the same level as male technicians, but this was voted down in court on account of the 'evaluation not being thorough and fair'. The Swedish midwives were disappointed, but not surprised. Earlier in the winter of 1996, Swedish nurses and physical therapists – the vast majority of whom are women – went on strike to demand a 20 per cent salary increase. They too were unsuccessful. The costs for the public coffer would clearly be great if jobs performed by women in health care and social services were compared to jobs performed by men. Today 'all Swedes have to tighten their belt', but it comes as no surprise to feminists that women have to tighten theirs more.

JämO has a fairly high public profile and supports all kinds of projects concerned with sexual equality in public life. In 1992 all employers with over ten employees had to submit plans for sexual equality which *JämO* was charged with scrutinizing. According to *JämO* these plans need improving. It has looked at plans produced by organizations with a responsibility to lead or influence Swedish society at large, including half of the local authorities and most political parties, unions, employers associations and large mass media corporations. The results showed that 90 per cent of these organizations have not made a proper inventory of their own work place and that their plans are vague and 'lack concrete policies and measurable goals' (*Jämsides* 1996. 1: 10).

Why are these plans so vague and what is their ideological content? The basis for all Swedish sexual equality plans is a 'peace-agreement' between the sexes (Eduards 1995: 59). Sexual equality concerns relationships between men and women, but in Swedish public life the content of these relationships is glossed over. Gender analyses are totally absent. Plans state the importance of utilizing both sexes to make work places more varied and rich. They also state that sexual equality (and plans for sexual equality) are important for democratic reasons. Linköping University's plan (1995), for example, states that *jämställdhet* has both a quantitative and qualitative aspect. In quantitative terms, sexual equality means that women and men should be evenly distributed in all areas of public life. In qualitative terms, sexual equality means that the experiences, know-how and values of both women and men are made to influence and enrich all spheres of society. The plan insists that women and men – as groups (*sic!*) – have 'equal rights, obligations, opportunities and possibilities within all essential aspects of life. A sexually-equal society is a society where the current biased work and power distribution between the sexes is abolished' (Linköping University 1995: 1). According to the plan, equality between women and men will constitute the basis for 'increased welfare in both a limited and an enlarged sense' (ibid.: 1).

Hernes (1984) argued that the Scandinavian welfare model is corporatist and that labour-market organizations and state institutions are strong compared to parliament and political parties. In the former men dominate and gender awareness is still quite absent. Issues of sexual equality have instead been 'adopted' by political parties and the Swedish parliament. *Jämställdhet* as a concept was coined by the Swedish Liberal party (which had a very large female constituency), but was adopted in the 1970s by the Social Democrats and became part and parcel of the Swedish welfare model. In this perspective, *jämställdhetsplaner* (plans for sexual equality) can be regarded as a device for political control by parliament on to reluctant organizations dominated by men. Yet political imposition can never be more than partial in Sweden. There are various ways for reluctant representatives of public organizations to avoid debating issues of power behind these plans. One common way to defuse gender analysis is to view sexual equality as a simple problem, rather than a political issue. Alternatively a tradition of 'sensible' consensus ensures that an analysis of the structure of gender relations is generally lacking because this might undermine the peace agreement referred to by Eduards (1995: 59).

Most Swedes feel that Sweden is a country which has 'come far' in issues of sexual equality. They do not realize that today European Union legislation is being utilized to further *jämställdhet* in Sweden. Part of the self-image of many Swedes is that women and men are treated as 'equal' in the workplace. When confronted with facts and figures confirming the segregated labour market and male dominance in private corporations and public organizations there is, however, no consensus in interpretation. To many, this segregation is not due to inequality between men and women. Many feel that 'with time' imbalances will be redressed and more women will have 'powerful positions'. Others claim that 'women are reluctant to make careers' or that 'women have other priorities'.

Equality between the sexes is 'not a matter of opinion but a field of knowledge', according to many official documents. What this means is that *jämställdhet* is not an issue you can voice an opinion against (unless, as a Swede, you want to stay outside the moral universe of Swedishness).[9] To be a Swede you have to pay your dues to *jämställdhet*. Furthermore, in the Swedish perception, sexual equality develops naturally through time. It can always be stated as a future goal. Advocates of policies of *jämställdhet* argue that more 'equality' for women will also lead to more 'equality' for men. Through debates, discussions and education, 'more' equality can be achieved. Hence it is very difficult to pinpoint parameters against which sexual equality is measured in Sweden. I think that most Swedes consider women and men to be *both* the same and different (*lika och olika*). By treating understandings of sameness and difference as a field of knowledge, rather than as an arena for power struggle, conflicts can be contained. This is seen when analysing how sexual equality policy works within higher education.

HIGHER EDUCATION, POLICIES OF SEXUAL EQUALITY AND ISSUES OF GENDER

Public sector cuts have only recently affected higher education. Just as political consensus in Sweden holds that *jämställdhet* must be subject to public policy, the consensus is that higher education remains an effective investment for the welfare of society at large. There is a widespread belief that the early universal literacy in Sweden was instrumental in successful industrialization. While some critics claim that Sweden spends too little on higher education and that too few young people continue beyond secondary education, as a *sector* higher education is still privileged. Other critics remark that higher education has expanded because of the growing unemployment. Young people are kept on student loans because loans are cheaper than unemployment schemes or benefits. New colleges are being established throughout the country and local politicians are convinced that regional development depends on the presence of colleges and universities. In 1989/90 about 40 per cent of all 20–25-year-olds started higher education courses (SOU 1992.1: 49). Higher education in Sweden is mainly state-financed while counties and boroughs are responsible for certain health care degrees (like nursing). There is a long tradition of centralized state control in Sweden. Today, however, local authorities finance schools and the state is responsible for controlling the quality of education, rather than forcing local schools to follow central directives step by step. Universities have more autonomy in deciding how to use their funds.

Swedish higher education institutions have, as elsewhere in Europe, been heavily male dominated. From the early nineteenth century, upper secondary schools were established throughout Sweden and the state regulated and moulded them into preparatory schools for higher education. In 1862 the exam (*studentexamen*) which was required for university entrance was placed in the upper secondary schools rather than at the university. Women were barred from these (publicly financed) schools. In 1870 women could take the upper secondary school exam as private students and were allowed into the faculty of medicine, but could still not study theology, law or philosophy. Florin and Johansson (1993), in their study of culture, class and gender in the upper secondary schools in the pre-World War I period, view these schools as an arena for the formation of the new male bourgeoisie. The boys had a varied class background, but were disciplined into becoming the new elite. Class and gender struggles in the educational sector a century ago are illuminating because they throw light on developments in higher education in recent decades. Nineteenth-century upper secondary schools had far fewer pupils than universities recruit today, but struggles over control of these schools resembled current conflicts over issues of sex and competence.

Between 1875, when women were admitted to all faculties, and 1914, only 435 Swedish women obtained an academic degree (Florin and Johansson 1993: 184). Barred from public employment, many worked as teachers in private schools for girls. University trained women tried to organize themselves and used their political connections and media skills to enhance their positions, much like feminists today. The upper secondary school reform of 1927 finally gave girls equal access to all educational avenues. In the 1930s about 25 per cent of university students were women, and about 20 per cent of degrees were awarded to women. Only twelve women had a degree from graduate studies in 1937 (Elgqvist-Salzman 1995: 191). In 1994, 56 per cent of university entrants were women, and women obtained 56 per cent of first degree awards. Women constitute the great majority in most art and social science disciplines, and within teacher training colleges. Only among engineering students are men still the majority, but women constitute the majority of students as *undergraduates*. In 1994, 40 per cent of the new postgraduates were women; in 1985 only 30 per cent were women (Högskoleverket 1996: 33). Of those receiving a doctorate in the same year, 31 per cent were women. Of all senior lecturers in Sweden, only 21 per cent are women. Only 7 per cent of Swedish university professors are women. In the last decade these ratios have been fairly stable.

The present Social Democratic government and the earlier Conservative–Liberal coalition government have tried to address this sex imbalance in different and often contradictory ways. While lamenting the shortage of women studying for higher degrees in general, both agreed that more women must move from the public sector 'eating' professions to the 'feeding' professions in science and technology. Politicians and educational experts are worried that too few young people study engineering or technology. Here, the female potential remains untapped. However, the reasoning behind these arguments is seldom fully discussed.

All political parties agree that women's talents are wasted in the higher education hierarchy. A new report on directions for research funding in Sweden states that:

> Sweden needs to pledge its best resources of talent (*begåvn-ingsresurser*) to develop the welfare of the country and create new knowledge. It is a misuse of resources not to utilize fully the potential and reserve of talent (*begåvningsreserv*) that women constitute.

(SOU 1996.29: 279)

This vocabulary of social engineering is typical of Swedish policy-makers' faith in education as a means to development. Such rhetoric also underlines that women are morally obliged to educate themselves as much as possible for the good of the country. It is assumed that education simultaneously serves the interests of the nation and those of the individual. The present Social Democratic government now encourages Swedish women to continue higher education beyond degree level and has commissioned research to discern why women do badly in academic careers, and why only 100 out of 1,760 professors in Sweden are women.

In Sweden close links exist between women's studies in academia and research on sexual equality commissioned by the state. Very often the same (female) researchers act as experts to politicians and consider themselves as researchers in the academic field of women's studies. This close link between academics and policy-makers is a salient feature of Swedish public life (Eduards 1995: 57). Politicians need academic experts and use them to legitimate scientifically political decisions. Through these links researchers have been able to argue that resources are needed for their specialities. In every Swedish university, for example, there is a Centre for Research on Women and Women Researchers. These centres gather female researchers from various fields, give courses, or conduct research on women. All receive earmarked money from the Ministry of Education and every university has an employee coordinating projects aimed at *jämställdhet*. Money is also earmarked to support women doing postdoctoral research abroad, to invite foreign female, guest professors for work on issues of sexual equality in contemporary Sweden. These measures show how seriously the government takes sexual equality within the universities. Many women (and some men) are actively engaged in handling this mixture of 'pure' academic funds and projects aimed at more general support of women within the universities. While some critics claim that women are pampered, others claim that the cost of these efforts exceeds the benefit. To work on *jämställdhet* has become a career for some.

REACTIONS TO A GOVERNMENT BILL

In 1995 the Minister of Education prepared a bill for increased sexual equality in higher education. The bill, accepted by parliamentary majority in spring 1996, proposed that thirty new professorships and sixty new postdoctoral research positions would be established for the 'under-represented sex'. Universities had to pay for part of these positions and prepare lists for disciplines in which they were prepared to accept candidates. Even before the bill was passed, a heated debate began inside and outside academia. Interest focused on the professorships rather than the postdoctoral positions – although these were twice as many and more important for strategic career considerations. In the proposition (Prop. 1994/95.164: 34–6) the government argued that professors are important role models for students and younger researchers. Professors also influence areas of research and general research policies by being members of funding research councils. In addition, they provide 'experts and commentators in various situations' (1994: 34–5). The proposition further states that the gender imbalance in academic positions is only very slowly being redressed, 'therefore an extraordinary effort is needed to quickly achieve an important increase' (1994: 34–5) of female professors. The money pledged was to be a once-and-for-all effort. In the future, universities themselves had to make efforts towards redressing the sex ratio imbalance within existing budget limits.[10] When needed, the proposition stated, positive discrimination would be used. A position 'shall be filled by a competent candidate of the under-represented sex, even if this person is less qualified than an applicant of the other sex' (1994: 36). Knowing that this would create fury in many universities, the proposition continued by citing the sixteenth paragraph of the law on sexual equality that 'positive discrimination is permissible, if it is part of the efforts to enhance *jämställdhet* in work life' (1994: 36).

In sum, the government claimed that special efforts were needed to create more prestigious and influential posts for women in academia. By creating postdoctoral positions, more women would have a stepping stone in their careers and greater future chances to apply for professorships. But there was also an immediate need to create professorships for competent women. If men applied for such posts, qualified women would be chosen even if their qualifications were deemed 'lower'. The gap, however, could not be 'too great'. Positive discrimination was justified on the grounds of the general Swedish law of *jämställdhet*, whereby the knowledge and experience of both women and men are seen to contribute positively to all work places.

In the ensuing media debates there were no negative reactions from university power holders, nor from the research councils handling the university lists. At Linköping University, for example, each faculty prepared lists and the Vice Chancellor selected a special group to coordinate this work. Within universities there was haggling over which academic disciplines could claim to need 'under-represented' professors, but to the outside each university presented agreed lists. In that sense the universities followed their own interests. The new financial resources enabled them to get positions that they had probably planned for anyway. They had to find money themselves, but this ensured that suggestions were thought over and carefully calculated. Over 300 suggestions for posts were presented by the ten universities involved in the process.

But individual professors, researchers and so-called opinion-makers were not so easily charmed by the government's arguments. Many were outraged and claimed that the holy principle of academic freedom had been violated. It was the duty of academia to defend itself from political control. Others retorted that no university is totally free and that research funds carry no strings. In Sweden the link between academia and the state is very close, so why object in this particular instance? Governments frequently promote new research areas, often in cooperation with the academic community. Furthermore, it was retorted, private capital has become increasingly involved in academic funding in the last decade and none of those disciples with newly-sponsored professorships had objected. These professors are usually hand-picked, because they have 'unique competence' in a field of interest for both industry and the university, and all are men. Why, opponents asked, is discrimination permissible sometimes and not others?

Another argument against the bill was that excellence through competition is the hallmark of professorships and that standards would invariably be lowered as 'the best' would be by-passed. Both men and women claimed that women already in academic positions felt violated by the proposition. 'Others' would suspect that these women had obtained their jobs on 'second-rate' research. Critics also argued that to suggest that women are unable to reach the highest posts in the universities without help from the government devalues female competence. To this argument feminists replied that the real outrage was that so few women were professors in the motherland of sexual equality.

Those against the proposition implied that 'any woman' could become a professor just because of her sex. Against this argument others replied that women who were not 'formally competent' would not get these posts. Furthermore, the universities would not suggest posts in disciplines for which there were no qualified prospective female applicants. Finally, the ratio of female professors would only increase from 7 per cent to 8.2 per cent through this bill. The vast majority of professors would still be men.

The bill's opponents said that even if women were discriminated against in academia, 'a new discrimination' would not redress this unfairness. Why should men suffer because women suffered? Why should talented men be deprived of career opportunities? Women and men have the same opportunities for study and research, and with time the imbalance will go away if women choose to commit themselves to academic careers.

The intensity of feelings in these debates is in many ways remarkable. Sweden is going through its worst recession since the 1930s. Unemployment rates are enormous. Every day people are sacked from their jobs following huge public sector cuts. Why should a proposition suggesting *one hundred new jobs* within the framework of politically-accepted sexual equality policy create such enormous debate? There are many reasons. Among the political and economic elite, higher education is considered to be of national importance. Hopes and aspirations for future welfare are tied to the well-being of higher education. In a small country like Sweden, with a long tradition of centralized policy-making, educational reforms have been instrumental in shaping relations between state and citizens and in continuously producing elites. A hundred years ago, the upper secondary schools were the focus of elite debates over competence and qualifications, and women were initially barred from these schools as pupils and employees. Florin and Johansson (1993: 190–7) argue that Swedish men utilized various kinds of closure techniques to prevent women from obtaining equal access to educational capital. First women were considered intellectually incapable of pursuing higher education or becoming teachers in the upper secondary schools. They were said to be biologically unsuited for such activities. After the law was changed, this argument was no longer acceptable. Instead, other closure tactics were used. Women were given smaller salaries. Many men continued to fight hard to show that it was important that teaching remained a male profession in the upper secondary schools. If salaries given to men and women were to be equal, they would probably be lower, so men would shun the work and move elsewhere. The issue of qualification and competence gained new significance. Qualifications were not just a matter of formal degrees, which women had shown they were capable of gaining, good schools and hard discipline required the presence of *male* teachers, it was claimed. Manhood and leadership could only be taught to boys by male teachers, hence competence was indirectly believed to be tied to the sex of the teacher.

Current debates about the new professorships are obviously different, yet also similar. Few Swedes would dare to say that women are unsuitable as role models for the new university elite. But how 'competence and qualifications' are understood is quite similar. These concepts are taken as exact measurements: value-neutral, absolute and agreed by like-minded peers. When outsiders – be they ministers, 'experts', or 'public opinion' – push educational reforms which threaten the *imagined* autonomy of a tiny group of men (and today a few women), this group reacts by claiming the right and the competence to decide who is qualified to join the group. Swedish university professors are powerful figures within the university hierarchy, with influential connections to public and private corporate institutions in Sweden. But they have less power over others than the average general director and they do not earn much money. Because there are so few professors, it is very prestigious to be one. But in many disciplines this prestige rests on the illusion that one is selected among peers. Today, this group is not homogeneous in terms of political or educational ideology. Reactions among Swedish (male) professors are not uniform. Interestingly, while most professorships are within the faculties of medicine and technology, most voiced opposition – *and* support – to the proposition comes from representatives from the humanities and social sciences (who write more often in newspapers). Furthermore, these faculties have more acknowledged conflicts. Here, we find anxiety that academic autonomy and competence will be undermined by state policies. But we also find many academics who understand that educational policies are always part of wider political considerations.

Hence, the fights over the new professorships were very much symbolic, highlighting fissions within the higher educational institutions, but also showing that for many the policy of *jämställdhet* is acceptable in principle as long as the 'under-represented sex' accepts that the gender hierarchy must never be questioned. Opposition was greater where women were already well established and hence often compete with men for positions and funds, such as the humanities and social sciences. The government reasoned in terms of justice, fairness and 'tapping a potential' rather than taking a feminist position. But many non-feminists saw the bill as extremely threatening. As Nina Björk points out the proposition:

> opened a debate where it became obvious that people no longer were in agreement about the meaning of 'knowledge' and 'competence'. It opened up a debate where these concepts were discussed as conditioned by positions and perspectives. . . . [The Minister of Education's] proposition made visible our invisible ideology as an ideology – no wonder then the many and angry retorts.
>
> (1996: 169)

As a postscript to this debate, observers calculate that even with these new professorships, the 'under-represented sex' will need another century before a gender balance exists due to the extremely slow renewal of senior academic posts. Perhaps when the dust has settled, and when women have been installed into these posts, everyone will be exceedingly pleased. Those against will realize that the new professors (who are products of these institutions) are loyal, hard-working, dependable and *similar* to their male colleagues. Despite the fact that women (a handful) were helped along through state policy, I anticipate that even former opponents will argue that female and male professors have interests to defend in common.

A STATE-COMMISSIONED REPORT

'Traditional' welfare policy-making in Sweden is said to depend on consensus among various interest groups. One instrument to reach consensus is the proliferation of state-commissioned reports. Here, experts are selected by parliamentary committees or ministries to inquire into a particular field of policy-making. The reports are distributed to people who are asked to comment as representatives of their particular 'interest group'. The reports may also be read (and bought) by 'ordinary' citizens, who can reply to the commissioning body within the stipulated time. The handling of state-commissioned reports (*offentliga utredningar*) is perceived, both by the authorities, and by citizens at large, to be an essential part of Swedish democracy.[11] As a genre, the reports are no longer uniformly 'dry and bureaucratic', but usually follow specific procedures.

In December 1995 a 400-page report (SOU 1995.110) commissioned by the Minister of Education caused quite a commotion. The scope of the inquiry was on *measures for research on women, women's research and research on equality between women and men.* Long before its publication, the media and parts of academia had shown great interest in its content. The chief inquirer was a well-known feminist who, while working on the report, gave interviews and media appearances. The 'proper' Swedish style for experts is to keep as much out of the limelight as possible. The more sensitive the inquiry, the more need for experts to appear as impeccable civil servants and to 'anchor' their recommendations among as many interest groups as possible. Not so here. The style of the expert, coupled with the method of the inquiry and the content of the recommendations, antagonized many academics (both feminists and anti-feminists), politicians and opinion-makers. According to the report, the work was carried out by applying the analytical tools of 'women studies' to the field of higher education.[12]

The report claimed that 'traditional male disciplines' were supported at the expense of 'women's disciplines' thereby discriminating against women in higher education (SOU 1995.129: 21). It argued that women are indirectly punished 'as carriers of the values of care-taking, of social concern, interest in languages, aesthetic interests, etc., interests emanating from their being socialized as girls' (SOU 1995: 24). The experts ask why there is never a demand for men to undertake studies in humanities. They answer by remarking ironically that being a man is always correct, and where men flock it is right to be. Thus, decisions to empty humanities of resources and favour science and technology have been justified. This is deeply unfair, claims the report, because competition is higher where women gather. Higher grades are needed to enter studies that are popular among women, and when women want to compete for positions in academia, there are longer queues. Is this really in accordance with the law on equality between the sexes (SOU 1995: 24)?

The style of the report is varied. Some chapters are sub-commissioned from women scholars asked to explore particular aspects of women and higher education. Large sections are compilations of interviews with women scholars, academics and students. The tone of the commissioned experts is one of smug self-righteousness. The experts, like no one before them, are proclaiming truths. Power relations within the university are depicted as only a gender issue, and only the life of female academics is analysed as terrible and dismal.

The report makes various recommendations. One is to change the wording of one paragraph in the Higher Education Act. Equality between women and men should not only always – as stated today – be taken into consideration in the universities, but also *promoted*, according to the report (SOU 1995: 177). The experts recommend establishing a new national institute to coordinate, inform, inquire into and give funds to research on women and sexual equality. This institute should also act like a research council, taking a national responsibility to promote and enhance research on gender issues. The experts recommend that all university and college departments be asked to have special posts in the field of women's studies within five years. They also recommend that all university and college teachers take a course in basic gender theory.

Reactions to this report differed from earlier reactions to the bill concerning posts for the under-represented sex. Few inside or outside academia supported the recommendations, and most found its style highly biased. Many feminists initially worried that the report would produce counter reactions and that the issue of sexual equality in higher education would be buried for a long time. Most official replies, however, stressed that *jämställdhet* continues as an important issue. For example, Linköping University stressed that 'our critique is not aimed at the goals of supporting research on women and women's research, although we prefer to talk about gender research'. It continues:

> The report is a rather strange product, while certainly not uninteresting or bland . . . But the main report is difficult to respond to since analyses and suggestions are in no way linked together . . . Furthermore a great many of the recommendations show a total lack of understanding of how processes of change can and should be conducted.
>
> (Linköping University 1996: 3272/95)

Women engaged in the various centres for research on women

were not pleased. The report proposed that these centres lose their earmarked money and be required to give mandatory gender courses thus acting as 'gender-police'. Many women academics also pointed out that a 'women's perspective' in the basic sciences was easier said than done. Media debates were less sedate with accusations and counter accusations. Women who criticized the report for its lack of clarity or analysis of higher education were called 'naive victims' of male professors by the main expert.

Interestingly, no one has really discussed what I see as the report's basic ideological assumption. Women are depicted as essentially *different* from men. They are more caring, more humane, and have a more holistic perspective on life. A view is propagated by the experts that women flock to the humanities and social sciences because of these inherent qualities. The report contains no gender analysis of the historical developments of various disciplines. The report simply states that it is unfair that 'female' disciplines get less public money than 'male' science and technology. The report finally implies that more support for women to become professors, will somehow benefit the academic world and society in general.

'WE ARE ALL DIFFERENT'

In 1993, under the bourgeois coalition government, the Ministry of Education commissioned an inquiry under the heading of 'female and male in schools'. This expert group was to collect current knowledge (*kunskap*) on the importance of 'sexual belonging' (*könstillhörighet*) for the development and education of children and youth. With this information the group was to define the basis of equality between the sexes in school settings and suggest measures to spread knowledge on the importance of 'sexual belonging'. The slim 100-page report, called *We are All Different* was finished in 1994. It was widely distributed and accompanied by an anthology of articles where research on similarities and differences between boys and girls is presented in a popular form. The official report describes equality between the sexes as a pedagogical issue and a 'field of knowledge'.

In the report *jämställdhet* is very much coupled to future needs of knowledge and competence. The experts say that we are on the threshold of the 'information society'. In the future, we will have to educate our children not only for technical competence but competence in the interface between technology and social processes (Ds

1994.98: 8). Society (i.e. Sweden) is becoming more international and this puts new demands on the education system. We need more foreign languages and 'cultural understanding as a tool to increased contacts with the surrounding world' (Ds 1994: 8). Hence, we need to have good education in our native tongue to develop these skills. In future, we can expect that organizations will become more 'flat'[13], with more responsibility given to employees. In flat organizations new demands will be made on managements. Work-life is becoming more 'humanistic, team-oriented and with more creative leaders' (Ds 1994: 9).

In future, fewer opportunities will exist for unskilled labour. Increasingly, the young generation will work in fields requiring constant reschooling and relearning, therefore 'schools must function in a flexible way to meet the demands so that girls and boys can acquire competence' (Ds 1994: 10), and schools must take sex differences into consideration. Education must be accessible and of equal quality for both sexes.

The report states that today women and men are equal parts of the workforce, are both responsible for the support and well-being of children, but that they are not equal in terms of Sweden's work culture:

> Female knowledge and experience is lacking or is not utilized in many parts of society and what we can call 'male competence' is strikingly absent within traditionally female fields. Women are still an unused potential in the labour market. Yet our overview underlines that so called 'female competence' and 'female values' are in high demand today and will be of even greater demand in the future . . . Old, so-called traditional female values, stressing human relations, international interest and education, will be needed and valued in the society of the future.
>
> (Ds 1994: 10)

The experts stress that Sweden's educational system is undergoing great changes. These changes have to take into consideration our knowledge about differences between girls' and boys' constraints and possibilities. Girls and boys view education and the future differently. Research shows that girls think education will be very important for their future and a higher percentage than boys plan to continue at university level. Also, girls in more practical training programmes in secondary schools have a positive attitude towards higher education (Ds 1994: 11). The problem of today's school, the report says, is that sex (gender) is ignored completely. Schools are not suited for girls, but they are not suited for boys either, and issues of equality between the sexes are not satisfactorily part of the curricula. Hence, in future, *jämställdhet* has to be treated both as a field of knowledge (as laid down by the government) and as a question of teaching methods.

The report claims that the Education Act is consistently misinterpreted. Equal access to education regardless of sex means that gender is important and schools must be gender-aware. But what norm of similarity do schools take as their point of reference? Should girls be treated as similar to boys, or vice versa? The experts claim:

> Girls' and boys' 'slumbering capacities' must be stimulated at the relevant level of development. Schools must also complement and compensate that which girls and boys specifically need. Many boys, for example, need more training in verbal skills and a majority of girls need more training in their spatial capacity.
>
> (Ds 1994: 21)

The experts' position seems exceedingly confused. On the one hand, the report underlines that schools must be made aware of gender differences by regarding each child as either a girl or boy and meeting each pupil's needs. On the other hand, schools must help the girls or boys to make up for what they lack. This implies that the goal of education is to make 'girls' and 'boys' more similar, more alike. Yet the report states that in future more 'female' skills and experiences are needed for the flexible and internationalized work-life anticipated and the 'flat' organizations now emerging. The inquiry works on various levels of analysis. It makes sweeping generalization about future economic and organizational changes and speculates on what competences are needed in plans *for* the young generation. At the level of social relationships, it views gender as an important principle of organization to which schools must pay attention. Then, at the level of the pupils, it uses psychological models of child development to discuss compensation and stimulation. The result is an ahistorical and ethnocentric understanding of gender typical of official Swedish reports. Differences are dealt with but mainly to be either compensated for individually, or utilized for the future organization of work-life. Gender differences are basically inherent but *can* be, and *must*, according to the experts, be overcome through careful planning of educational methods.

In the anthology '*Of course we are different!*' accompanying the official report, all articles stress differences between schoolgirls and schoolboys. This is not surprising since the book is meant to create debate and be utilized by teachers and in teacher training colleges. Some of the experts, psychologists and psychiatrists, view the differences as inherent and grounded in biological and cognitive differences. The social science trained experts view differences more in terms of 'social factors'. Hence both 'nature' and 'nurture' views are represented. Yet, significantly, the main report also says that variations in 'behaviour', 'talent' and 'verbal skills' are greater *within* groups of boys and groups of girls than they are between boys and girls as general categories. Why, then, set an inquiry into motion stressing 'differences' between girls and boys, when other variables for 'difference' could have been chosen?

Common sense and experience tell Swedes there *is* some kind of difference between the sexes. We might disagree about the causes for difference but difference itself cannot be denied. This state-commissioned inquiry reflects, I think, the centrality of *jämställdhet* in Swedish policy-making which rests on the assumption that education can and should redress *unequal differences*. Policy documents, however, do not acknowledge that 'differences' can be constructed, understood and studied from many vantage points.

Teachers are important role models, according to the report, and schools need more male teachers. Girls 'need to see that men can work in female fields', and boys lack male teachers with whom they can identify (1994: 34). The question of committed, interested *and* gendered teachers is an interesting issue linked to the professional training of teachers. Commonly, educational experts and female teacher trainers view the 'uneven' recruitment into the teaching profession as a problem. The official supply estimate from Linköping University from 1996 states – under the headline of 'more equal sex distribution' – that the 'dominance of women in schools is probably a greater problem for equality between the sexes (*jämställdhetsproblem*) in society than male dominance in industry' (Linköpings universitets anslagsframställning 1996: 53). In the same section, it notes that only 17 per cent of technology students are female. Linköping University likes to stress its farsightedness in matters of *jämställdhet*. Equality between the sexes is seen as some sort of zero-sum game where there ought to be 'balance' everywhere. When such balance fails, the 'problem' is that not enough women make the right choices!

In 1995 a state-commissioned inquiry was made into the teaching training colleges in Sweden. The expert on *jämställdhet*, one of the special tasks of the inquiry, writes that in all teacher training colleges sexual equality is talked about, but often not much more. There is talk about the 'uneven sex distribution both among personnel and among students' (Högskoleverket 1991: 105). However, there are few concrete ideas for change. All colleges identified the lack of future male teachers as a problem. All interviewed saw the lack of career opportunities and the 'low salary and low status' of teaching as a reason why men do not want to become teachers (Högskoleverket 1991: 107).[14] In a few colleges, those interviewed also stressed that women must not take the blame for the sex ratio in the teaching profession. Educators and students in the teacher training colleges want more men because both sexes are needed as role models, and the work environment becomes better when both are represented in schools. The report continues:

> although the male students are always in a minority in the colleges it is not unusual that they dominate the student groups in terms of making themselves heard (just like boys in schools). Male students are also active in the student unions, etc., and many male student representatives took part in the discussions for this evaluation.
>
> (Högskoleverket 1996: 113)

The evaluator concludes that although the teacher training colleges are numerically dominated by women, the content of the curricula as well as teaching methods show that male values are dominant (ibid.: 115).

The reports on *jämställdhet* in schools and teacher training colleges make rather dismal reading. According to Swedish law, compulsory schools have to enhance equal opportunities between women and men, as noted earlier. Policy-makers, politicians, educators and citizens at large are concerned about the educational system. Swedes believe it is possible to change people through education. Within these systems, however, women take it upon themselves to devalue their contributions. They want more men involved, and actively help their male colleagues to positions of more influence and power. In the controversial state-commissioned inquiry discussed above, the main expert claimed that male dominance in higher education is expressed through 'male disciplines' getting more attention and funds. 'It is right to be where men are.' When scrutinizing *jämställdhet* in education documents this clearly stands out. In order for an institution to be 'right', men have to be there, to populate it and state their opinions. Both men *and* women agree to this. Men are not, like women, an 'untapped potential' for the development of the nation. They are the norm.

CONCLUSIONS: SEXUAL EQUALITY POLICY, HIGHER EDUCATION AND 'FREE CHOICE'

Debates about policies of *jämställdhet* in Sweden's higher education and schools today can be analysed from many points of view, but a gender analysis highlights the paradoxes of social engineering in which policies of sexual equality become instruments of cooptation or even repression. These policies, it can be argued, make women feel that 'the state' cares, hence luring women into education, which is deemed good for the nation. Thus, women continue, much more than men, to be the victims of state policies: obedient citizens who accept the rhetoric of 'good for the nation, good for all'. Women symbolically represent the childlike citizens who need to be told what decisions to make in order to be brought into the world of the grown-ups – that is, of the men.

Another perspective is to stress the change in Sweden from social engineering and general welfare programmes to a model where 'the market' is utilized as a metaphor also for state–citizen relationships. Viewed this way, it can be argued that citizens today are free to make the *right* choice. If women persist in flocking to fields of higher education where career opportunities are few and salaries are low, they must take responsibility for their choices. The struggle over 'right choices' between feminists and educationalists represents a response to this change.

Another perspective reveals how educational reforms shape state–citizen relationships and how such reforms produce elites. In this perspective the 'traditional' corporate society has not totally disappeared. Policies of *jämställdhet* are helped along by governments and political parties but they are seldom implemented by employers and often neglected by unions where women's influence is negligible. In the field of education, however, where the political influence is great, plans and projects to enhance more equal opportunities have to be paid attention to. The intersection between policies of *jämställdhet* and higher education is interesting because it highlights the ambiguities of policy-making and interpretation. Higher education is future-oriented. Students are educated for the future. *Jämställdhet* policies, on the other hand, often implicitly debate and rework the past. Historical developments are constructed, the past is recreated to set the agenda for the present. The intersection between education and *jämställdhet* can hence also be viewed as a symbolic arena where the participants in the debates try to cope with questions of loss and change, and struggle for future power and influence.

Jämställdhet is not yet contaminated by the failures associated with the traditional state welfare model, hence it is a fairly safe subject for debate in Sweden, unlike issues of class inequality and ethnic inequality. In these latter, 'difference' and 'similarity' are also salient concepts used to make and interpret policy. Class inequality has not been much discussed in the last decades in Sweden, yet recruitment to higher education is still very much confined to those from middle- and upper-middle-class backgrounds. Ethnic inequality is not yet seriously debated in Sweden despite massive immigration in recent decades. Within teacher training colleges, for example, very few students have a cosmopolitan background although all Swedish classrooms contain children with non-Swedish parents.

Essential differences and similarities are assumed in most Swedish *jämställdhet*-policies. In some contexts, similarity is stressed. It is assumed that women and men have similar obligations to society and to the family, and similar rights as individuals. Women and men are equally capable. But women and men are assumed different, in that they make different choices, talk in different ways and have different perspectives on science, life and politics. However, different strategies are employed when 'difference' and 'similarity' become the criteria used to make and interpret policy. By not really making equality between women and men into an analysis of gender, *jämställdhet* is malleable and can be moulded into various shapes and sizes. 'Difference' and 'similarity' are never scrutinized as concepts and never analysed as mirroring each other.

Policies of equality between women and men will continue to be privileged in Sweden because *jämställdhet* today is used and thought of as a uniquely Swedish invention in the cultural politics of transnational identities. Through policies of *jämställdhet* Swedish women and men can paradoxically say: 'We are different, we make a difference and our policies are different' within a European Union where centralized 'similarity' is shaped and fostered.

NOTES

1 All translations from Swedish are my own. I have tried to render the Swedish into intelligible English, but at the same time retain the rhetorical qualities of the texts.

2 The Swedish word *likhet* can mean both 'equal' and 'alike' and 'similar'. The conceptual fusion between similarity and equality in Swedish has successfully been utilized in politics during the construction of the 'folk home'.

3 1.2 million people migrated from Sweden to America up until the 1930s and 1.7 million people have migrated to Sweden in the post-World War II period (Lundh and Ohlsson 1994: 10–11).

4 See Rosendahl 1985 for anthropological analysis of the ideals of *folkhemmet* in a small community.

5 For an account of the Swedish national bourgeois in the nineteenth century and the virtues described as 'typically Swedish' (e.g. punctuality, cleanliness, love of Nature) see Frykman and Löfgren 1987.

6 A well-known propagator of the 'eaters'/'feeders' dichotomy is Bo Södersten, a professor of economics and former member of parliament for the Social Democratic party. He claims that women's work in the public sector is 'unproductive' and that industrial male workers are paid too little (*Dagens Nyheter* 1995: 4). Södersten is, at the same time, chairman of the university teachers' union.

7 Finland has (1993) 39 per cent female members of parliament, Sweden and Denmark both have 33 per cent, and Germany and Spain have 21.5 per cent and 14.2 per cent respectively (Hedlund 1993:109).

8 International comparisons are difficult to make, but according to Hedlund (1993: 95, 108) 1–2 per cent of the 'top-leaders' in British industry are women, and in Spain 10.5 % of the general director positions are filled by women.

9 Hence, Swedes, in general, are convinced that immigrants, especially from outside Europe, need to be educated into the Swedish ideals of *jämställdhet*.

10 The government pledged 25 million Swedish crowns (c. £ sterling 2.5 million) for the professorships and researchers for a period of three years.

11 The principle of public access (*offentlighetsprincipen*) to all official documents is highly cherished in Sweden and the lack of this principle in the European Union was one major argument against Sweden's membership.

12 'Women studies' (*kvinnoforskning*) as a concept includes both a feminist perspective and research on, as well as by, women. Typically, in public and academic debates, very little distinction is made between various aspects of *kvinnoforskning, jämställdhet*, and gender research.

13 In Sweden 'hierarchy' is studiously avoided as a concept in many official inquiries.
14 For similar debates in Eastern and Central Europe, see Einhorn (1993:124).

REFERENCES

Books and articles

Björk, Nina (1996) *Under det rosa täcket*, Stockholm: Wahlström and Widstrand.
Eduards, Maud (1995) 'En allvarsam lek med ord' in *Viljan att veta och viljan att förstå*, Sou 1995.110, Utbildningsdepartementet, Stockholm: Nordstedts.
Einhorn, Barbara (1993) *Cinderella Goes to Market: Citizenship, Gender and Women's Movements in East Central Europe*, London: Verso.
Elgqvist-Salzman, Inga (1995) 'Kvinnor i utbildningslandskapet – en utbildningsforskares reflektioner' in *Viljan att veta och viljan att förstå*, Sou 1995.110, Utbildningsdepartementet, Stockholm: Nordstedts.
Florin, Christina and Johansson, Ulla (1993) *'Där de härliga lagrarna gro'*, Kristianstad: Tiden.
Frykman, Jonas and Löfgren, Orvar (1987) *Culture Builders: A Historical Anthropology of Middle Class Life*, New Brunswick: Rutgers University Press.
Hedlund, Eva (1993) *Kvinnornas Europa*, Borås: DN förlaget.
Hernes, Helga Maria (1984) 'Women and the welfare state. The transition from private to public dependence' in Harriet Holter (ed.) *Patriarchy in a Welfare Society*, Oslo: Universitetsforlaget.
Hirdman, Yvonne (1989) *Att lägga livet till rätta*, Stockholm: Carlssons.
Lundh, Christer and Ohlsson Rolf (1994) *Från arbetskraftsimport till flyktinginvandring*, Kristianstad: SNS Förlag.
Olsson, Sven E. (1990) *Social Policy and Welfare State in Sweden*, Lund: Arkiv.
Rosendahl, Mona (1985) *Conflict and Compliance: Class Consciousness among Swedish Workers*, Stockholm: Stockholm Studies in Social Anthropology.
Södersten, Bo (1995) 'Women's salaries are too high', debate article in *Dagens Nyheter*, 30 April: 4, Stockholm.

Official reports, documents and newspapers

Forskningsfinansieringsutredningen (Report of financing higher education), SOU 1996: 29 (Official Inquiries of the State).
Frihet, ansvar, kompetens (Freedom, responsibility and competence), SOU 1992: 1.
Grundskollärarutbildningen (1995): en utvärdering (Teacher training for the

mandatory schools (1995): an evaluation), Högskoleverkets rapportserie 1996: I R.

Jämsides nr. 1, 1996.

Kvinnor och män i högskolan (Women and men in higher education), Högskoleverkets rapportserie 1996: 13 R.

Linköpings universitet Anslagsframställning, 1997–1999 (Supply estimates for Linköping University 1997–1999), Linköpings universitet 1996.

Linköpings universitet: Yttrande 1996 Dnr 3272/95 (Reply from Linköping University to official report).

Linköpings universitet: universitetets jämställdhetspolitik (The policy of equality between women and men at Linköping University) 1995.

Svenska Dagbladet 11 April 1996.

Utbildningsutskottets betänkande: Jämställdhet (The Parliamentary Committe on Education) 1994/95: Ub U 18.

Vi är alla olika: en åtgärdsrapport om jämställdhet i skolan som en pedagogisk fråga och ett kunskapsområde ('We are all different': a report for measures on equality between women and men in schools as a question of teaching methods and a field of knowledge), Utbildningsdepartementet (Departmental report) Ds 1994: 98.

Viljan att veta och viljan att förstå: kön, makt och den kvinnovetenskapliga utmaningen i högre utbildning (The will to know and the will to understand: gender, power and the challenge of women's research in higher education), Utbildningsdepartementet SOU 1995: 110.

Visst är vi olika! ('Of course we are different') Utbildningsdepartementet, 1993.

Chapter 6

The cultural politics of populism
Celebrating Canadian national identity

Eva Mackey

In the late twentieth century despite talk of transnational cultural forms and global economic systems, conflicts around national identity continue to fill the world's stage.[1] Further, salient political contests often occur *within* nation-states, and around differing conceptions of citizenship (Hall and Held 1989; Hall 1993). Many nation-states have witnessed an increase in both movements of an intolerant and 'populist' majoritarian Right as well as the assertive identity politics of minorities. Within this conflicted field, as Chatterjee points out, some of the fundamental tenets of Western liberalism are being questioned (1995: 11). For example, in India, as well as in Ontario, Canada, the Right have gained power through mobilizing precisely the key concepts and images thought to be the prerogative of the left, such as images of populism and the 'people'.

National identity is what Greenfeld calls modernity's 'fundamental identity'. She argues that 'the specificity of nationalism derives from the fact that in its framework the source of identity, whether individual or collective, is located within a "people" which is seen as the bearer of sovereignty, the central object of loyalty, and the basis of collective solidarity' (1996: 10–11).[2] Perhaps, therefore, it is not surprising that the term 'the people' evokes powerful and emotive, yet also ambiguous and contested images. Whereas in traditional leftist thought 'the people' call up images of a politicized popular class struggling for freedom and equality against an exploitative ruling class and its state apparatus, in New Right discourse 'the people' are constructed as a natural and non-political category of authentic citizens who resist the 'political correctness' of radicalized minorities and the meddlesome 'nanny state'. As neo-conservative parties are elected and form governments, policies

which draw on these discourses have become increasingly institutionalized.

As noted elsewhere in this book, anthropological studies of identity formation and nationalism have tended to focus on subnational
units, minorities and marginal peoples. They have also tended to
emphasize the (often quite recent) 'inventedness' (Hobsbawm 1983:
1–14) of these social collectivities. Yet nations are equally 'imagined
communities' (Anderson 1991), constructed through mass communications, mass rituals and state institutions of education and
culture. These processes of creating identity at a national level typically involve 'cultural politics' whereby attempts are made to
institutionalize a particular ideological notion of 'the people' in
order to create new types of citizens and subjects, and new categories of 'insiders' and 'outsiders' (Hall and Held 1989; Foster
1991).

Although the role of nationalist intellectuals in the construction
of national identity has received much critical attention (Nairn
1981: 329–63; Anderson 1991), the state has also been extensively
involved in this task, making the creation of identity in nations and
in regions a specific and named site of government policy (cf. Shore,
this volume). For example, in 1992, the Secretary of State of the
federal government of Canada had a 'National Identity and Special
Events Task Force'. This Task Force was responsible for planning
and organizing events explicitly designed to promote Canada's
national identity, particularly the celebrations of the 125th anniversary of Canada's formation as a nation. In 1992 the ruling party of
the government of Canada was the Progressive Conservative Party
and, as I discuss below, a key feature of its celebratory policy was its
use of populist imagery.

This chapter examines the cultural politics of how 'the people'
were represented in government policy aimed at the construction of
national identity in Canada during 1992. I seek to problematize
axiomatic assumptions and key concepts of policy, examine their
links to coexisting discourses, and document how these concepts are
mobilized politically by the people concerned, and how they function as 'organizing principle[s] of society' (Wright and Shore 1995:
30). I use this approach to examine Canada's 125th anniversary
celebratory policy, focusing on the cultural politics of a nexus of
key concepts concerning notions of 'the people' and 'populism'. I
ask, how are these concepts mobilized to define inclusion, exclusion
and belonging in the Canadian nation?

MULTICULTURALISM, CONSTITUTIONAL CRISIS AND CELEBRATIONS

Canada, during the past thirty years, has often been called a nation in 'crisis'. In part, the reason for this can be traced to historical conflicts between the different regional and cultural groups that make up the nation. Canada is a settler colony, and to simplify its complex history, first French and then English colonists extracted resources from, and then settled on, land previously inhabited by Native North Americans. In the struggle between these two colonial powers the English emerged as the victors, making one set of immigrants the dominant population. After Confederation in 1867 it was assumed that Canada's Native peoples would either become extinct or assimilate to the dominant European culture. In order to manage the differences between the nation's cultural groups, and to build the nation, eventually the French minority were accorded a modicum of constitutional rights, and European immigrants were encouraged (Trigger 1986; Harney 1989: 51–98; Palmer 1991; Whitaker 1991; Bumsted 1992a, 1992b; Francis 1992; Smith 1993: 50–77; Mackey 1996).

Since World War II, Canada has been defined by high levels of state intervention in culture, and has constructed a national identity based on the notion that Canada is tolerant to multiple forms of cultural and racial difference. Since the rise of the 'Quiet Revolution' of Quebec separatism in the sixties, the Canadian state has attempted to manage the conflict between the rest of Canada and Quebec, and Canada and its other minorities, through initiatives to create constitutional change as well as official policies of bilingualism and 'multiculturalism'. Multiculturalism is defined in official government discourse as a 'fundamental characteristic of Canadian heritage and identity'. Canada is often described as a 'cultural mosaic' (in which minority groups may maintain their cultural identities) rather than an assimilationist US-style 'melting pot'. Yet, despite this mythology of pluralism, white English-speaking Canadians have economic and cultural dominance. Canada is commonly described as having different kinds or categories of Canadian. These groups are 'First Nations' (Native or Aboriginal) peoples, the two 'Founding nations' (the English and the French), and finally 'ethnocultural' groups.[3] The hierarchy of belonging in these categorizations of difference is betrayed by the fact that white Anglophone Canadians often consider themselves simply 'Canadians' or '*Canadian*-Canadians', whereas other groups are marked by difference from this implicit norm (Mackey 1996; see also Moodley 1983; Breton 1988: 27–44; Lewycky 1992: 359–97; Satzewic 1992).

In the 1980s and 1990s, conflicts over culture, nation and race increased in Canada, and discourses of national belonging became more racialized. Canada saw growth in the activism of minority groups, as well as increasingly xenophobic and populist forms of nationalism spoken in the name of democracy and 'the people'. During 1992, political crises brought issues of identity to the forefront of Canadian politics. Canada's Native peoples had become a strong political force, and during 1992 were pressuring the government to implement a system of 'Aboriginal self-government'. Other minority groups were challenging the white Anglophone dominance seen to underlie multiculturalism (Mackey 1995, 1996). Quebec was beginning to speak again about separatism. At the same time, Canada was experiencing a 'white backlash' to these gains made by minorities.

The plans for celebrating Canada in 1992 took account of these conflicts. Many nations planned to celebrate the 1992 Columbus quincentenary, sponsoring extravagant celebratory displays to promote nationalism and stimulate international trade and global tourism. At the same time, Aboriginal and black North and South Americans sought to use the occasion instead to mark 500 years of resistance to European imperialism (Harvey 1992; Mackey 1996: 12–13). As early as 1988, the Canadian government set up a committee, made up of representatives from 'ethnocultural groups', Native people and Quebeckers, to make proposals on how to celebrate Columbus (Special Committee 1989). However, these potentially controversial official Columbus celebrations were jettisoned by the government in the early stages of planning. Instead, the federal government decided that in 1992 Canada was to have national celebrations of the 125th anniversary of its formation as a nation – the 'Canada 125' celebrations. These celebratory plans were part of a complex political manoeuvre by the federal Progressive Conservative government. They were intricately linked to the constitutional changes which the Progressive Conservative government was trying to initiate at the same time. In Canada, since the end of World War II, the Liberal Party had had nearly complete control of the federal government. Canada had defined itself by a social collectivist, protectionist philosophy, and policies of bilingualism and multiculturalism. However, in 1984, Canadians elected a majority Progressive Conservative federal government, led by Brian Mulroney. As with other Conservative governments, such as those of Margaret Thatcher and Ronald Reagan, two of their most central projects were the severe reduction of state power, spending and intervention, and the related aim of a more market-oriented, less protectionist capitalism (Simeon 1988: 25–47; Bashevkin 1991: 107–8; Feaver 1993; McBride 1993). Mulroney's government entrusted itself with the mission of 'the "reconstruction" of Canadian society and politics' (Gollner and Salee 1988: 21).

Part of this reconstruction involved attempts to create national unity through changing Canada's constitution. Beginning in 1989, the Progressive Conservatives began their 'Unity Agenda' of 'national reconciliation' which included the controversial Meech Lake Accord, and the Spicer Task Force (Cairns 1991; Milne 1991; McBride 1993; Vipond 1993: 231–9; Webber 1994). Each of these constitutional debates evoked calls of Canada's 'identity crisis'. In 1992, these 'crises' came to a head and the federal government attempted again to redesign Canada's constitution. The Conservatives set up the Beaudoin–Dobbie Commission, which made the Canadian constitution the subject of innumerable public hearings, debates and contests, culminating in the agreement known as the Charlottetown Accord, which was the subject of a national referendum in October 1992.

The 1992 celebrations were developed within this political context and in tandem with the political programme of the Conservatives. An employee of the government's National Identity and Special Events Task Force, Ronald Dagleish,[4] said that the cele-brations were one of twenty-six versions of 'identity and unity related projects' developed by the Task Force between 1989 and early 1992. The government had never had any intention of having Columbus celebrations. In fact, he admitted they had formed a committee of representatives of minority groups (the Columbus Committee) just so that they could say they had 'studied the sucker'. However, they never seriously intended to go through with the celebrations. Celebrations of Columbus, even critical ones, were simply too controversial. Further, in the specific political context of Canada's crisis (and the fact that 1992 could be an election year), forging and reinforcing national unity was a much more important issue and therefore it 'made more sense' to celebrate Canada's anniversary.

Planned at the highest levels of government, the celebration of the Canadian nation was an intensely political strategy, imbricated in a web of political events and repercussions. Further, the plans themselves changed as the political context shifted. Each day, and each week, as the complex political situation in Canada developed, the National Identity and Special Events Task Force, Dagleish told me, responded by inventing new and different plans for the celebrations. As the Conservative Party's popularity began to plummet in public opinion polls, the most important strategic issue was to make the government appear legitimate. Dagleish said that celebrating Canada during this time of political crisis, was 'dangerous'. The answer to this danger and problem of legitimacy was a policy designed to make the celebration of Canada appear 'populist', 'participatory' and non-political.

KEY ASPECTS OF CELEBRATORY POLICY

The mandate to have the celebrations appear populist and non-political had two facets. The first was institutional. Dagleish said that the government felt that the idea of celebrations 'brought to you by the government' would not 'go down well', during the recession Canada was experiencing and because of the sinking popularity of the Conservative Party. Therefore, rather than have government run the celebrations through a crown corporation, they formed the 'Canada 125 Corporation'. This was a private corporation, at 'arms length' from the government, and with no legal ties to the crown. The government gave money to the corporation to spend on the festivities. However, the celebrations were explicitly designed to be perceived as *not* organized *by the government*. This privatized version of celebrations was seen by Dagleish to be on the 'cutting edge' of 'event marketing'.

This move to private sponsorship, and private/public 'partnership' based on the model of 'event marketing' in big sporting events such as the Olympics is a reflection of neo-conservative ideologies of privatization and government 'down-sizing'. In the final celebratory plan, the government intended that businesses would facilitate this apparently non-political patriotism, through their sponsorship of activities. The federal government supplied only fifty million dollars, a minuscule amount compared to the immense government investment in the centennial celebrations in 1967, which I estimate at almost a billion and a half 1992 dollars (Mackey 1996: 112). The rest of the funding was to be raised through corporate sponsorship.

If companies donated funds, goods or services, their logos would appear on advertising materials and Canada 125 merchandise, and their names would be associated with the good feelings the celebrations were expected to arouse. These activities included companies such as Avis rent-a-car contributing free car rentals for one of the programmes, or a bus line or airline donating free trips for regional exchange programmes. It might also include Canada Dry supplying ginger ale for a National Neighbourhood Party (see Mackey 1996 for description).

Corporate sponsorship was also intended to help create a fiction of 'non-political' and populist nationalist celebrations, not 'brought to you' by the (political) government, but created through a combination of business sponsorship and 'grass-roots' activities. In these celebratory plans, therefore, government was constructed as 'political', and the celebratory policy was intended to erase government presence. Canada 125, on the other hand, presented business interests, as 'non-political' and non-partisan. An early advertisement for 'Canada 125' announced that any activity, to receive Canada 125 sponsorship, had to be 'non-controversial, non-partisan, and apolitical'. It described Imperial Oil (Esso) Canada as the sponsor of the Canada's national celebrations (Canada 125 Corporation 1992a). The federal government had privatized the country's national celebrations in order to appear non-political, non-partisan and populist.

In tandem with business sponsorship, the second facet of the 'populist' approach was that 'Canada 125' would focus on *local* celebrations of nationhood – creating or 'piggybacking' on existing local festivals community events. If a small town regularly held a summer community festival, Canada 125 hoped to have them register as a Canada 125 activity. Canada 125 Corporation would not directly give funds to local communities, although they might donate flags and banners. They promised, however, that they would 'facilitate' links between corporate sponsors and local communities. If a small town wished to have a beer tent in their festival, for example, Canada 125 promised to help link the local community with a potential corporate sponsor, such as Molson Breweries. The local community might get a discount, or even a donation, and the corporation would have its name associated with the local community, and with celebrations of the nation. The idea of piggybacking on local events was not only a means of reducing spending, it was also intended to bolster the appearance of celebrations of 'the people' as opposed to 'the government'.

According to Bill Sunfield, a spokesperson for Canada 125, its design was intended to promote a political agenda of patriotism and unity to support the federal proposals in the referendum, while presenting itself as the 'voice of the people'. It could only work, in Sunfield's words, if it could 'be unity without even being unity'. From the early planning stages, Canada 125 Corporation mobilized a conceptual division between political and non-political patriotism, and between politicians–government–the state and 'the people'. From the outset, according to Ronald Dagleish, the corporation would not support anything seen as 'political'. 'Political' was anything promoting divisions or controversy. He mentioned that they would not support political or controversial issues such as euthanasia, abortion, capital punishment, Oka warriors, or Lesbian and Gay Pride Day. The idea was to make the celebrations something to 'bring Canadians together' in a more 'personal' way by promoting 'person-to-person contact' and community activities. Indeed, in my discussions with planners and strategists in the Canada 125 campaign, the phrases 'non-political', 'grass roots', 'people focus', 'face-to-face', 'real Canadians', recurred with striking frequency. The celebrations, according to Dagleish, were intended to make people see that 'we [Canadians] are nice people', and that 'we have something in common'. They were designed to make people remember that in 'our neighbourhoods' and families we are good people – 'it is *politicians* who fight, not *us*'.

A key feature, therefore, of the Canada 125 celebratory policy is that it revolves around a conceptual opposition between 'the government' and 'the people'. 'The people' are presented as the site of authentic and non-political patriotism, whereas government involvement must be erased because it is perceived as divisive, political and manipulative. Ironically, it is the government itself which uses this opposition in an attempt to legitimate itself.

NON-POLITICAL PATRIOTISM AND CIVIL SOCIETY AS DIAGNOSTICS OF POWER

The reason why the government was denying its role in the Canada 125 celebrations, and why it was conspiring in the seemingly contradictory populist attacks on the 'meddlesome government', was because of the symbolic weight attached to popular conceptions of nation and state. As Handler (1988: 7) points out, 'the state' usually has negative connotations, associated with rational, instrumental organization, whereas 'the nation' is conceived of as something inherently wholesome, sentimental and less calculating. The former is typically regarded in pejorative terms as a necessary evil, whereas the latter, like the idea of 'community', is always deemed to be something natural, good and authentic. In nationalist logic, the source of authentic nationhood is seen to originate in 'a people', and ideally the state should reflect this authentic and natural 'nation'.

The Conservative mobilization of the idea of nation as the realm of 'the people' draws on historical conceptions of 'civil society', as well as the notion of the 'public'. These interlinked concepts are central to European political thought and practice, to the development of modern liberal nation-states, to ideas of democracy and to European political traditions (Taylor 1990). The notion of civil society, as originated by Locke, developed into 'a picture of human social life in which much that is valuable is seen as coming about in a *pre- or non-political realm*, at best under the protection of political authority, but by no means under its direction' (ibid.: 105).[5] Taylor contends that the later development of the idea of a self-regulating economy, and the notion of an autonomous 'public' with an opinion, give body to the Lockean idea that society has 'its own *identity* outside of the *political* dimension' (ibid.: 107–9). The connected language of 'the people', as in the phrase 'We, the People' (epitomized in the American War of Independence and the doctrine of Thomas Paine) takes the notion of civil society and links it to nationhood and self-determination. It draws on the idea that 'the people have an *identity*, they have a purpose, even (one might say) a will, *outside of any political structure*. In the name of this identity, following this will, they have the right to make and unmake these structures . . . This has become a commonplace of modern thought' (ibid.: 111).

Yet, as Foucault's work on governmentality (1991: 87–104) and subjectivity (1986: 229–42) reminds us, the conception of civil society as an 'autonomous order which confronts and experiences the state as an alien, incursive force' is implausible (see Gordon 1991: 34). Chatterjee points out that Foucault's concept of governmentality allows us to see this opposition between the state (as a domain of coercion) and civil society (as a zone of freedom) as in fact a 'liberal doctrine' (Chatterjee 1995: 32). 'The people' is a political, and hence contested, discursive construct (Hall 1981: 227–40).

Using Foucaultian notions of governmentality and subjectivity, I suggest that rather than take the opposition between these realms as 'common sense', it is more useful to explore how the conceptual distinction between them is mobilized and crossed over, to explore these categories as 'diagnostics of power' (Abu-Lughod 1990: 42) integral to the formation of subjectivities and identity.

Indeed, as I have discussed, these categories which construct civil society as a non-political realm of naturalized national identity opposed to the manipulative and political state are used by the government itself to attempt to legitimate its political programme and transform notions of national identity. It draws on common-sense liberal axioms, thereby naturalizing a particular view of national identity and attempting to reinforce particular forms of power.

NATURALIZING IMAGERY, CELEBRATORY TABOOS AND INVENTED SYMBOLS

Indeed, in much political discourse (Right or Left) it is a common-sense assumption that in theory, if not in practice, it should be 'the people' – defined here as 'civil society' and as a non-political realm – who should define and legitimate political authority. It is common sense that 'society has its own *pre-political life* and *unity* which the political structure must serve' (Taylor 1990: 111).

The nation, therefore, is often constructed with naturalizing imagery. As Anderson points out, the nation is often described:

> either in the vocabulary of kinship (motherland, *Vaterland, patria*) or that of home (*heimat*) . . . Both idioms denote something to which one is naturally tied. As we have seen earlier, in everything 'natural' there is always something unchosen . . . And in these 'natural ties' one senses what one might call 'the beauty of *gemeinshaft*'. To put it another way, precisely because such ties are not chosen, they have about them a halo of disinterestedness.
>
> (1991: 143)

Indeed, the recurring images of families, local celebrations, 'face-to-face' and 'grass roots' in the Canada 125 strategy were an attempt to make Canadian unity and patriotism natural, common sense and non-political.

In an effort to naturalize the idea of unity and patriotism as a non-political, non-governmental (and hence legitimate) phenomenon,

Canada 125 carefully strategized around their celebratory policy. First, they avoided using 'political' language and symbols of the state. Unity, as a keyword in political debate, and therefore a 'political' term, was literally erased from the language and programming of Canada 125. Bill Sunfield, a spokesperson for Canada 125 Corporation, said that words such as unity 'were *taboo* words for us'. Other Canadian symbols such as Canadian flags or maple leaves were also 'taboo' because people might see them as 'political'.

Further, these designers of patriotic policy consciously manipulated and created new patriotic symbols, strategically designed to distance commemoration from politics, and to present the celebrations as 'grass roots'. Sunfield explained that Canada 125 created its own logo, a 'new Canadian symbol', which had 'its own symbolic meaning'. He said there was 'a conscious attempt' to stay away from traditional Canadian symbols such as the Canadian flag, 'to fulfill the mandate that we were asked to fulfill'. New 'media vehicles' were invented and used by the Canada 125 Corporation to project these images. The most important were 'tabloids': information pamphlets which were put in almost all the homes in Canada in five editions over the spring, summer and autumn of 1992 (Canada 125 Corporation 1992b, 1992c, 1992d). Compared to some of the very glossy and highly produced patriotic advertising put out by governments and corporations during 1992, the tabloids, printed on newsprint, have a more gritty, less expensive, feel to them. They were designed to show what 'ordinary Canadians' were doing to celebrate Canada 125. As well as advertising Canada 125 merchandise, they also had listings of local, regional and national events. Sunfield said the tabloids were important because they listed local events that were very important to the corporation because they gave it:

> credibility, that was *proof that Canadians were doing something*. And we felt *the most credible thing* that we could do in this tabloid is to *have Canadians tell Canadians* what they are doing. Nothing from the *top down*. These are all *real Canadians*, and these were all real things that were happening. And again it was *Canadians telling Canadians* [EM's emphasis].

The tabloids had an opening section in which descriptions of patriotic activities were described in 'the voice of the people'. These 'human interest' stories about 'real Canadians' were specifically designed to inspire sentimental and naturalized feelings of patriotism.

WHICH PEOPLE?

There were also innumerable inconsistencies in the government's approach to the politics of celebration, at times verging on the absurd. However, these inconsistencies reveal modes of inclusion and exclusion in definitions of 'the people'. For example, the Secretary of State's theme song for the 125th anniversary was 'For Love of This Country'. It was played innumerable times on television ads celebrating Canada's 125 anniversary, sung by a girl who looked suspiciously like Mila Mulroney, the Prime Minister's wife. This song was originally commissioned by the Conservative party and first presented at a fund-raiser in Montreal in December 1991 (Winsor 1992b). It is difficult to maintain the fiction of non-partisan celebrations in this context.

Further, Canada 125 Corporation refused to give official recognition and rights to use the Canada 125 logo for a publication focusing on gays and lesbians entitled 'A Family Portrait: Gay and Lesbian Canada 1992'. David Roman, who initiated the Lesbian and Gay project, was told by Canada 125 that they routinely refused outside use of the logo. One of the other members of the project, Sandra Pate, tested the decision by sending in a fictional application. Pate, owner of a toy poodle named Butch, entitled her proposal 'The Joy of Toys: Toy Poodle Owners of Canada'. It was quickly approved by Canada 125 (Swainson 1992). When interviewed, Brian Barrett, a spokesperson for Canada 125, said the poodle approval would be rescinded as soon as possible. 'We're not infallible. This isn't the Vatican, you know. We're celebrating the country, we're not trying to tear it apart . . . anything controversial we're staying away from' (Swainson 1992).

Hitherto, in government rhetoric and programmes, and in the statutory Canadian Charter of Rights and Freedoms, multiculturalism had been defined as an inherent characteristic of Canadian national identity. Now, Canada 125, in trying to be non-political, implicitly constructed multiculturalism as *political*, and therefore not of the *real Canadian people*. Sunfield said that Canada 125 always made an effort to present Canada in a 'representative' way – 'You never saw a tabloid without an Asiatic person or a black person'. They did not, however, make any effort to '*promote*' multiculturalism because 'that would have been a *political* stand, and we didn't want to have any political connotations'. Further, Canada 125 did not support a project for a new 'multicultural' version of the national anthem because it might be seen as too 'political'. Other insiders from Canada 125 spoke about the internal politics of the organization. They suggested that even people hired with the mandate of including diverse populations in the celebrations were 'stonewalled' within the organization and excluded from major decisions. They were seen as too 'political'.

COEXISTING DISCOURSES

Government involvement in the celebrations took place within the wider context of Canada's political and constitutional 'crisis', and other strategic interventions designed to manage it. The Canada 125 plans were made during constitutional negotiations. The celebrations took place during the lead up to, and the campaigns for, the referendum on the Charlottetown Accord on 26 October 1992.

Even before the agreement was reached and the referendum date declared, the government drew together what one journalist called the 'sinews of a powerful communications organization', a 'propaganda machine', under order of the Communications Committee of the Cabinet (Winsor 1992a, 1992b). All government departments had been ordered to use their communications divisions to 'reinforce national unity' (ibid.). With a combined budget for television advertising expected to be over $100 million, the federal Department of the Secretary of State, the Ministry of Multiculturalism and Citizenship, the Department of Industry and the Department of Tourism created television advertising campaigns intended to promote national identity and unity. Winsor describes the 'feel-good' campaigns with war-like images: 'a major build-up of capacity to use communications and research as major artillery in the battle for Canadian (especially French-Canadian) hearts and minds' (ibid.). Further, during this time many businesses took it upon themselves to engage in what I call 'corporate nationalism' – using advertising to make statements about the necessity of unity in the country and referring to Canada's 125th anniversary and the constitutional debates. The Bank of Montreal put out a special full-colour eighteen-page insert for newspapers and magazines, entitled 'A Portrait of Canada', to celebrate Canada's 125th anniversary and the bank's 175th anniversary. On 1 July 1992 the 'Canada Day' edition of *Maclean's*, Canada's national news magazine, had several examples of 'corporate nationalism'. On the inside cover, the Chairman of the Board of the Investor's Group, speaks of his commitment to Canada as the son of immigrants, and the need to 'stand up on behalf of Canada'. The Canadian Imperial Bank of Commerce paid to have a sixteen-page discussion of the Constitution placed in the centre of this Canada Day edition of *Maclean's*, entitled 'The Constitutional Debates: A Straight Talking Guide for Canadians'.

On 26 October 1992, Canadians of voting age were asked to vote in a referendum on the Charlottetown Accord, answering 'Yes' or 'No' to the question 'Do you agree that the Constitution of Canada should be renewed on the basis of the agreement reached on August 28, 1992?'[6] Thus, during the fall of 1992 the media was a battleground of contested visions of Canada, and explicit attempts to influence voters (Mackey 1996).

The campaigns were very different. The Yes side, centralized and high profile, was supported by elites and money. The No campaign, dispersed and underfunded, was described as a form of 'Guerrilla warfare' (Jeffrey 1993). The Yes side was characterized as having a 'top-down' strategy and the No side having a 'bottom-up' strategy, coming from the 'grass roots' (Delacourt 1992a). In fact, in a manner similar to the celebratory policy, both sides of the referendum campaign tried to present themselves as populist and of 'the people'. The 'yes' campaign, for example, had a strategy that entailed attempting to erase government involvement in their campaign and tried to have it endorsed by 'ordinary Canadians'. Further, they prioritized business sponsorship, assuming this would be seen as non-political.

When the Charlottetown accord was first announced, it seemed virtually impossible that the public would not support it. However, on voting day eight weeks later, the Charlottetown Accord was rejected in the referendum. To many commentators, it seemed 'the people' had risen from the flames and shown the great distance between the 'elites' and 'ordinary Canadians'. The rejection was considered by many to reflect 'an underlying current of popular rebellion', and was called a 'popular uprising' (Jeffrey 1993).

The 'people', and their opposition to 'the politicians' and the 'government', became the main storyline in most versions of the referendum narrative. Jeffrey calls this the theme of ' "the little people" against the elites' (1993: 11). Many articles in the press, supported by authoritative graphs of poll results, showed the weakening of the Yes side ('the elites' who supported the Accord) and the strengthening of the No side ('the people' who rejected the Accord).

These articles had titles such as 'Loss of Faith' and 'The Deep Divide' (Delacourt 1992b).[7] Many saw the rejection of the Accord as a massive rebuttal of the Conservative party and politicians, and a moment in which 'the Canadian people' found their unified and true democratic voice. Others saw the campaign result as the 'harbinger of a new kind of democracy for Canada' (Gwyn 1992).

The discourses which coexisted with the celebrations of Canada 125, therefore, had a great deal of similarity with them, in that 'the people' were the subjects and the objects of advertising and propaganda. Furthermore, as in the Canada 125 policy, in the referendum coverage 'the people' were increasingly defined as 'non-political' Canadians – not immigrants, or people of colour, or lesbians and gays, or even women who were often defined as 'special interest groups' and not 'ordinary Canadians' (see Mackey 1996).

'THE PEOPLE' AT THE WALLACEFORD PUMPKIN FESTIVAL

Wallaceford is a quiet town of about 2,500 people, located in a tobacco farming area. It has a central core with many old and beautifully kept houses. The town is populated mainly by people of British and French background, as well as Belgians and Ukrainians (many of whom came to the area to grow tobacco). It has few 'visible minorities' (government terminology for racial minorities). The pumpkin festival I attended was an annual event begun ten years earlier, and in 1992, in combination with Canada 125, was the biggest they had ever had. It was estimated that over 40,000 people attended the festival over the course of the weekend.

The pumpkin theme of the festival was woven together to create an environment of 'old-fashioned family fun' – a nostalgic sense of the long-lost ideal small town at Halloween in autumn. When I entered the town at dusk on the Friday evening, houses and shops and street lamps were all decorated with corn stalks and jack-o'-lanterns. It even smelled like autumn and falling leaves, and it glowed with oranges and harvest colours. Most of the houses were decorated, some in an outrageous manner, reaffirming the sense that this was 'genuine' and not simply commercial and tourist-oriented. There was a sense that this was the authentic and non-alienated *gemeinshaft* of community.

The festival featured no ceremonies with politicians or national anthems, and no 'multicultural' tables, even at the craft fair, although imported goods were included. The fireworks had a Canada 125 theme, with the new multicultural version of the national anthem playing while colours filled the sky. The parade included a number of floats sponsored by local and national businesses such as Bell Canada, and a Canada 125 float which played theme music from the 1967 centennial celebrations. The only 'ethnic' float, sponsored by local Ukrainian-Canadians, celebrated Canada 125 and 100 years of Ukrainian settlement in Canada.

The idea of 'the local' as the site of non-political patriotism was central to the Canada 125 policy. They thought that erasing government involvement and highlighting businesses and local festivals would make the celebrations appear non-political. In fact, as in the Wallaceford Pumpkinfest, many of the local festivals were not focused on celebrating the 'multicultural' nation, but became primarily celebrations of unmarked and yet normative local white identity, seen as *Canadian*-Canadian identity (see Mackey 1996: Ch. 6). Further, at the Wallaceford Canada 125 Pumpkinfest, the idea of authentic and unified locality and the opposition between activities seen as political and non-political was mobilized by the organizers to exclude some community members from the festival itself.

Sounding almost like a Canada 125 advertising brochure, one of the organizers of the festival, Donald, told me innumerable times over the course of the weekend festival how his town was 'old-fashioned', and 'friendly', and how 'everyone worked together'. Like many other people in Wallaceford and other small towns, he suggested that it was the smallness and friendliness of the town which made it possible for them to have such a successful and pleasant festival. Painting a picture of community respect and consensus, he told me that in Wallaceford 'nobody interferes or forces anybody else's opinion. Everyone's opinion is respected'. He mentioned that there had been a small problem in town recently, but that he wasn't sure he wanted to talk about it.

As well as describing the lack of conflict in the town, he also detailed some of the decision-making and policy-making processes of the festival organizing committee:

The Pumpkinfest committee has maintained an attitude [that] we want to be totally *politically unbiased*. We don't want to, for example, put something in our parade that would be for the Yes or No vote. We are looking for total *impartiality*. We actually a couple of meetings ago issued a *policy*, we need a policy here, there's bound to be an issue come up at some time in the future, maybe this year or next year, some controversial type issue. We [had a] discussion at great length, and we ended up passing the motion that there should be nothing in the parade or any other event in the festival which would be in *bad taste*. We went through the wording. We didn't want anyone to express any *political* views; we ended up settling on wording that said '*in bad taste*' which would be up to the *discretion of the committee*, which would give *us* a little more *flexibility*, and *that's just the attitude of Wallaceford*, more *flexibility*, more *understanding*. For example, if somebody came with a float for the parade that said something we didn't like, that we thought was a controversial statement they would be politely asked to [stay out or change the message] [EM's emphasis].

Donald continued, 'We want *everyone's opinion respected*. We don't want our pumpkin festival used as a venue for any *controversial* issues of any sort'.

We return here to the notion of the 'non-political' as a model of consensus, and the institutionalization of this axiom in policy. Paradoxically, the exclusion of politics and controversy (both phenomena resulting from differences of *opinion*) is presented as a result of the committee and Wallaceford having respect and understanding for different *opinions*. Embedded within this rationale is the assumption that the community is, or should be, non-political. More importantly, *policy-making* at the local level of the pumpkin-fest parade, in a similar way to policy-making regarding national identity at the federal level in the Canada 125 Corporation, *institutionalized* the exclusion of 'politics' and controversy in order to create and defend a particular version of 'community'. This version of community also defines and limits norms of behaviour which become requirements of 'belonging'.

In fact, the 'controversy' that Donald had not wanted to talk with me about was the reason the festival committee made the new policy which outlawed 'bad taste' and controversy. A woman from Wallaceford had recently charged one of the 'respectable men' of the town with raping her at a school picnic twenty years earlier. A women's shelter in a larger town close to Wallaceford had been supporting the woman in her court case. In response, some townspeople had set up an anonymous fund to defend this man. At this point the fund contained contributions of over $20,000. The woman's shelter had wanted to have a float in the parade. The festival committee refused them on the basis of 'politics' and 'bad taste' after the policy meeting Donald described. People in the town were apparently still worried that the women from the shelter would show up and disturb the pumpkin festival.

When I asked Donald about the controversy, he said the fact that the town set up the support fund for the accused rapist was an indication of the kind of positive community spirit they have in Wallaceford. 'Even though the man was sentenced by a court', he said, 'Wallaceford stands up for its community members.' He added that this was unique and wonderful and showed what a great community Wallaceford was. 'No matter what happens, we stick up for our community members', Donald assured me.

Donald's expressions of local 'community logic' reflects, in microcosm, the opposition between 'the people' and 'politics' in the policy of Canada 125 and the coexisting discourses in the referendum campaigns. A nexus of conceptually linked ideas (the local as the site of natural consensus and community, and the opposition between political and non-political) have been mobilized to create ideas about authentic and non-authentic community or national identity – and hence about who is included and excluded in the ideal Canadian community. This form of identity construction excludes people seen as divisive and political (lesbians and gays, Oka warriors, people who raise 'women's issues'). It reifies a set of norms (*pace* Foucault) which act to categorize and isolate social deviants.

In Wallaceford, Donald expressed pride in how his community defends its own, how it sticks together no matter what. However, the woman who created the 'problem' had also lived in Wallaceford her whole life. But in one fell swoop, she is effectively constructed as outside the community because of her 'politics', and she is therefore not deemed deserving of the defence, respect or community spirit, which the accused rapist receives. As in notions of 'tolerance' to difference at a national level, difference is not allowed if it threatens the imagined community non-political *gemeinshaft*. People who embody forms of political difference perceived to threaten community consensus are cast outside the bounds of 'community' and nation. Like Donald, those left inside the bounds of 'community' – the political nature of their actions erased in a bubble of self-congratulatory 'non-political' authenticity – may even feel proud of what they perceive as the natural and authentic community

solidarity and consensus that remain. The notion of the non-political as the model of community consensus, drawing on key modern
liberal frameworks such as civil society, when embedded in policy at
local and national levels, allows both the exclusion of difference and
the construction of innocence.

POPULISM AND LOCALITY AT THE BROOKSIDE RAISE-THE-FLAG DAY

The conceptual opposition between political and non-political
patriotism was apparent in the town of Brookside, at a Raise-the-
Flag day ceremony, held on 26 September 1992, a month before the
referendum on the Charlottetown Accord. It was at the core of
some conflict between the mayor and members of the women's
service club which had organized the event.

Brookside is a small town approximately one hour outside of a
large urban centre. Similar to many other small towns of its kind,
its population is mostly white English-speaking Canadians. There
are few Francophones, Native people, people of colour, or groups
who explicitly define themselves as 'ethnic' in a politicized sense. At
the Raise-the-Flag day, the mayor of Brookside had wanted to use
the ceremony to have speeches promoting the 'Yes' side in the referendum. Mary, one of the organizers, had protested, arguing that
patriotism should not be enmeshed with politics. She wanted the
occasion to be without political speeches and to focus on the children of the town. She was already concerned that the ceremony
would be interpreted as 'political', because in a ceremony they had
had a few weeks earlier, there had been heckling from passers-by on
that theme.

Mary, when I interviewed her about the Brookside event,
conceived of the government as a 'political machine' trying to
'brainwash' and 'ram' the Charlottetown agreement 'down people's
throats'. She also proposed a naturalized division between politicians and the 'real' Canadian people. Although Mary had organized
the Raise-the-Flag day and was planning to vote Yes in the referendum, she explained that there was a big difference between 'the
government' and 'the community'. She commented on her feelings
about the referendum and the way it had been handled:

> I just think it's really sad that people are making it a government
> issue. And it's the country. It has *nothing* to do with the *govern-*

ment. The government has nothing to do with the country. We are a nation and we are making this a political issue and it's not a political issue.

These phrases of Mary's – 'the government has nothing to do with the country', and 'we are a nation and it's not a political issue' – are strikingly similar to the recurring themes of the Canada 125 strategy and the coexisting discourses. Indeed, Mary's statements draw on the idea of the nation and its people (civil society) existing outside of, and in opposition to, the manipulative realm of government and party politics. Mary argues for a more natural and less manipulative understanding of the nation and its problems. Similar to the Canada 125 policy and advertising, the idea of 'non-political' patriotism was linked to naturalized images of 'ordinary people' – families, mothers, children and communities. Mary discusses Canada's crisis:

To me it [Canada] feels like it's an ailing mother who's dying and the kids are all there fighting over what they are going to get out of it. They have the strength to help her, and bring her back. Maybe she won't be as strong as before, but she will be there for them. They have that power to help her and they're not doing anything, that's what it feels like to me. And if they would just stop fighting and nurture this ailing mother back to health. . . . It just scares me.

Mary's metaphor of the ailing mother in need of nurturing while the children bicker is compelling. It makes her critique of the government and what she calls 'special interest groups' commonsensical and very powerful. Who could gainsay that children should not argue while their mother dies? It is an image that defies disagreement if accepted on its own terms. The naturalized images of Canada as a family continue:

I've often felt that Quebec has been acting like a spoiled whiny brat. They want to leave home and they get to the point where the parents say, 'Just go, now you're on your own, if you need us call us, we'll always be here for you but go on out and give it a try, I hope you don't die.' There has to come a point where you can't tolerate it. Yeah, I think Canada's pretty close to that but, maybe it's getting, I don't know, politicians seem to ruin it. The issue is so much more grass-rooted than the way they have approached it. I think if you actually got all the people in

Canada together, if you got a mother of two children from Quebec to sit down with me in my living room, or a bunch of moms, or an aerobic class . . . Take that Quebec aerobic class and bring it together with an aerobic class in Toronto [and] you're gonna find out that a lot of people have a lot of things in common.

Mary's naturalized images of families, children and ordinary people make the abstract, complex and distant project of national politics understandable in an apparently common-sense language. Over and over again in the coverage of the constitutional debates, the press used these kinds of family metaphors. The coherence and mobilizing power of these images emerge from naturalized understandings embedded within them. Yet, these common sense, familial metaphors also delegitimate Quebec and the other groups demanding recognition in the constitutional discussions, and do so without even addressing the issues at hand. Simply by using the term 'whiny brat' for Quebec, Mary makes their demands seem illegitimate, ridiculous and childish. The image also infantilizes Quebec's aspirations for sovereignty, suggesting that the federal government should be like strong and knowing parents, parents who would discipline this unruly child.

More to the point, however, the government, politicians and 'interest groups' are constructed as a 'small number' of manipulators *dividing* the country, while the 'ordinary people' are seen to understand and know how to promote *unity*. Unity of all the differences, finding things in 'common', being able to 'get together and agree', is seen as natural and good, whereas division and disunity are seen as unnatural and bad. The naturalness of the unity of the nation is again created through a populist, familial and highly gendered image: the group of mothers with children at an aerobic class. The 'people', *ordinary* people in families with children, *know* how to solve the problems of the country, based on their experiences in families and communities. This is just plain 'common sense'. Indeed, these characteristics of the naturalized realm of 'the people' are similar to the definitions of 'civil society' I have discussed above. Civil society is seen as the source of the *unified* and *non-political* identity of society.

As I discuss above, the Canada 125 policy was also built on the notion of 'the local' as site of authentic non-political patriotism. For some people at small town festivals, notions of local place and community became the framework to express ideas of national belonging which limit and define 'Canadian' to mean white, small town Canadians and others who do not create problems. In Brookside, I asked Ron (a man in his early forties, wearing a 'Proud to be Canadian' T-shirt) why his town seemed to be so patriotic. He answered:

> I think it's more a sense of pride and Canadianship in a smaller community, as opposed to a larger place like Toronto. I opened the [*Toronto*] *Sun* this morning and the first thing that caught my eye was a full page of a Greek Minister [doing something for Raise-the-Flag day]. That's fine if you don't mind that – if you do it to yourselves – *but is that really Canadian?* Unfortunately, I think it is in Toronto, I think that's what being Canadian is in Toronto. In a town the size of Brookside, *this* is Canada; getting kids to sign a flag.

This striking comment about being 'really Canadian' was followed by similar descriptions of small town life, in opposition to the big city.

> In a place like Toronto there isn't that sense of being one big family, it's seventy-five different families. It's easier to get ourselves into a project like this because, given what we know, and are known around the community . . . There's something nice about walking along the street and being able to say 'Hi' to a few people or stand by a window and talk. In Toronto, if you say 'Hi' to someone, they wonder what's wrong with you.

Ron's romanticization of small town life, with its face-to-face contact, could be interpreted as a defence against the increasing urbanization and alienation of postmodern global living. This is the naturalized nation as *gemeinshaft* described by Anderson (1991) above. However, Ron's discourse is not simply positing the superiority of small town over city living. He is mobilizing a notion of locality in a discourse of national inclusion and exclusion. The naturalizing imagery of nationalism (the nation as family and local community) is mobilized to create boundaries of exclusion. He suggests that in Brookside, because they know each other, they can be 'one big family', whereas in Toronto they are 'seventy-five different families'. Family, in this moment, means cultural sameness. Toronto is implicitly set up as multicultural and, therefore, incapable of being 'really Canadian', whereas the small town is more Canadian. Here, concepts and images also embedded in Canada 125 policy – face-to-face contact and the local as the site of authentic national identity – are used to exclude 'multicultural' others from belonging in the nation.

Finally, Ron thinks that the government is destroying the country because of its political motives and 'political correctness' – especially their promotion of multiculturalism and other 'Balkanizing' factors. The government, too, is opposed to the sincerity and authenticity of small town non-political patriotism:

EM   On some of the Canada 125 ads they have a lot of multicultural shots . . .

RON   Politically correct.

EM   What do you mean?

RON   That's not a good word in my vocabulary. I use it as sarcastically as possible. Remember when we were talking downtown and I was talking about little events put on by a community. I was saying that small was more sincere than the big-scale stuff and the million dollars spent on fireworks. Well that's how those ads come across to me. Politically correct scenarios where everyone is singing smacks to me of political statements. Whereas a bunch of people giving out a cake in downtown with friends and neighbours walking by, we are here because we want to, making fools of ourselves because we want to. Not because we want to be politically correct.

In this passage, multiculturalism is equated with a manipulative and 'political' large-scale government campaign, and opposed to the sincerity of his local and all-white Raise-the-Flag day. In discussing the referendum, Mary also makes a series of oppositions in which, as I discussed above, the government and politicians 'brainwash' and 'ram through deals'. For Mary, it was also 'special interest groups' that were seen to inhabit the divisive political universe of manipulation, machination and bickering.

Ron and Mary's sense of locality – their non-urban, non-multicultural homes and their defence of the *gemeinshaft* of knowing and being known – is also the secure and authentic jumping-off point which allows them to propose that their identities *are*, or *should* be, *the* authoritative and authentic national identity. Their community became opposed to the political and manipulative patriotism of the government, and the un-Canadianness of urban multiculturalism. Further, both see themselves rejecting, and even resisting, the manipulations of politicians and the government. However, their discourses of belonging utilize strikingly similar frameworks to those of the government, at least in terms of definitions of authentic Canadianness. Paradoxically, the opposition between political and non-political patriotism allowed Mary and Ron to construct themselves as rebels against the very politicians and government which used the same populist images in order to influence them.

LEGITIMACY AND COMMON SENSE

The paradox that 'local people' felt they rebelled against the Conservative government, although using similar conceptual frameworks, raises a key issue. If we assess the Conservative celebratory policy in terms of whether it succeeded in helping to legitimate the government and their constitutional initiatives in the short term, it was a miserable failure. The Charlottetown Accord failed in the referendum, Prime Minister Brian Mulroney resigned as a result of that failure, and the Conservative Party was brutally defeated in the next election. Yet, many of the key frameworks I have discussed informing the policy and the Conservative agenda have gained legitimacy and increased social space. The press spoke (and still speaks) of the rejection of the Charlottetown Accord and the Conservatives as a 'populist' rebellion, even a new and unprecedented form of Canadian 'anti-elite' consciousness. To those of us schooled in Left politics, the idea of the people resisting the Conservative party is compelling. Yet, while the Conservatives may have been ousted, the even more extreme right and 'populist' Reform Party gained political ground and is now only a few seats short of being the official opposition. Further, the programme of the governing federal Liberals has shifted to the right. Ontario, the province where the festivals I have discussed took place, elected a Progressive Conservative provincial government which now slashes social services and fights unions in the name of 'the people'.

Indeed, the kinds of 'local people' central in Canada 125 discourses have become a defined, marked, and increasingly powerful, political force. Recently, the telephone area codes of such small town, mostly white, communities which surround Toronto have been changed to 905 in order to accommodate increased population. The press, accounting for the political clout of this population, has begun to speak of 'The 905 Revolution' (Delacourt 1995). The term 'revolution' also plays on the election slogan of Mike Harris, the new Progressive Conservative Premier of Ontario, who described his programme as a 'common-sense revolution'. Indeed, Harris was elected, according to results, primarily because of his ability to mobilize and speak to the concerns of voters such as these. Thus, people similar to those highlighted in the Canada 125 policy have become a defined and politically powerful population of voters, a specific 'public' which is addressed and responded to by political parties. The '905 revolution' is based on anti-government sentiment, opposition to taxes, replacement of the word 'citizen' with 'taxpayer', a belief in individual rights, and anti-immigrant and anti-minority sentiment (ibid.). Further, people such as these are increasingly, in political discourse and electoral politics, considered the 'ordinary Canadians', the democratic majority, whereas other groups are increasingly defined as 'special interest groups'.

This chapter has shown that the key term 'the people' is a site of political and discursive contest, and that key political actors shape and manipulate these terms for their own ends and institutionalize particular notions of identity and belonging in policy. Despite the fact that the policy failed in terms of legitimating the federal Progressive Conservatives in 1992, key features and conceptual frameworks of the policy linked to the concept of an exclusionary 'populism' have become 'common sense' and have more political and social space and legitimacy. The notion of the nation and the community as made up of a non-political and natural 'people' draws on notions of 'civil society' and 'the popular' which are fundamental to Western modernity and the development of 'the nation'. Significantly, it is through using these liberal categories that the Right has been able to successfully appropriate the conceptual ground of left and liberal democratic discourse, as they have in Britain (see Hyatt this volume) and in India (see Chatterjee 1995). These key assumptions are mobilized in Conservative policy to redefine citizenship and to naturalize the exclusion of some citizens from notions of national belonging, doing so without direct reference to culture, race, sexual preference and gender. This is successful because they draw upon common-sense oppositions between political and non-political forms of identity.

NOTES

1 This chapter draws on doctoral research based on fieldwork done during

1992 (Mackey 1996). Funding for the project was provided by the Commonwealth Scholarship Commission, the Social Sciences and Humanities Research Council of Canada and the Royal Anthropological Institute through the Emslie Horniman Anthropological Scholarship Fund and the Radcliffe-Brown Fund. I would like to thank Brian Street, Mary Millen, Rahnuma Ahmed, Rebecca Garret and Susan Reinhold for their intellectual inspiration and unstinting support for the project. I am grateful to Cris Shore for his comments on earlier drafts, and to Sue Wright for her comments on this chapter, and for her generous and ongoing support for my work.

2 Greenfeld continues, '[T]he specificity of nationalism is conceptual. Its foundation – and the only factor without which it cannot develop – is the presence of this particular concept of the "people" and the idea of the "nation" in which it is implied' (Greenfeld 1996: 10–11).

3 Of course, none of these groups are homogeneous. It should be pointed out that there are salient differences between 'ethnocultural' groups. White European immigrants, for example, were and are able to assimilate or partially assimilate into the dominant white Anglophone culture, and thereby become unmarked as 'ethnic'. More recent immigrants, often 'people of colour' – or 'visible minorities', in government parlance – do not have this option. For a more in-depth discussion of the cultural politics of multiculturalism in Canada, see Mackey (1996).

4 All people interviewed for this research have been given pseudonyms.

5 Civil society is usually considered to include areas of social life which are 'organized by private or voluntary arrangements between individuals and groups outside of the *direct* control of the state' (Held 1992: 73).

6 The Charlottetown Accord was a proposal for radical amendments to the Canadian Constitution. In more than sixty clauses it proposed changes to approximately one-third of the existing Constitution, including, *inter alia*, the definition of Quebec as a 'distinct society,' renewed commitment to official language minorities, reform of the House of Commons and Senate, a new division of powers between regional and federal governments, recognition of the inherent right of Canada's Aboriginal peoples to self-government, and amendments to the formula enabling constitutional changes to be passed (Jeffrey 1993; Mackey 1996).

7 Feature stories in *Maclean's* magazine on 12 and 19 October 1992 and 2 November 1992 all examine this issue. Articles such as 'The psychology of anger: Canadians are lashing out at the elites', by Nora Underwood (1992: 21) and 'What happens next?', by Anthony Wilson Smith (1992: 12–14), both examine this populist rejection of elites. 'Breaking down the vote' (ibid.), a report of the voting after the referendum, says that the failure of the Accord 'amounted, in effect to a massive repudiation by Canadian voters of the country's political and economic elites, the vast majority of which supported the agreement'. Alan Fotheringham's article in *Maclean's* (1992: 76), entitled 'A fury that found its voice', implies the rejection was a decision to 'rebel'. (For a more detailed discussion of the Charlottetown Accord and the Referendum campaigns, see Mackey 1996.)

REFERENCES

Abu-Lughod, Lila (1990) 'The romance of resistance: tracing transformations of power through Bedouin women', *American Ethnologist* 17 (1): 41–55.

Anderson, B. (1991) *Imagined Communities: Reflections on the Origin and Spread of Nationalism* (revised edition), London: Verso.

Bashevkin, Sylvia B. (1991) *True Patriot Love: The Politics of Canadian Nationalism,* Toronto: Oxford University Press.

Breton, Raymond (1988) 'The evolution of the Canadian Multicultural Society: the significance of government intervention', in A. J. Fry and C. Forceville (eds) *Canada: Canadian Mosaic. Essays on Multiculturalism,* Amsterdam: Free University Press.

Bumsted, J. M. (1992a) *The Peoples of Canada: A Post-Confederation History,* Toronto: Oxford University Press.

—— (1992b) *The Peoples of Canada: A Pre-Confederation History,* Toronto: Oxford University Press.

Cairns, Alan C. (1991) *Disruptions: Constitutional Struggles, from the Charter to Meech Lake,* Toronto: McLelland and Stewart.

Canada 125 Corporation (1992a) 'We're looking for some big ideas'.

—— (1992b) 'Canadians Say it Loud and Clear!', Canada 125 tabloid, April 1992.

—— (1992c) 'Happy Birthday, Canada!', Canada 125 tabloid, July 1992.

—— (1992d) 'The Celebrations Continue!', Canada 125 tabloid, August 1992.

Chatterjee, Partha (1995) 'Religious minorities and the secular state: reflections on an Indian impasse', *Public Culture* 8 (1): 11–39.

Delacourt, Susan (1992a) 'No appears stronger over long haul', *Globe and Mail* 19 October 1992.

—— (1992b) 'Loss of faith: the referendum campaign has exposed a great divide in Canada's political system', *Globe and Mail,* 24 October 1992.

—— (1995) 'The 905 revolution', *Globe and Mail,* 25 November 1995.

Feaver, George (1993) 'Inventing Canada in the Mulroney years', *Government and Opposition* 28 (4): 463–78.

Foster, Robert J. (1991) 'Making national cultures in a global ecumene', *Annual Review of Anthropology* 20: 235–60.

Fotheringham, Allan (1992) 'A fury that found its voice', *Maclean's* 2 November 1992: 76.

Foucault, Michel (1986) 'Disciplinary power and subjection', in Steven Lukes (ed.) *Power*, London: Basil Blackwell.

—— (1991) 'Governmentality', in Graham Burchell, Colin Gordon and Peter Miller (eds) *The Foucault Effect*, Hemel Hempstead: Harvester Wheatsheaf.

Francis, Daniel (1992) *The Imaginary Indian: The Image of the Indian in Canadian Culture*, Vancouver: Arsenal Pulp Press.

Gollner, Andrew B. and Salee, Daniel (1988) 'Introduction: a turn to the Right? Canada in the post-Trudeau era', in Andrew B. Gollner and Daniel Salee (eds) *Canada Under Mulroney*, Montreal: Vehicule Press.

Gordon, Colin (1991) 'Governmant rationality: an introduction', in

Graham Burchell, Colin Gordon and Peter Miller (eds) *The Foucault Effect: Studies in Governmentality*, Hemel Hempstead: Harvester Wheatsheaf.

Greenfeld, Liah (1996) 'Nationalism and modernity', *Social Research* 63 (1): 3–40.

Gwyn, Richard (1992) 'No to accord was also no to old-style politics', *Toronto Star* 27 October 1992.

Hall, Stuart (1981) 'Notes on deconstructing "the Popular"', in Raphael Samuel (ed.) *People's History and Socialist Theory*, London: Routledge and Kegan Paul.

—— (1993) 'Culture, community, nation', *Cultural Studies* 7 (3): 349–63.

Hall, Stuart and Held, David (1989) 'Citizens and citizenship', in Stuart Hall and Martin Jaques (eds) *New Times: The Changing Face of Politics in the 1990s*, London: Lawrence and Wishart, 173–88.

Handler, R. (1988) *Nationalism and the Politics of Culture in Quebec*, Madison: University of Wisconsin Press.

Harney, Robert F. (1989) ' "So Great a Heritage as Ours": immigration and the survival of the Canadian polity', in Stephen R. Graubard (ed.) *In Search of Canada*, New Jersey: Transaction Publishers.

Harvey, Penelope (1992) 'Discovering Native America', *Anthropology Today* 8 (1): 1–2.

Held, David (1992) 'The development of the modern state', in Stuart Hall and Bram Gieben (eds) *Formations of Modernity*, Cambridge: Polity Press.

Hobsbawm, Eric (1983) 'Introduction: inventing traditions', in Eric Hobsbawm and Terence Ranger *The Invention of Tradition*, Cambridge: Cambridge University Press.

Jeffrey, Brooke (1993) *Strange Bedfellows, Trying Times*, Toronto: Key Porter Books.

Lewycky, Laverne (1992) 'Multiculturalism in the 1990s and into the 21st century: beyond ideology and utopia', in Vic Satzewic (ed.) *Deconstructing a Nation: Immigration, Multiculturalism and Racism in '90s Canada*, Halifax: Fernwood Publishing, 359–97.

Mackey, Eva (1995) 'Postmodernism and cultural politics in a multicultural nation: contests over truth in the "Into the Heart of Africa" controversy', *Public Culture* 7 (2): 403–32.

—— (1996) 'Managing and imagining diversity: multiculturalism and the construction of national identity in Canada', D.Phil. thesis in Social Anthropology, University of Sussex (unpublished).

Maclean's (1992) 'Breaking Down the Vote', 2 November 1992: 18–19.

McBride, Stephen (1993) 'Renewed federalism as an instrument of competitiveness: Liberal political economy and the Canadian Constitution', *International Journal of Canadian Studies* 7–8: 187–205.

Milne, David (1991) *The Canadian Constitution*, Toronto: James Lorimer.

Moodley, Kogila (1983) 'Canadian multiculturalism as ideology', *Ethnic and Racial Studies* 6 (3): 320–31.

Nairn, T. (1981) *The Break-up of Britain: Crisis and Neo-Nationalism*, London: Verso.

Palmer, Howard (1991) *Ethnicity and Politics in Canada Since Confederation*, St John, N.B.: Canadian Historical Association.

Satzewic, V. (1992) 'Introduction', in V. Satzewic (ed.) *Deconstructing a Nation: Immigration, Multiculturalism and Racism in '90s Canada*, Halifax: Fernwood.

Simeon, Richard (1988) 'National reconciliation: the Mulroney government and federalism', in Andrew B. Gollner and Daniel Salee (eds) *Canada Under Mulroney*, Montreal: Vehicule Press.

Smith, Susan (1993) 'Immigration and nation-building in Canada and the United Kingdom', in Peter Jackson and Jan Penrose (eds) *Constructions of Race, Place and Nation*, Minneapolis: University of Minnesota Press.

Special Commitee on Canadian Participation in the 1992 International Anniversary of Christopher Columbus's first voyage to the Americas (1989) 'Report to the Minister of State: Multiculturalism and citizenship', unpublished document obtained from the Secretary of State.

Swainson, Gail (1992) 'Poodles win Canada 125 logo rights but gays don't', *Toronto Star* 9 August 1992.

Taylor, Charles (1990) 'Modes of civil society', *Public Culture* 3 (1): 95–118.

Trigger, Bruce G. (1986) 'The historian's Indian: Native Americans in Canadian historical writing from Charlevoix to the present', *Canadian Historical Review* LXVII (3): 315–42.

Underwood, Nora (1992) 'The psychology of anger: Canadians are lashing out at the elites', *Maclean's* 12 October 1992.

Vipond, Robert C. (1993) 'Constitution making in Canada: writing a national identity or preparing for national disintegration?' in Vivien Hart and Shannon C. Stimson (eds) *Writing a National Identity: Political, Economic and Cultural Perspectives on the Written Constitution*, Manchester: Manchester University Press in association with Fulbright Commission.

Webber, Jeremy (1994) *Reimagining Canada: Language, Culture, Community, and the Canadian Constitution*, Kingston and Montreal: McGill–Queen's University Press.

Whitaker, Reg (1991) *Canadian Immigration Policy Since Confederation*, St John, N.B.: Canadian Historical Association.

Wilson Smith, Anthony (1992) 'What happens next?' *Maclean's* 2 November 1992.

Winsor, Hugh (1992a) 'The high cost of feeling better', *Globe and Mail*, 26 May 1992.

—— (1992b) 'Bidding to quicken the patriotic heart beat', *Globe and Mail*, 28 May 1992.

Wright, Sue and Shore, Cris (1995) 'Towards an anthropology of policy: morality, power and the art of government', *Anthropology in Action* 2 (2): 27–31.

Chapter 7

Governing Europe
European Union audiovisual policy and the politics of identity

Cris Shore

> Europe, the stage for the two greatest conflicts of the century, has – in creating the Community – invented a new form of government in the service of peace.
>
> (Commission of the European Communities 1995a: 5)

ANTHROPOLOGY, IDENTITY AND THE POLITICS OF COMMUNICATION

Anthropologists have long studied identity formation, ethnicity and nationalism as 'micro' or local-level phenomena. They have paid detailed attention to the symbols and 'invented traditions' upon which these are based and the social contexts in which they are embedded. They have also analysed the myriad ways in which identities are organized and articulated and their complex relations to social boundary markers such as race, religion, language and ideology – and how these are constantly challenged and recreated in the practice of everyday life. However, the anthropological focus on identity formation has typically concerned itself with subnational units, minorities and marginal peoples (Chapman et al. 1989: 17). Relatively seldom have anthropologists 'studied up' beyond the subnational level to document how larger-scale collectivities are forged by *policy*, or how policy functions as an instrument for constructing mass identities. Oddly, this task has been left largely to historians, sociologists of nationalism and media and communications theorists. I say 'oddly' because at the heart of attempts to construct nations lie processes of fundamental concern to anthropology: mobilizing rituals and symbols, manipulating heritage, rewriting history, creating new boundaries of inclusion/exclusion, reclassifying peoples (as 'citizens', 'subjects' and 'outsiders') – all of which pertain to the 'politicization of ethnicity' and its obverse, the 'ethnicization of polity' (Grillo 1980). State-formation, nation-building and nationalism are therefore inherently *anthropological* phenomena, deeply implicated in the politics of identity formation (Anderson 1983; Gellner 1983; Shore and Black 1992, 1994).

However, whereas identity formation has tended to be perceived as a cultural process shaped either by macro historical forces or, following Hobsbawm and Ranger (1983), by the manipulative actions of inventive entrepreneurs and freelance agents, the approach developed here takes *policy* as the framework for analysing these processes and as a site of contestation between rival discourses over the identity to be forged. Developing this 'policy perspective', this chapter explores two questions.[1] First, why do European Union ('EU') elites attach so much significance to communication policy as a factor in European integration and are there parallels here with the role of communications in the history of nation-state formation? Second, what light can analysis of European Union communication policy shed on the way different systems of governance are being constructed and contested within Europe today?

Taking up the first question, a prerequisite for the emergence of the modern nation state was not only the existence of an elite of administrators and intellectuals enthused with national conscious-ness, but the communication technologies necessary for spreading and amplifying the nationalist message.[2] 'The new middle class intelligentsia of nationalism', as Tom Nairn (1977: 340) put it, 'had to invite the masses into history; and the invitation-card had to be written in a language they understood'. To use Althusser's termi-nology (1971), the masses had to be 'interpellated' and 'hailed' as national subjects before the nation state could become a political reality. Mass communications – combined with taxation, education and conscription – were the primary agents of modernity that helped achieve this; shifting people's loyalties away from the parochialism of village life and the universalism of great empire towards the new, and often revolutionary, ideas of 'nationhood' and 'citizenship'.

As most theories of nationalism suggest, communications are central to the construction of large-scale social identities (Deutsch 1966; Gellner 1983; Schlesinger 1991). Paradoxically, they also play a critical role in breaking down established collectivities, as witnessed in former Yugoslavia where the different nationalist media were particularly instrumental in setting the stage for the 'ethnic cleansing' and subsequent Balkanization of that once multi-ethnic state (Bowman 1994: 152–6). Recent revolutions in communication technologies may also be contributing to what Mestrovic (1994) calls the 'Balkanization of the West': the fragmentation of those older identities associated with modernity and based on class, gender, religion, occupation and nationality – all of which were once seemingly contained under what Gellner (1983: 1) called the 'political roof' of the nation state. Yet modern communications have also created new possibilities for *supranational* political institutions (including those of the European Union), and for forms of cultural pan-nationalism hitherto unknown (Smith 1992). This paradox, which reflects something of the 'condition of postmodernity', has major implications for the future of the nation state and for European Union policies for promoting social cohesion and integration among the peoples of Europe.

AUDIOVISUAL POLICY AND EUROPEAN INTEGRATION

Since its inception in the 1980s, the audiovisual policy of the European Union has generated intense debate and controversy among both academics and politicians.[3] In part, this reflects the important place the media occupy in all modern societies, lying as they do 'at the heart of the major economic, industrial, cultural, social and technological challenges facing us' (CEC 1995b: 5). Yet it also reflects the high expectations European Union officials and politicians place on the media industries as political tools for furthering European integration. Stripped to its essentials, the European federalist (or 'constructivist')[4] argument is that television, broadcasting and film are not simply commercial services requiring regulation within the single European market, but cultural agents for creating a collective 'European consciousness' among Europe's divided nations. Indeed, broadcasting is thought to be a particularly effective instrument for reinforcing the European values and 'cultural identity' upon which integration depends (Vasconcelos et al. 1994: 60).

The assumption here, which echoes contemporary theories of the nation state as 'imagined community' (Anderson 1983) or type of 'narrative' (Bhabha 1990), is that the mass media could provide the 'social glue' necessary for welding Europeans into a cohesive body-politic or 'demos'. 'The idea', as Kevin Robins comments, 'is that transnational media will give rise to transnational publics who will then begin to imagine the new community of Europe' (Robins 1994: 81). A self-recognizing *European* public would also lend much needed authority to those institutions of European governance, particularly the European Commission, whose legitimacy largely rests upon its claim to serve the (hitherto ill-defined) 'European interest' (Soledad-Garcia 1994). The European Commission typically portrays itself as 'custodian of the European interest', 'guardian of the treaties', 'engine of European integration' and even 'future government of Europe in waiting' (George 1985; Spence 1994: 90). However, if there is no such thing as a 'European people' or self-constituting 'European public' – as is currently the case – then such claims ring hollow. To put it another way, if the newly constituted category of 'European citizenship' does not translate into 'European consciousness' or a new kind of 'European subjectivity', then the self-denominated political needs and reasons of European Union institutions simply become a new version of *'raison d'état'*.

For European officials and Euro-federalists the new Europe must therefore be forged at the level of ideas and images as well as institutions: the former providing the ideological building blocks and legitimacy for the latter. This idea of 'transcending' the nation state in Europe by creating supranational institutions, although contested by some member states, is typically justified in terms of the EU treaties themselves. The rationale that drives European Union policy may be economics,[5] but the longer-term goal enshrined in its founding treaties, and repeated in the 1992 Maastricht Treaty, was political: to 'forge an ever-closer union among the peoples of Europe' (CEC 1983: 113, 1992a: 2). The creation of what the Commission calls a 'European audiovisual space' not only satisfies the commercial logic of the single European market programme, for EU policy makers it also provides a vehicle and 'mobilizing metaphor' (see Shore and Wright, this volume) for transforming the 'technocrats' Europe' of legal treaties and economic transactions into a popular 'people's Europe' (another mobilizing metaphor) in which European citizens share common rights and a collective sense of identity and belonging. With its capacity for creating myths 'which then become collective dreams and enter the history of a people', concludes the Commission's think-tank on audiovisual affairs, 'the audiovisual sector could become the ideal instrument to consolidate the process of European integration' (Vasconcelos et al. 1994: 60, 63). However, these assumptions about the integrative role of the mass media are questionable. Closer analysis of European Union audiovisual policy reveals radically different and conflicting discourses at work among member states concerning cultural identity and governance in Europe.

TELEVISION WITHOUT FRONTIERS: FROM 1984 GREEN PAPER TO 1989 DIRECTIVE

The history of the EU's audiovisual policy can be charted from June 1984 with the publication of the Commission's influential Green Paper, 'Television Without Frontiers' (CEC 1984). The aim of this 342-page document was to set out draft rules for the creation of a single European market in broadcasting and media services. These included proposals for regulating advertising standards, copyright and programming, as well as measures for promoting new media technologies and the distribution of programmes throughout the Community. The Green Paper promised 'free skies over Europe' by eliminating commercial restrictions on information flows, abolishing barriers arising from the different technical standards operating in different countries and the establishment of an overarching broadcasting framework of pan-European norms and rules. In effect, harmonization meant simultaneously liberalizing yet 'Europeanizing' standards in order to create the 'level playing field' necessary for the single European market to operate, with a corresponding emphasis on enhancing profits, market share, competition, economies of scale and rationalization. As a result, the single market was perceived to move 'hand in hand with an erosion of the *cultural* dimension upon which the European public service tradition has been based' (Burgelman and Pauwels 1992: 169).

While espousing free-market principles, the European Commission (under pressure from France) therefore set up a series of countervailing measures to protect the European film and TV industries from the effects of opening up the market. Briefly, these included a series of European sponsorships, subsidies and pump-priming initiatives, such as the various 'MEDIA' programmes (Measures to Encourage the Development of an Audiovisual Industry). From a purely commercial perspective the European media industries appeared weak, fragmented and under threat from global broadcasting giants (Burgelman and Pauwels 1992: 171). Fears of competition from America and Japan had earlier galvanized the Commission into promoting a new private sector strategy to meet this challenge. The idea was that if national champions in the media industries could expand their operations, this would create a sufficiently large market to stimulate a recovery throughout the European consumer electronics industry – which the Delors Commission was particularly eager to promote (Ross 1993). When this strategy failed, the idea of the 'European champion' emerged. The problem here though was that pan-European television channels also failed because of the linguistic insularity of the television market: as many advertisers have found to their cost 'cultural and consumer symbols do not translate well across borders' (Davis and Levy 1992: 471).

A further aim of the Green Paper was perhaps more relevant to the idea of European governance: to set out the Commission's claim for jurisdiction in the audiovisual field. This was particularly controversial for while the Commission's competence in regulating services was accepted unequivocally, its competence to regulate in 'cultural' matters was fiercely disputed (Gavin 1991: 42; Davis and Levy 1992: 272). Moreover, the Treaty of Rome had given the Commission no legal competence to intervene in the cultural sector. Acknowledging this in his first speech as Commission President to the European Parliament in 1985 Jacques Delors declared that:

> the culture industry will tomorrow be one of the biggest industries, a creator of wealth and jobs. Under the terms of the Treaty we do not have the resources to implement a cultural policy; but we are going to try to tackle it along economic lines. . . . We have to build a powerful European culture industry that will enable us to be in control of both the medium and its content, maintaining our standards of civilization, and encouraging the creative people amongst us.
>
> (Delors, cited in Collins 1993: 90)

The Commission was therefore operating a *de facto* cultural policy long before the Maastricht Treaty of 1992 gave it the legal right to do so. European Union officials were claiming authority over far greater domains of governance than the Treaties originally allowed for. Significantly, the Commission's Green Paper defended Community intervention in audiovisual matters on the grounds that although broadcasting embraces many *cultural* activities, insofar as these are carried out for 'remuneration' they can be deemed economic activities, and hence fall squarely within the category of 'goods and services' covered by existing European Community law

(CEC 1984: 6–7; 1994: 2).[6] In order to extend the Commission's scope and influence, the cultural industries and broadcasting services were thus redefined as 'commercial' enterprises. However, they were later reclassified as 'cultural services' again when American negotiators insisted that, as *commercial* enterprises, they be included in the GATT talks on world trade (much to the chagrin of the French government which had long sought to exploit the definitional boundary between culture and commerce in its efforts to continue subsidizing France's media industries).

Within the Commission, two political currents were clearly discernable on this and other policy issues. One is neo-liberal, *laissez faire* and conservative, the other is broadly social-democrat, interventionist and grounded in a predominantly French model of centralized state planning (or *dirigisme*). Knowing that appeals to free-market economics alone would not guarantee sufficient support to enable the proposal to be translated into law, the neo-liberals within the Commission (who were the prime movers behind the Green Paper) tried to 'sell' its liberal doctrine of an integrated Community broadcasting market to the interventionists by claiming that the single market would strengthen the European audiovisual industry in the face of the American and Japanese challenge *and* assist the growth and dissemination of European culture (Collins 1993: 11). In short, they appealed to a sense of 'Euro-patriotism' against generally perceived threats from the non-European other.[7]

If, as anthropologists have often shown, the identity of a group of people crystallizes most sharply in situations of adversity and threat, then clearly fears about US and Japanese cultural imperialism were not shared equally among different member states. It took five years of protracted negotiations over the degree of harmonization needed for achieving a single Community broadcasting market before the long-awaited Directive on Television Broadcasting was agreed in October 1989. Not surprisingly, this reflected the compromise between neo-liberalism and *dirigisme* necessary for securing a qualified majority vote in support of the Directive (Collins 1993: 13). The Directive spoke of 'coordinated action' for three objectives: 'the establishment of the rules of the game, promotion of the programme industry and mastery of new technologies' (CEC 1990: 33). 'Coordinated action' meant, *inter alia*; creating a common market in television broadcasting and programme supply, stimulating the audiovisual sector in restricted language areas and in countries with a low production capacity (particularly Belgium, Holland and Denmark), establishing minimum standards for television advertising and sponsorship (especially for tobacco and alcohol advertising), instituting a 'right of reply' and prohibiting programmes which threatened the 'physical, mental or moral development of minors'.

However, the most controversial aspect was Article 4. This required that 'Member States shall ensure where practicable and by appropriate means, that broadcasters reserve for European works . . . a majority proportion of their transmission time, excluding the time appointed to news, sports events, games, advertising and teletext services' (CEC 1990: 18). This call for a 'European content quota' and an effective 49 per cent ceiling on broadcasting foreign programmes – inserted at France's insistence[8] – immediately provoked accusations of protectionism from US representatives at the GATT world trade negotiations, prompting threats of American reprisals. Broadly speaking, the American interpretation was correct: imposing quotas on the amount of 'non-European' programmes allowed in any European country was a protectionist strategy – and, as the world's largest exporter of films and television programmes, America had most to lose from any system designed to limit access to European markets. However, the article contained a legal loophole in its wording. The 'where practicable' caveat meant that the provision carried no juridical force whatsoever; it 'merely gave expression to a political desire' which member states could ignore should they so wish (Burgelman and Pauwels 1992: 169).

CREATING A 'COMMUNITY OF EUROPEANS': THE POLITICS OF MEDIA POLICY

Beyond the rhetoric of the single European market, European federalists and the *dirigiste* camp sought to use audiovisual policy as a vehicle for promoting 'social cohesion' and 'European consciousness'. Guiding this strategy was the belief that a stronger 'European identity' was needed to overcome Europe's divisive legacy of nationalism and to buttress the technical aspects of integration, and the belief that this could be developed by promoting 'cultural Europeanness'. During the late 1980s, therefore, the idea of creating such a 'European identity' gained momentum among Europe's technocratic elites, particularly those officials employed in

DGX, the Commission's Directorate for Audiovisual and Cultural affairs.[9]

Despite the enthusiasm for European integration reported in the Commission's own *Eurobarometer* polls, evidence elsewhere suggested widespread indifference and cynicism towards the European Union. With persistently low and falling turnouts in successive European elections and the near-disastrous 1992 Danish and French referenda on ratification of the Maastricht Treaty, the Commission was clearly failing to engage the support of its would-be citizens. Meanwhile, popular media stereotypes continued to portray the Commission as a remote, meddlesome, unelected bureaucracy zealously trying to regulate everything from exchange rates and national borrowing levels, to the shape of cucumbers and the permitted noise levels for lawnmowers. While some officials argued for greater transparency and openness within European Union institutions to head off criticism and win over sceptics, the Commission concluded that the EU's problems were largely matters of image and identity. The solution it proposed was to organize a series of public relations exercises and 'information campaigns' designed to promote greater awareness of the European Union and convince people of its merits (see Adonnino 1985; de Clercq 1993). The hope was that creating a more accessible 'Citizens' Europe' would generate political spill-over in the form of greater popularity (and legitimacy) for EU institutions.

Significantly, therefore, the 1984 'Television Without Frontiers' proposal was published in the same year as the European Community launched another important cultural initiative: the 'People's Europe' campaign. This aimed specifically at forging 'European consciousness' through a series of practical and symbolic measures. Foremost among these was the creation of a new repertoire of Euro-symbols to express European identity and citizenship (Shore 1993, 1995). These included a new European passport and flag (a circle of twelve gold stars on a blue background), a European anthem (taken from Beethoven's 'Ode to Joy' and described as 'particularly representative of the European idea' (Adonnino 1985; Fontaine 1991)); European car number plates, twinning arrangements, sports competitions and honorary awards; the creation of 'European cities of culture'; and a new European calendar with special 'European years', 'European weeks', and commemorative public holidays marking significant moments in the history of European integration, including the accession of Spain

and Portugal and Robert Schumann's birthday on 9 May (designated official 'Europe Day').

Initially, the Commission saw cross-border television as a key
instrument for forging 'Europeanness'. As Schlesinger observes
(1994: 29), this was 'an exemplary instance of a rationalist approach
to cultural management'. EU officials were effectively arrogating to
themselves the role of social engineers and cultural brokers – a
political role seemingly at odds with their formal status as apolitical
'public servants'. After 1992, however, the Commission was given
official jurisdiction over cultural affairs with the inclusion of Article
128 of the Maastricht Treaty. This calls on the Community 'to
contribute to the flowering of the cultures of the Member States'
while 'bringing the common cultural heritage to the fore'. In addition to a stipulation that 'the Community shall take cultural aspects
into account in its action under other provisions of this Treaty', the
Article (CEC 1992a: 13) lists four specific objectives:

- improvement of the knowledge and dissemination of the culture
  and history of the European peoples;
- conservation and safeguarding of cultural heritage of European
  significance;
- non-commercial cultural exchanges;
- artistic and literary creation, including in the audiovisual sector.

This emphasis on promoting Europe's 'common cultural heritage'
and defending the 'core values' of 'European civilization' are recur-
rent themes in Commission discourse. Their influence can be seen in
numerous policies and practices, from EU 'information' pamphlets
and 'cohesion funds', to 'targeted socio-economic research' and
student exchange schemes ('ERASMUS', 'SOCRATES',
'TEMPUS'). As Ray Pahl (1991) notes, underlying Commission
thinking is a constant quest for 'social cohesion' – a preoccupation
which recalls the naive consensus model of society and uncritical
view of power typical of the outdated functionalist paradigm of
Western social science. The ideological assumption underpinning
the Commission's policy agenda is that European citizens must inte-
grate and 'cohere' around supranational European institutions –
which are, by definition, more advanced and progressive than their
national counterparts – in order to transcend the parochialism of
their national sentiments and reach the higher plain of European
consciousness. In many respects, this is simply an extension of its
earlier policy of *engrenage* – the practice of bringing national

bureaucracies together so that civil servants would acquire the habit of approaching problems from a 'European' perspective – to the whole population of Europe. Paradoxically, the assumption that cultural and political identities must be congruent if institutions are to have legitimacy echoes a fundamental principle of *nationalist* thinking. The idea that citizenship must be identical with the boundaries of the state (summed up in the slogan 'one nation, one state') has long been championed by ultra-nationalists (Gellner 1983: 134) – against whom the European Union often defines itself.

For European Union elites, therefore, pan-European television offered the potential for creating a collective European consciousness while simultaneously providing a bulwark against the menacing tides of globalization and commercialization threatening to drown 'European values' and 'European civilization' under a carpet of wall-to-wall 'Dallas' (Morley and Robins 1990; Collins 1993: 90). Fear of 'Americanization' is another recurring motif in European Union discourse (Baget-Bozzo 1986; Barzanti 1992; Burgelman and Pauwels 1992; Schlesinger 1994: 33). While this is usually expressed in the language of commerce (i.e. the dangers of European industry losing its competitiveness or share of world markets), it is often combined with xenophobia and chauvinism about European cultural supremacy and fears of foreign contamination. It is striking how metaphors of 'purity' and 'danger' characterize much of the language used in debates about protecting Europe's heritage and identity. For example, Roberto Barzanti, Chair of the European Parliament's Youth and Culture Committee described the single market as a ' "Trojan horse" for the Americanization of European culture' (Collins 1994: 91). Using the plight of the native American Indians as a metaphor for European culture, French film director Bertrand Tavernier delivered an equally emotive plea to the European Parliament: 'We cannot allow the Americans to treat us as they did the Redskins' (*Financial Times*, 18 September 1993: 7).

Exactly what this fragile but distinctive 'European' culture consists of, or why it needs to be protected from harmful foreign influences, are value-laden notions that reveal important aspects of the way 'culture' has become politicized in European Union discourse. They also reflect a peculiarly static and conservative conception of culture as something bounded, integral and integrating – a view similar to the outmoded anthropological models of the 1950s. Even the Commission's own think-tank of audiovisual experts criticized the Commission for adopting an 'environmental approach' to Europe's audiovisual industries, one that treated film and television production as 'if it was a "species on the verge of extinction" that had to be protected from industrial predators' (Vasconcelos et al. 1994: 12). Furthermore, the 'European culture' depicted in EU discourses on Europe typically emphasizes an elitist, intelligentsia view of *haute culture* (Schlesinger 1994: 321). It also rests on a Catholic conception of European unity: the idea that there exists an essential Europe whose heritage lies primarily in classical civilization, the Renaissance, Enlightenment thinking, Reason, Progress, Science, individualism and liberal economics. These elements are seen as providing the 'core values' that underpin the 'European culture-area'. This view, common among European policy makers, is shared by some social scientists and academics. For example, Helen Wallace (1991: 654) talks of European 'core values' – including 'democracy', the 'rule of law', the 'military will to defend pluralism', 'consensus building practices', 'parliamentary institutions', 'private property' and 'the market' – but fails to specify in what ways these 'European values' differ from so-called 'American values', or from those harmful imported values which are supposedly threatening European culture. According to this interpretation, globalization is an alien invention which has nothing to do with European culture, commerce or institutions.

Most of these self-congratulatory cultural attributes were used as the basis for the 1979 'Declaration on the European Identity' signed by the EC heads of state. Similar notions about what makes Europe culturally distinctive are echoed in what Anthony Smith (1991: 174) calls the 'patterns of European culture':

> The heritage of Roman law, Judeo-Christian ethics, Renaissance humanism and individualism, Enlightenment rationalism and science, artistic classicism and romanticism, and above all, traditions of civil rights and democracy, which have emerged at various times and places in the continent – have created a common European cultural heritage and formed a unique culture area straddling national boundaries and interrelating their different national cultures through common motifs and traditions.

The problem with historiography of this kind is that it offers a highly selective, uncritical and largely 'sanitized' version of the past; one that offers a jingoistic celebration of Europe's achievements whilst ignoring the darker side of European modernity; most notably, Europe's legacy of slavery and colonialism, fascism, the holocaust, anti-semitism, imperialism and religious bigotry.

BEYOND THE NATION STATE? EU AUDIOVISUAL POLICY AND SUPRANATIONALISM

A key assumption underlying EU audiovisual policy was that transnational TV and radio broadcasting would somehow promote these European 'core values', thereby cementing ties and stimulating solidarity among Europeans, while weaning them from the ideological grip of nationalism which still binds them to their exclusive nation states. Significantly, this thinking echoes classical theories of nationalism, particularly those of Deutsch, Anderson and Gellner, all of whom stress the importance of establishing an integrated field of social communication as a precondition for forging national (or 'supranational') consciousness.

The history of nation-state formation provides interesting insights for understanding European integration. As Anderson (1983) argues, the European nation state is an 'imagined community' structured largely by nationalist elites. Yet the most important agents for forging and diffusing nationalist consciousness were *cultural*: the museum and the map, the newspaper and the novel. These latter two were particularly salient: as products of an emergent print capitalism they helped, perhaps more than anything else, to undermine the intellectual foundations and authority of the feudal, monarchic *ancien régime*. These elements combined to create new ways of conceptualizing the fundamental categories of thought such as time, space, history, the self, and the individual's relationship to systems of power and authority. In short, the new print media not only gave rise to the supremacy of vernacular languages over the old sacred script languages, they also helped to forge a new kind of distinctly 'national' subjectivity and consciousness, diffusing among the masses a new image of themselves as 'national citizens' rather than simply parochial or imperial subjects – what Eugene Weber (1977) called the transformation of 'peasants into Frenchmen'.

During the 1980s, the Commission appeared to be emulating this model at a pan-national level in order to turn nationals into 'Europeans' and transform the European Community into a community of Europeans. However, the idea of creating a European 'core culture' which could be amplified and diffused via the media and cultural industries, although initially popular among architects of European integration, soon became discredited when national politicians saw pan-Europeanism in television and popular culture as a threat to their own authority and national cultures. Furthermore, taken to its logical conclusion, the nation-state model of integration presupposes a common or dominant language – which in the European Union's case is rapidly becoming English. This was never likely to be accepted by Britain's European partners, particularly France whose linguistic hegemony within EU institutions had largely been accepted. According to one senior official, the French government under Pompidou had insisted on Britain agreeing not to challenge the supremacy of the French language in this respect, and had tried to make this a condition of Britain's entry to the EEC.[10] The Commission's initial emphasis on creating 'cultural unity' was therefore replaced with the more politically acceptable theme of cultural pluralism and 'unity in diversity'. This formula of words was subsequently incorporated into Article 128 of the Maastricht Treaty, although EU cultural policy has never reconciled this 'celebration of cultural difference' with the perceived need to define and promote a common European culture.

Clearly, European Union cultural policies are sites of conflicting interest and contradictory goals. But these policy debates reflect not only competing agendas and ideologies (neo-liberal and *dirigiste*), but two radically different visions of Europe's future: the former minimalist and nationalist, based on the idea of sovereign nation states coming together around limited intergovernmental structures; the latter maximalist and federalist, based on the idea of superseding the nation states and creating supranational institutions of governance, broadly following the federal model of Switzerland or the United States. During the 1980s, France and Britain came to represent the two most extreme positions of *dirigisme* and liberalism (and *supranationalism* and *intergovernmentalism*) respectively. Moreover, these positions could also be loosely mapped on to different Directorates within the Commission (Collins 1994: 92). Four different Commission General Directorates ('DGs') claimed an interest in audiovisual affairs. Two of these, DG III (at that time, Internal Market and Financial Affairs) and DG IV (Competition) were traditionally liberal and free-market in orientation, while the other two, DG X (Information, Communication, Culture) and DG XIII (Telecommunications and Information Industry) were notably both interventionist and Francophone.

However, despite the European Commission's claim to be building a union that will supersede nationalism (and all European commissioners upon taking up their post pledge allegiance to the Community), national interests and sectoral rivalries continue to be prime factors behind these conflicting policy positions. Britain's support for a free market without state aid, for example, can be explained by the fact that the UK's audiovisual industries generally had a much healthier international balance of trade than other European countries and were much better placed to benefit from internationalization and deregulation. British industry also benefited from English being the world's most important *lingua franca*. Furthermore, Britain's relaxed attitude to deregulation reflected the fact that, like Germany (and unlike France), it hardly has a national film industry left to defend from foreign competition. France by contrast, with its highly protected film industry and the declining worldwide influence of the French language, was the most vociferous advocate of EU intervention and regulation of the European audiovisual market.

What is interesting when exploring the discourses through which these positions are articulated, is the way that 'Europeanism' was mobilized to promote different national interests. For Britain, the single European market was consistent with the policies and ideals of the Conservative government. For France, the arguments most frequently advanced in support of regulation and intervention were that globalization poses a threat to French cultural identity – a view also echoed by some of the smaller EU countries. Former Prime Minister Edouard Balladur summed up France's position in almost Manichean terms:

> I say we should leave this to the market, but only up to a certain point. What is the market? It is the law of the jungle, the law of nature. And what is civilization? It is the struggle against nature.
>
> (*Financial Times*, 31 December 1993, cited in Wolf 1994)

The problem for the French government, which like the Commission enjoys the status of being at the metaphorical 'heart of Europe', is that protectionism at national level is illegal under the terms of the EC treaties. The concepts of a 'level playing field' and free competition are central tenets of the single market now enshrined in the *acquis communitaire* of EC law. For this reason, France (like other member states) has consistently sought to use European Union legislation to promote domestic policy priorities.

USING TV AS THE CULTURAL ARM OF NATION-BUILDING: FLAWS IN EU STRATEGY

The problem for both France and its allies in the Commission is that their managerialist approach to 'culture' contains fundamental flaws. First, the idea of using television as an instrument for nation-building reflects an outdated public-service model of broadcasting, one that fails to acknowledge the increasingly fragmented, global and commercialized reality of the modern media landscape (Schlesinger 1994: 30). In the 1950s, national broadcasting corporations like the BBC may have become a rallying point for ideals of 'Britishness' and a standard form of language ('BBC English'), but the post-war socio-economic conditions that allowed these national champions to exert their cultural hegemony no longer pertain. There is now far more competition for television audiences and the supremacy public service broadcasting once enjoyed is increasingly being diminished by private television stations and cross-border commercial cable and satellite broadcasting. Second, the EU model is also based on naive and discredited assumptions that a unilinear and causal connection exists between media consumption and collective identity formation – what Morley and Robins (1995) call the 'hypodermic model' of media imperialism. This model wrongly constructs audiences as passive recipients of televisual images and ideologies, devoid of agency or critical faculties. In fact, studies show that most audiences reinterpret audiovisual messages in active, complex ways, invariably filtering these images through the prism of their own conceptual categories and cultural values (Ang 1985; Morley 1992). For example, the same episode of 'Dallas' means different things to an audience of French children as it would to American teenagers or Japanese businessmen. Finally, European-content-quotas and regulation of the cultural sector not only threatened to provoke a trade war with the EU's partners (who accused it of pursuing 'Fortress Europe' policies), it also violated the commercial principles at the heart of European Union laws and treaties themselves.

European identity, cultural nationalism and the GATT talks

The question of European Union audiovisual policy became a major issue of contention during the Uruguay Round of world trade liberalization talks during the early 1990s. The United States

insisted that audiovisual services be included in the GATT negotiations. The French government, supported by Spain and Ireland,
argued that the special public service nature of the audiovisual
sector meant that it should be treated as a 'cultural exception' and
therefore exempted and protected under GATT rules. Significantly,
the Commission had argued precisely the opposite case only a few
years earlier when it redefined the European audiovisual sector as a
'commercial' concern in order to make it a legitimate domain for
EU intervention.

Despite this apparent inconsistency, 'cultural exception' was the
negotiating formula adopted by the European Commission to
protect Europe's cinema, video and broadcasting industries from
foreign competitors. This formula would allow EU countries to
reserve screening time for indigenous productions of films and television programmes and regulate transmission and technologies. To
strengthen its negotiating position, the French government mobilized its cultural elite to defend the cultural sector and lobby the
Commission. On 28 September *Le Monde* and other French
national newspapers published a plea, signed by 4,400 actors,
producers and authors, to keep (*sic*) 'Europe's cultural identity'
from being submerged in the GATT negotiations. Gerard
Depardieu added his voice to this, declaring that France's cinema
constitutes 'our identity', while director Claude Berri insisted that
'Europe's cultural identity will die' if culture is not exempted from
the GATT agreement (Buchan 1993b: 3). The German director,
Wim Wenders, painted an equally apocalyptic future for European
culture, warning that 'Europe will become a Third World continent'
dominated by 'American values and American ideas' if the cultural
industries are not protected (Gardner 1993a: 21). Finally, following
his own warnings that 'the survival of our culture and pluralism are
at stake', France's minister for culture, M. Toubon, announced that
his government would never sign a GATT deal that covers, however
marginally, the audiovisual industry (Buchan 1993a: 7).

The controversy was further soured by the success of Steven
Spielberg's Hollywood blockbuster *Jurassic Park*, which dwarfed
Germinale at the box office – France's most expensive cinematic
venture to date – and confirmed not only the vulnerability of the
French cinema industry, but also the growing appeal of American
films to French audiences ('Cola versus Zola' was how the *Economist*
magazine caricatured the conflict). Despite huge state subsidies of
over $245 million annually to promote the French film industry, by

1993 American films accounted for 60 per cent of cinema entries, double the proportion a decade earlier. Were it not for the introduction of strict quotas for French television requiring that at least 60 per cent of programmes be of European origin (of which two-thirds must be French) American programmes would probably have dominated television in France too (*Economist*, 1993a: 21).

The complaint from the French film industry, however, was that Americans dislike dubbed or subtitled films and that French films therefore find it virtually impossible to get a foothold in the US market. American films, by contrast, arrive in the European market at cut-prices, having already paid off most of their investment costs by sales at home, and are bought up by French commercial television networks. This has led European cultural elites to accuse America of 'cultural dumping'. For its part, the *Wall Street Journal* compared French demands for censorship with those of the pro-Fascist Vichy government fifty years ago (*Economist*, 1993b). The head of the Motion Picture Association of America went further in debunking EU claims to be defending European culture: 'If you equate Europe's game shows and talk shows with Moliere and Racine, then that's about culture. But the culture issue is a transparent cloak, and I want to disrobe Europe on this' (Dodwell 1993: 6). Carla Hills, America's GATT negotiator, rejected the 'cultural specificity' argument telling the French government: 'Make films as good as your cheeses and you will sell them'. Equally revealing was the emotional response of Delors to this argument:

> I would simply like to pose a question to our American friends: do we have the right to exist? Have we the right to preserve our traditions, our heritage, our languages? How will a country of 10 million inhabitants be able to maintain its language – the very linchpin of its culture – faced with the universality which satellites offer? Doesn't the defense of freedom, elsewhere so loftily proclaimed, include the effort of each country . . . to use the audiovisual sphere to ensure the protection of their identity?
>
> (Cited in Burgelman and Pauwels 1992: 176)

This discourse constructs film and television as the core of both European culture and national identity – and something exempt from commercial considerations. These are debatable (and essentialist) assumptions. But America's argument that the audiovisual sector should be treated as just another industry is equally questionable. At one level, Delors' discourse about cultural defence and inalienable rights revealed the sensitivity and apparent vulnerability much of France's political elite feel about their national identity – and the self-conscious, chauvinistic way the French government sees French language and national identity as implicated in each other. A more sophisticated chauvinist argument is that language shapes thought: watch CNN news and you begin to take on an American view of the world.[11] But French political elites are equally aware of the commercial importance of the audiovisual sector – and the gains from maintaining its carefully constructed rampart of quotas and domestic subsidies. As the Head of the French Gaumont chain put it, 'Without Westerns, blue jeans would not have invaded the world' (Buchan 1993a: 7).

The point is that television and cinema bring with them important commercial spin-offs, particularly in the spheres of advertising and marketing. The separation of culture and commerce at the level of theory (already problematic) becomes increasingly controversial at the level of practice. As arguments over European Union audiovisual policy and the GATT negotiations indicate, the boundary between these domains is frequently manipulated for political ends. Indeed, audiovisual products are America's second biggest export to the EU – worth some 3.7 billion dollars in 1992, compared to EU audiovisual exports to the US of only 388 million dollars (Collins 1993: 100; *Economist* 1993a; Gardner 1993b: 4). While M. Toubon denied charges of 'anti-Americanism', like his predecessor Jack Lang – who vigorously denounced 'American cultural imperialism' at the 1982 UNESCO conference in Mexico – his message was that American imports are a threat to European (and Gallic) civilization. Hollywood, he said, is 'a war machine, a state within a state' which has 'already captured nearly 60 per cent of the French cinema market and an average of 80 per cent in Europe, and is voracious for more' (Buchan 1993a: 7). The GATT negotiations were therefore concluded without agreement on audiovisual services – a position hailed as a victory by the French government.

Developments since the 1990s

Since its introduction in 1990, the Television Without Frontiers Directive has been broadly respected, although French governments have consistently campaigned for a tougher revised directive that would legally compel EU member states to guarantee that 51 per cent of materials broadcast are 'European works' (itself a highly problematic concept to define given the global nature of the audio-visual industries). This view was also shared by the European Parliament's cultural committee, by the former Portuguese commissioner for audiovisual affairs, and by the Greek Minister for Culture, Melina Mercouri, who publicly vowed to 'fight Hollywood' in defence of 'our European ideal' (Brock 1994: 13). Throughout 1995, as the EU was drawing up revisions to the Directive, France continued its diplomatic campaign for stricter rules, greater financial aid, and the removal of the words 'where practicable' from the stipulation on European quotas. During the EU summit in Cannes in May 1995 the French prime minister proclaimed that 'defence of European culture' would be a major priority of his government,[12] and pressed for an Ecu 200 million EU-wide fund from the European Investment Bank to underwrite European film productions (thereby protecting the industry against Hollywood imports).[13] Both of these proposals were duly incorporated into the Commission's draft proposal.

After protracted negotiations, EU culture ministers eventually reached a unanimous compromise in November 1995. Contrary to the Commission's recommendation, the existing text for broadcast quotas would be maintained with no major modifications, and the directive's scope of application would not be widened to cover new audiovisual products such as electronic publishing, video-on-demand and internet-type services. However, by announcing its decision three months before the European Parliament could deliver its verdict, ministers had broken new EU rules governing the 'co-decision' procedure giving Parliament the right to express opinions on certain policy matters. As one senior Council official admitted, this was not an accident but a calculated risk, the assumption being that if ministers gave a clear lead, the European Parliament would probably follow. Instead, infuriated MEPs subsequently tabled 225 amendments to the draft directive and, at their plenary in February 1996, overturned the Council's compromise by voting for mandatory quotas and an extension of the directive to new interactive audiovisual services. At the time of writing, this disagreement between Parliament and Council had not been resolved, although all indications were that the Council's position would probably triumph. To most observers it seemed that months of anguished debate and detailed committee work had produced an amended 'Television Without Frontiers' Directive virtually identical to the 1989 Directive. The only novelty was greater clarity concerning definitions such as 'television advertising', 'tele-shopping' and 'European works'. France succeeded in drawing support for a doubling of funds for the EU's 'MEDIA 2' programme (thus providing 400 million ecus for film production, training and distribution), but its campaign to regulate the 'European content' of broadcasting, although popular among MEPs, failed to win support from fellow member states in the Council, or from Commission president Jacques Santer. As one Commission official described it, 'quotas are a French obsession, not a European one' (Tucker 1995: 2). This again raises questions about the rationale underlying calls for the defence of 'European culture' and 'the European interest'. It also highlights just how ambiguous and malleable are these concepts.

It is equally questionable whether EU attempts to 'Europeanize the audiovisual sector' have actually helped European integration or, instead, exacerbated national rivalries and divisions by exposing the difficulties of trying to reconcile contradictory national interests with an even more abstract 'European interest'. Furthermore, the goal of circulating more European-made programmes around the Union has not happened to any significant degree. The vast majority of 'foreign' films broadcast by European television stations are American and only 4.5 per cent, on average, are produced in other European countries. As the European Union's Committee of audiovisual experts concluded, 'if Europe has a common film culture, it is that of American films' (Vasconcelos et al. 1994: 60, 71). What the Commission describes as 'Hollywood's war-machine' and a threat to European identity would appear to be, ironically, one of the few genuinely pan-European popular culture experiences that contribute to a shared sense of European identity.

Apart from the series called 'Eurocops', attempts to create pan-European television audiences have met with little success either. Perhaps the most significant insight from these debates is not whether 'European culture' is at risk from foreign competition or from Europe's failure to create pan-national television audiences, as many EU supporters claim, but the way that these 'Europeanist' discourses are used to promote the political interests of both Euro-federalists and their more nationalist adversaries. To borrow Edwin Ardener's (1971: xliv) metaphor, 'Europe' and 'culture' have become 'blank banners': icons linked to no specific programme which can be appropriated for different aims, including policies of cultural chauvinism and economic protectionism.

CONCLUSION

Using European Union audiovisual policy as a case study, this chapter set out to examine the conflicting policy paradigms and ideological agendas that shape the European Union. It argued that audiovisual policy provides clues to deeper organizing principles governing the direction and scope of European integration – conceptual and cultural as well as political and pragmatic. Different policy positions clearly indicate where each member state stands in relation to competing visions of Europe. They also reveal some of the major fault lines that run through the European Union, divisions which recur in other policy debates – from agriculture and competition to social policy and economic and monetary union – as well as globally. But the confrontation between neo-liberal and *dirigiste* approaches is also a conflict between two radically different models of European governance; intergovernmentalism and supra-nationalism. Contrary to how it is often depicted, this division is not between recidivist nationalists and progressive Europeans. *Both* models are underscored by nationalist thinking: the former approach broadly reflecting a market model of governance most closely associated with the British New Right, the latter reflecting the centralized, interventionist tradition of French government and administration. In each case, the interpretive framework within which EU issues are considered continues to be national rather than European. As Ruane (1994) notes, even ideas of superseding nationalism are conceptualized through the prism of nationalist thinking and reflect different nationalist traditions.[14]

During the mid-1980s, when the EU's audiovisual and cultural polices were initiated, the Commission succeeded in giving the Community a sharper sense of purpose and direction and a stronger political identity. However, national self-interest remained a key element underlying both neo-liberal and *dirigiste* agendas. The 'European culture' invoked in debates on audiovisual policy must be seen as a contested discourse, one that is typically inflected and reinterpreted to suit the domestic and ideological interests of national governments. 'Europeanness', to echo Schlesinger (1994), has itself become 'a new cultural battlefield'. Being 'at the heart of Europe' and 'good Europeans' are mobilizing metaphors full of cultural capital which most national governments try to appropriate, and over which they vie for hegemony.

That Britain's Conservative government should champion *laissez faire* capitalism and deregulation is hardly surprising. More curious, perhaps, is the rationality underlying the *dirigiste* approach of France and much of the Commission. As I have argued elsewhere (Shore 1995), the Commission's characteristically French administrative outlook reflects a typically technocratic, managerial and 'Jacobinist' approach to government, not only in its emphasis on interventionism, regulation and control from above, but also in its belief in vanguard leadership and its elitist attitude towards the (as yet 'un-Europeanized') masses into which it seeks to instil 'European consciousness'. The language with which the Commission portrays itself – as 'engine of integration' and 'custodian' of the European interest – reinforces this heroic self-image and sense of mission. Delors summed it up succinctly. Speaking on French television in 1990, he declared that he was, 'with my colleagues in the Commission, the trustee of European history' (cited in Grant 1994: 136).

As Spence (1994) observes, the Commission's self-image has important implications for policy-making. It also raises questions about the Commission's status as a truly 'supranational' body, independent of national bias or sectional interest. In theory, the Commission acts as an 'honest broker', defending the Community interests and holding the ring against national rivalries. Its members are required by statute to be independent 'beyond doubt', and its decisions are intended to reflect a 'European viewpoint'. But 'European viewpoint' and 'European interest' are themselves highly ambiguous and contested concepts. Even within the Commission some senior officials argue that institutional Europe is a 'dangerous fiction' and that 'there is no such thing as the Community interest' (Connolly 1995: 391). Schlesinger recently dismissed the EU's idea of engineering a collective identity, arguing that there is 'no predominant cultural nation in the EU that can become the core of the would-be state's nation and hegemonize Euro-culture' (Schlesinger 1994: 321). However, it is less hegemonic models of *culture* as models of *governance* that are at stake here. Under Delors, the European Commission, with its French administrative model and *dirigiste* philosophy, came to embody even further many of the characteristics of the French system of government. To what extent this may have compromised the Commission's neutrality and its claim to be promoting the 'European interest' is a question for another chapter.

Finally, returning to the theme of anthropology and policy, this study has tried to show how a 'policy focus' can provide a useful tool for analysing those macro-level organizations and institutions of governance that influence contemporary social and political life at the micro level. However, to understand how policy works we must examine not only the 'culture[s] of the policy professionals' (Donnan and MacFarlane 1989: 8) but also the broader political agendas or meta-narratives through which policy is construed, and the different interests, actors and agents that constitute the 'policy field'. In this case, the study of audiovisual policy becomes a study of conflicting ideas about European identity and culture. It also highlights the way discourses on Europe are implicated in issues of national identity and why, for the reasons outlined above, the European Union is unlikely to succeed in its attempts to utilize the audiovisual industries as vehicles for constructing the 'imagined community' of Europe or a European state-nation.

NOTES

1 This chapter is based on fieldwork undertaken in Brussels between 1992–3 and 1995–6. I would like to thank the Nuffield Foundation and the Economic and Social Research Council (project R000236097) for their generous help in supporting this research and for enabling me to learn about European politics first-hand.

2 For interesting analyses of the role of intellectuals in the formation of nationalist movements, see Anderson 1983; Hechter and Levi 1979; Nairn 1977.

3 Publication of the 1984 Commission Green Paper 'Television Without Frontiers' can be taken as marking the beginning of the policy. However, Collins (1993: 92) dates its inception to the earlier European Parliament 'Hahn Report' of 1982 which first proposed using European Community broadcasting policy as an instrument for achieving the political goal of 'ever closer union' in Europe. For useful reviews of debates over European communications policies, see Collins 1993; Davis and Levy 1992; Robins 1994.

4 I use these terms to denote those individuals or groups that profess allegiance to the ideals of European federalism and supranationalism espoused by pioneers of European political integration such as Jean Monnet and Altiero Spinelli.

5 Article 3 of the 1957 Rome Treaty which established the European Economic Community referred explicitly to 'an internal market characterized by the abolition, as between Member States, of obstacles to the free movement of goods, persons, services and capital' (CEC 1983).

6 The 1989 Directive on Broadcasting was thus justified by – and conceived within – Articles 57 (2) and 66 of the Rome Treaty (CEC 1990: 15).

7 This interventionist stance, encouraged particularly by Delors,

'meshed nicely with the revival of European Community industrial policy in the 1980s' (Davis and Levy 1992: 471). The result was heavy investment by the Commission in the development of High Definition Television (HDTV).

8 However, as French officials would argue when pushed on this point, the architect behind the Directive was a British official in Directorate-General 10.

9 'European identity' also became an important theme explored by the 'Forward Studies Unit', the think-tank created by Delors in 1989.

10 Fieldwork interviews with staff from DG IX (Administration), June 1993.

11 This partly explains why the state-owned broadcasting authorities of France, Italy, Spain and Switzerland recently injected new capital into a loss-making, multi-lingual company called 'Euronews TV' broadcast twenty hours a day. Significantly, the European Parliament voted to supplement this with a generous contribution of 4.3 million ecus (*Economist*, 5 February 1994).

12 The previous year, M. Balladur, launching a new language law prohibiting the use of certain 'foreign' words or phrases by public sector organizations, had declared the protection of *French* culture and identity a political priority of his government (Buchan 1994: 2).

13 The Spanish Commissioner for audiovisual policy, who supported this initiative, went even further and spoke of creating a 'Hollywood in Europe' (Barber and Tucker 1995: 2).

14 This is evidenced vividly in the contradictory national interpretations given to the word 'federalism'.

REFERENCES

Adonnino, Pietro (1985) 'A people's Europe: Reports from the Ad Hoc Committee', *Bulletin of the European Communities, Supplement 7/85*, Luxembourg: Office of Official Publications of the European Community.

Althusser, Louis (1971) *Lenin and Philosophy and Other Essays*, London: Verso.

Anderson, Benedict (1983) *Imagined Communities: Reflections on the Origins and Spread of Nationalism*, London: Verso.

Ang, Ien (1985) *Watching Dallas*, London: Methuen.

Ardener, Edwin (1971) 'Introduction: social anthropology and language', in E. Ardener (ed.), *Social Anthropology and Language*, London: Tavistock.

Baget-Bozzo, Gianni (1986) *Report on the Information Policy of the European Community* (Doc A-111), Luxembourg: Office of Official Publications of the European Community.

Barber, Lionel and Tucker, Emma (1995) 'France seeks EU fund for film industry', *Financial Times*, 29 April 1995: 2.

Barzanti, Roberto (1992) *New Prospects for Community Cultural Action (Draft Report for the European Parliament)*, Brussels: Office of Official Publications of the European Community.

Bhabha, Homi (ed.) (1990) *The Nation and Narration*, London: Routledge.

Bowman, Glenn (1994) 'Xenophobia, fantasy and the nation: the logic of ethnic violence in former Yugoslavia', in V. Goddard, J. Llobera and C. Shore (eds) *The Anthropology of Europe*, Oxford: Berg.

Brock, George (1994) 'Mercouri prepares for Elgin battle', *The Times*, 7 January 1994: 13.

Buchan, David (1993a) 'Lights, camera – reaction', *Financial Times*, 18 September 1993: 7.

—— (1993b) 'Plea to defend Europe's cultural identity', *Financial Times*, 29 September 1993: 3.

—— (1994) 'Balladur declares war on Franglais', *Financial Times*, 9 March 1994: 2.

Burgelman, Jean-Claude and Pauwels, Caroline (1992) 'Audiovisual policy and cultural identity in small European states: the challenge of a unified market', *Media, Culture and Society* 14: 169–83.

Chapman, Malcolm, McDonald, Maryon and Tonkin, Elizabeth (1989) 'Introduction', in E. Tonkin, M. McDonald and C. Chapman (eds) *History and Ethnicity*, London: Routledge.

Collins, Richard (1993) *Audiovisual and Broadcasting Policy in the European Community*, London: University of North London Press (European Dossier Series No. 23).

—— (1994) 'Unity in diversity: the European single market in broadcasting and the audiovisual, 1982–92', *Journal of Common Market Studies* 32 (1) (March): 89–102.

Commission of the European Communities (CEC) (1983) *Treaties Establishing the European Communities*, Luxembourg: Office for Official Publications of the European Communities.

—— (1984) *Television Without Frontiers. Green Paper on the Establishment of the Common Market for Broadcasting especially for Satellite and Cable*, COM (84) final, Luxembourg: Office for Official Publications of the European Communities.

—— (1990) *The European Community Policy in the Audiovisual Field. Legal and Political Texts*, Luxembourg: Office for Official Publications of the European Communities.

—— (1992a) *Treaty on European Union Signed at Maastricht on 7 February*, Luxembourg: Office of Official Publications for the European Communities.

—— (1992b) *New Prospects for Community Cultural Action: Background Report*, ISEC/B26/92, London: Commission of the European Communities.

—— (1994) *Information, Communication, Openness: Background Report*, ISEC/B25/94, London: Commission of the European Communities.

—— (1995a) *Commission Report for the Reflection Group. Intergovernmental Conference, 1996*, Luxembourg: Office for Official Publications of the European Communities.

—— (1995b) *Report on Application of Directive 89/552/EEC and Proposal for a European Parliament and Council Directive Amending Council Directive 89/552/EEC*, COM (95) 86 final, Luxembourg: Office for Official Publications of the European Communities.

Connolly, Bernard (1995) *The Rotten Heart of Europe*, London: Faber and Faber.

Davis, Howard and Levy, Carl (1992) 'The regulation and deregulation of television: a British/West European comparison', *Economy and Society* 21 (4): 453–82.

De Clercq, Willy (1993) *Reflection on Information and Communication Policy of the European Community*, Brussels: European Commission (DGX).

Delors, Jacques (1985) 'Address to the opening of the European Parliament 12 March 1985. Commission Programme for 1985', *Debates of the European Union* OJ No. 2324.

Deutsch, Karl (1966) *Nationalism and Social Communication: An Inquiry into the Foundations of Nationality* (2nd edition), Cambridge MA: MIT.

Dodwell, David (1993) 'World trade news: US opts to bide time on audiovisual battle', *Financial Times,* 15 December 1993: 6.

Donnan, Hastings and McFarlane, Graham (eds) (1989) *Social Anthropology and Public Policy in Northern Ireland*, Aldershot: Avebury.

Economist (1993a) 'Taking cultural exception. Europe's entertainment gap', 25 September 1993: 328.

—— (1993b) 'Cola v. Zola: Europe's creative projectionists', 16 October 1993: 329.

—— (1994) 'Cultural Protectionism: Television of Babel', 5 February 1994: 330.

Fontaine, Pascal (1991) *A Citizen's Europe*, Luxembourg: Office of Official Publications of the European Communities.

Gardner, David (1993a) 'World Trade News', *Financial Times,* 14 October 1993: 21.

—— (1993b) 'EC agreement on formula to protect European culture under Uruguay Round', *Financial Times,* 6 November 1993: 4.

Gavin, Brigid (ed.) (1991) *European Broadcasting Standards in the 1990s*, Oxford: NCC Blackwell.

Gellner, Ernest (1983) *Nations and Nationalism*, Oxford: Blackwell.

George, Stephen (1985) *Politics and Policy in the European Community*, Oxford: Clarendon.

Grant, Charles (1994) *Delors. Inside The House That Jacques Built*, London: Nicholas Brealey.

Grillo, Ralph (1980) 'Introduction', in R. D. Grillo (ed.) *'Nation' and 'State' in Europe: Anthropological Perspectives*, London: Academic Press.

Hechter, Michael and Levi, Michael (1979) 'The comparative analysis of ethnoregional movements', *Ethnic and Racial Studies* 2 (3): 262–74.

Hobsbawm, Eric and Ranger, Terrence (eds) (1983) *The Invention of Tradition*, Cambridge: Cambridge University Press.

Mestrovic, Stjepan (1994) *The Balkanization of the West*, London: Routledge.

Morley, David (1992) *Television Audiences and Cultural Studies*, London: Routledge.

Morley, David and Robins, Kevin (1990) 'No place like heimat: images of home(land) in European culture', *New Formations* 12: 1–24.

—— (1995) 'Cultural imperialism and the mediation of Otherness', in A.

Ahmed and C. Shore (eds) *The Future of Anthropology: Its Relevance to the Contemporary World*, London: Athlone Press.

Nairn, Tom (1977) *The Break-Up of Britain*, London: New Left Books.

Pahl, Ray (1991) 'The search for social cohesion: from Durkheim to the European Commission', *Archives europeen de sociologie* 23: 345–60.

Robins, Kevin (1994) 'The politics of silence: the meaning of community and the uses of media in the New Europe', *New Formations* 21: 80–101.

Ross, George (1993) 'Sliding into industrial policy: inside the European Commission', *French Politics and Society* 11 (1): 20–44.

Ruane, Joseph (1994) 'Nationalism and European Community integration: the Republic of Ireland', in V. Goddard, J. Llobera and C. Shore (eds) *The Anthropology of Europe*, Oxford: Berg.

Schlesinger, Philip (1991) *Media, State and Nation. Political Violence and Collective Identities*, London: Sage.

—— (1994) 'Europeanness – a new cultural battlefield?', in J. Hutchinson and A. D. Smith (eds) *Nationalism*, Oxford: Oxford University Press.

Shore, Cris (1993) 'Inventing the "People's Europe": critical perspectives on European Community cultural policy', *Man. Journal of the Royal Anthropological Institute* 28 (4): 779–800.

—— (1995) 'Usurpers or pioneers? EC bureaucrats and the question of "European consciousness"', in A. P. Cohen and N. Rapport (eds), *Questions of Consciousness*, London: Routledge.

Shore, Cris and Black, Annabel (1992) 'The European Communities and the construction of Europe', *Anthropology Today* 8 (3): 10–11.

—— (1994) '"Citizens' Europe" and the Construction of European Identity', in V. Goddard, J. Llobera and C. Shore (eds) *The Anthropology of Europe: Identities and Boundaries in Conflict*, Oxford: Berg.

Smith, Anthony D. (1991) *National Identity*, Harmondsworth: Penguin.

—— (1992) 'A Europe of nations – or the Nation of Europe?', *Journal of Peace Research* 30 (2): 129–35.

Soledad-Garcia, M. (ed.) (1994) *European Identity and the Search for Legitimacy*, London: Pinter.

Spence, David (1994) 'Staff and personnel policy in the Commission', in G. Edwards and D. Spence (eds) *The European Commission*, Harlow: Longman.

Tucker, Emma (1995) 'Vision fades for fortress Europe', *Financial Times*, 18/19 February 1995.

Vasconcelos, A-P., Cotta, M., Balmaseda, E., Stucchi, G., Fleischmann, P. and Putnam, D. (1994) *Report by the Think-Tank on the Audiovisual Policy in the European Union*, Luxembourg: Office for Official Publications of the European Union.

Wallace, Helen (1991) 'The Europe that came in from the Cold', *International Affairs* 67 (4) October: 648–64.

Weber, Eugene (1977) *Peasants into Frenchmen: The Modernization of Rural France, 1870–1914*, London: Chatto and Windus.

Wolf, Martin (1994) 'A fortress would be no defense', *Financial Times*, 15 December 1994.

Part III

Policy as political technology

Governmentality and subjectivity

Chapter 8

Reform and resistance
A Norwegian illustration

Halvard Vike

INTRODUCTION

This study explores the relationship between reform and resistance in Ulefoss, a Norwegian industrial community in south-eastern Norway.[1] In 1989 the municipal administration launched an ambitious attempt to reorganize care for the elderly. The overall aim was to reduce the emphasis on institutional care and develop more flexible services at reduced costs. The new policy was to materialize from a comprehensive and inclusive planning process which was to create political consensus and link this to goal-oriented administrative action in an unambiguous way.

The reform provoked strong reactions in the community and a serious political conflict followed from it. This conflict was particularly strong within the local branch of the Labour Party in Ulefoss. In this chapter, I describe this conflict with respect to an antagonistic relationship between different kinds of knowledge. Although the reform process involved representatives from all major political parties in the municipality, the most active and devoted promoters of the plan were municipal administrators. For them, the promotion of the plan was closely related to the question of how to make people understand that the plan pointed at the right solutions and that it depicted the correct means to achieve them. The criticism was directed at the administrators' role as experts and the plan as a privileged terrain for their knowledge.

Focusing on these reactions as a form of resistance, I explore the way in which they were linked to a struggle for *the right to know* in alternative terms and the means with which the struggle was carried out. The opponents introduced *morality* as their major means of resistance. This served as an efficient weapon, and even though the opponents failed to develop an alternative policy, their practical resistance served as an efficient display of basic symbols of the local political tradition: *sunn fornuft* (common sense), individual experience and the ideal of *å stå sammen* (standing together). These contributed strongly to undermine the legitimacy of bureaucratic authority as well as the idea of objective knowledge as anchored in individual, formal competence. The opponents introduced concrete persons and their intentions as the focus of concern.

At the time of the reform, it was commonly known that the problem of elderly care involved major disagreements in Ulefoss. Clearly, the ambitious reform became controversial because it was based on the assumption that the existence of a multitude of contradictory values and political interests in the community could be overcome by rational government. The plan portrayed elderly care as consisting of quantifiable elements within a flow of (municipal) resources which was to be acted upon on the basis of unambiguously defined means–ends relations. The plan made an authoritative symbolic representation of the essential properties of a segment of the population – the elderly – and the apparatus which was to serve them. As a very important part of the process, politicians were called upon to add legitimacy to the plan and to take responsibility for it. In return, they were presented with a vision of proper care for all the elderly in the municipality.

In the first part of this study I will specify the analytical terms in which this process of reform and resistance may be understood. This discussion is focused on 'moral economy', a concept through which I seek to relate the moral dimension of social relations which constitute the political field in Ulefoss, to a new, rational form of governance. In the context of this case study, the relationship between the moral dimension and rational governance takes an antagonistic form. This antagonism, I argue, rested on contradictory perspectives of society. While the promoters of the plan sought to operationalize morality so as to make it subject to administrative control (in terms of proper formal standards of care, knowledge, rights and administrative procedures) in line with the categories of individuals and resources, the opponents foregrounded the significance of morality as a quality of the political community and as an aspect of social relations in a broad and concrete sense.

Following this discussion of the terms in which the conflict was conducted, I present the plan (*eldreplanen*), its content and its rationale, and introduce the characteristics of the community and its social history. I seek to conceptualize the local branch of the Labour Party in Ulefoss as a normative environment which allows its members to control each other and negotiate matters of power with reference to moral symbols according to which behaviour is evaluated. This constitutes the framework for my discussion of political resistance. I seek to understand this resistance in terms of *moral economy* (Scott 1985), and I relate this to Marx and Weber's perspectives on rationalization and differentiation in the modernization process.

MORAL ECONOMY AND POLICY

In various contexts it has been shown that morality may serve as a resource for those who are the victims of power, as 'weapons of the weak'. Scott (1985) defines morality as a system of norms which may be translated into transactional claims by poor peasants in their struggle to maintain their position within the local economy. He carefully explores various forms of 'everyday resistance' which may vary from practical sabotage and foot-dragging, to the insistence that tradition and kinship chart relations of reciprocity between the rich and the poor and represent a common moral standard which is threatened by the rich. Scott has shown how, by mobilizing these notions of a moral economy, the poor may influence the effects of increasing inequality.

The concept of moral economy may serve as a tool for understanding the way in which a given society reproduces itself morally and what people do to maintain or establish what they consider to be a preferable social balance when direct political action is not on the agenda. Thus, in a sense, morality and norms function as means of regulation in the same way as material resources and means of exchange. What they regulate is of course not 'justice' in an absolute sense, but rather the relationship between people's ideas of a reasonable social order and what we may call social performance.

Moral discourses are metadiscourses of power and legitimacy, and are in no way reducible to 'culture'. In the present discussion, I depict a social context in which problems of social change and increasing institutional complexity are fundamental. As a consequence, my own interest in the concept of 'moral economy' concerns the relationship between morality and rationalization in local politics.

In his book *Weapons of the Weak*, James Scott has shown, in a situation of increasing social differentiation and class formation in a previously relatively homogenous Malaysian community, how the moral framework of the community works ideologically. For the marginalized peasants, the traditional order which is objectified in various images of 'the remembered village' serves as a means for preventing their relations to the landowners from becoming purely commercial in the strict, economic sense. For the peasants, their whole existence depends on their ability to present themselves as 'necessary labour', 'close kin' and 'fellow villagers' vis-à-vis the landowners in a situation where their labour power is no longer needed. The landowners, on the other hand, attempt to rid themselves of such claims now that they do not need to attract industrious tenants to farm their land. Their strategies involve attempts at 'stretching the truth', for instance, by complaining that poor people are 'lazy'.[2]

Normative discourses, such as the one so well analysed by Scott, involve much more than 'social games'. In this particular Malaysian case, 'norms' may be perceived as aspects of a class discourse. Furthermore, as an 'economy', the moral discourse involves its own currency. The poor peasants of Sedaka may take home victories from the normative arena which, for the time being, may reduce the significance of their material marginalization. Yet there is a strong link between the world of material marginalization and 'normative devaluation'. Thus, from an analytical point of view, it is essential to ask not only how people play games, but also which actions are legitimate for what kinds of people under what kinds of conditions. We may also ask what determines the conventionalization of norms and goals themselves. As Lukes (1981) has shown, Durkheim did not only conceptualize morality as rules with relation to sanctions and obligations, he also saw morality as a set of beliefs. From such a perspective, morality is not only a question of how people relate to rules. Morality may also serve as ideals which may provide vehicles for the realization of people's desires (Archetti 1991).

The attempt in Ulefoss to reconstruct a sense of tradition by investing it with a moral insistence on the fundamental importance of maintaining party and community unity can be seen as a parallel to the struggle among the peasants of Sedaka. The opponents to the reform process in Ulefoss were unable to compete with the reformers over the means of (political) production: for instance, they were never able to argue that the calculations in the reformers' documents were wrong. However, the opponents of the reform were

well equipped for the struggle over the meaning of these calculations – that is to say, the motivation behind them and the morality
of their application. Their resistance involved attempts to influence
the mode of communication in the formal arenas to which the
reform was marketed and to bring it 'out on the streets', that is, into
informal arenas.

At the same time, the resistance involved appealing to major
symbols in Labour Party discourse (common sense, standing
together, equality) which, because at a general level everyone
stressed their importance, were generally seen by members as
somehow beyond politics. It is important to stress that, as moral
symbols, these ideas were used – in the context of Ulefoss at least –
more as a means for regulating the morality of the political process
than as a tool for solving more practical policy problems through a
rational linking of political decisions to administrative action. In
this sense, morality as experience and as a system of knowledge is
different from instrumental rationality, particularly in the sense that
it is deeply anchored in social processes and not subject to a decontextualized logic of means and ends.

THE PLAN

The municipal plan to reform elderly care was initiated in 1987
when it was realized that a combination of demographic and financial changes put the municipal health and welfare services under
severe pressure. Another basic stimulus for the planning process was
an increasing awareness of the need for decision-making innova-
tions at the municipal level. In particular, this awareness was
concerned with budget control and the question of how to make the
decision-making process stable, predictable and efficient.

Compared to previous types of municipal planning, *Eldreplanen*
was considered special in several respects. One important difference
was related to the need to make firm priorities. While earlier plans
had been heavily influenced by the ambition to collect background
information, *Eldreplanen* was adjusted to the will to produce action.
A key element in the strategy to make a practical plan was the
emphasis on establishing hierarchies of political goals, as well as
specifying the means that were considered relevant to them.
Through these goals, the plan stressed that it was important that all
elderly people had their 'physical, psychological, social, and spiri-
tual needs' satisfied. This was to be achieved through five objectives:

that elderly people should have confidence that the municipality would do everything in order to satisfy changing needs; that all elderly people should be given the opportunity to live in their own homes as long as they want to; that the elderly would be given the possibility to take responsibility for their own lives; and that health personnel would be properly educated. The last goal dealt with organizational matters internal to the health department and stressed the idea of 'co-operation and fellowship'.

Significantly, while the members of the committee, who represented all the political parties in the municipality, were supportive of the hierarchy of goals, problems started when the last part of the plan was discussed. The last part considered practical matters and outlined a political programme. First, the programme specified how to achieve the goal of more open elderly care. This included apartment complexes, activity groups, facilities in community centres and support to make it easier to live at home. Second, the programme offered a solution to the financial problem. This involved closing down the old people's home in Ulefoss, *Holla Trygdeheim* and strengthening the 'open' elderly care system. This proposal aimed to reduce total expenditure considerably at the same time as adjusting the health service to the various needs of the elderly more adequately, including intensive care. Those in need of intensive care in the future, it was proposed, would be properly taken care of in an institution located in the neighbouring community of Lunde. This institution is more modern than *Holla Trygdeheim* and reorganization would increase its capacity for intensive care from 62 patients to about 70.

According to the document, among the 52 'patients' at *Holla Trygdeheim*, 22 were in need of intensive care. The remaining 30 'patients' were healthy enough to manage themselves, provided that they had a functional apartment. The total cost of the old institution corresponded to approximately 25 per cent of the municipality's welfare budget. Politically, the proposition to close down *Holla Trygdeheim* became by far the most central issue in the *eldreplan* controversy, and it created a great deal of frustration and aggression among people in Ulefoss. At an early point, it became clear than a substantial number of people were intensely concerned to preserve the institution which was located physically and symbolically in the middle of Ulefoss.

Until the document was released in the spring of 1989, all parties were in general political agreement in about its main elements. Only the Elderly's Council was hesitant about giving unanimous support, preferring to wait until the public hearing was over. There was little disagreement concerning the need for reform; nor did anybody argue against the overall goal of increasing the *trygghet* (security) of the elderly. Although the plan aimed at a total reorganization of municipal elderly care, the controversy focused almost exclusively on one, single question: the fate of *Holla Trygdeheim*, the old people's home in the centre of Ulefoss. The reformers – the municipal administration and leading politicians – considered the home to be a very non-rational and expensive institution and the major obstacle to more efficient and rational care. Among the larger part of the local population, however, the institution was seen as an important symbol of decent elderly care and community solidarity. Hence the idea of closing it down mobilized a great deal of frustration and aggression in Ulefoss.

At a very early stage, it became clear that the whole plan, as well as the prestige and legitimacy of the municipal administration, rested on the single premise that the old people's home had to be closed down. This struggle to prove that the premise was 'correct' included popular mobilization against the municipal administration and certain local politicians. Conflicting views and expectations concerning the nature and function of politics, as well as the skills necessary to be qualified as a participant in the political process, were brought to the surface. Both the form of the struggle and the agenda were transformed in the course of the conflict.

Since the aim of the plan was a complete financial and organizational revision of the care of the elderly as a whole, the issue became at the same time one of finding concrete solutions to this more encompassing challenge. This became a problem of major importance, since those who insisted that the old people's home in Ulefoss should be preserved never offered any alternative to the plan as a whole. As a result, they came under heavy attack from the reformers who were especially concerned about the combined effects of long-term planning and budget control. Instead of responding to this attack on its own terms, the opponents switched their emphasis to one of morality.

In the *Eldreplanen* document, *the elderly* were depicted as a category of people whose potential for activity and self-realization was suppressed by the existing elderly care system based to a great extent on big institutions. Consequently, the whole system needed revision. Most of the elderly, it was said, were not particularly sick.

This view evoked little discussion and seemed to be generally accepted. However, they were also said to be much more economically well off than commonly believed. This statement was certainly not equally well received by the elderly themselves, who connected this to the elderly-as-a-burden attitude and the fear that administrators wanted to get their hands on their private resources. This fear was stimulated by statements made by administrators and leading politicians, stressing that most elderly people are really 'quite wealthy'. Such claims were substantiated by statistical figures and projections which showed that within a few years the 'elderly wave' would hit the municipality particularly severely. In short, the audience was presented with the scenario of a progressive accumulation of severe problems which might be controlled only if rational action was taken before too long. The head of the health and welfare department put it in these terms:

> Do we make the right priorities? Do the elderly distribute their money to their children and let the municipality pay for everything? How is the money in the health care budget used? Care for the elderly counts for over seventy per cent [of the municipal budget]. If we were able to get more money, it ought not be the elderly, but children and youths who should have it.

In the eyes of the opponents, this kind of argument threatened their picture of the elderly as an essentially weak group. Thus, at party meetings and elsewhere, the complaint that the administrators had found that the elderly were 'too expensive' for the municipality became quite frequently expressed. Among those of the elderly who participated in political discussions, it became increasingly important to stress that they in fact were not economically well off at all. Witnessing elderly people shouting at public meetings that they could not afford to buy their own flats – which many were supposed to do according to the plan – usually had a very strong effect on the audience.

THE CONTEXT: A NORWEGIAN INDUSTRIAL COMMUNITY

The community of Ulefoss is located in the southern part of the county of Telemark in south-eastern Norway, and is the capital of the municipality of Nome. The population of Ulefoss slightly exceeds 4,000, thus constituting more than half of Nome's population of 7,500.

The community is partly separated (economically, socially and culturally) from the surrounding agricultural areas. Ulefoss developed as a result of the sawmill activities which were established in the sixteenth century at the waterfall which gives the community its name. This industry has been one of two key elements in the economic development of Ulefoss and, until it was closed down in the 1970s, it provided the basis of the structure of ownership, power, settlement and social relationships in general.

The other significant economic factor in the development of Ulefoss was the establishment of the ironworks in the middle of the seventeenth century. In 1847 the Cappelen family – still the biggest private employer in Ulefoss – took over the ironworks. The family modernized iron production, which remained a stable source of profit as well as a source of income for a large number of people in the community for more than 150 years. Two basic characteristics of the social history of Ulefoss should be stressed: first, the relative stability of class relations and paternalistic power, which were present as early as the seventeenth century, and second, the transformation of the political organization and representation of this structure during the post-war era.

The local Labour Party, established in 1890, became a major influence in the community in the mid-war era, as did the labour unions. At the municipal level, these two traditions of labour mobilization in Ulefoss joined forces and successfully pursued 'parliamentary' ends. The Labour Party has controlled the mayorship of the municipality continually since 1935, and throughout most of this period it has also controlled the municipal assembly. Until quite recently, the Labour Party not only constituted a secure majority and a source of working-class influence, it also represented a stable ideological horizon and a symbol of heroic achievement, of growth and equality both nationally and in the community. Since the Second World War, the Labour Party tradition has not been one of resistance against capital and local power, but one of peaceful cooperation.

Today, the electoral base of the party seems to be diminishing. As the effects of increasing inequality, unemployment, difficulties in controlling the economy and bureaucratization become visible (paradoxically at a time when the Labour Party power in national government seems secure) many members view the ideological tradition as inadequate, and find that internal conflict is increasing. For party members, common identity and common interests are no longer easy to identify. Faced with new administrative tasks and administrative expertise in all areas of political decision-making, it is harder to see how 'traditional' political solutions apply. A major divide is developing within the party between the grass roots and the ideological conservatives, on the one hand, and the party elite, on the other. To a considerable extent, the latter relies on the expertise of the local municipal administration, which, because it involves itself heavily in the local political process, has provoked much irritation and protest in the community.

DECISION-MAKING AND THE LABOUR PARTY IDEOLOGY

One of the more interesting and challenging tasks for the anthropologist in contemporary capitalist society is to understand how institutionalization, for instance bureaucratization, influences social practice. The question is particularly relevant to the study of local political processes, because of their dual, and thus ambiguous, nature: political legitimacy depends both on informal relations in which ideological and personal credibility is generated, and on the ability to achieve concrete results. The latter is secured by institutionalized, and thus formal, procedures of decision-making and administration. In local politics in Norway, the relationship between formal, rational administration and the informal aspects of political participation seems to be one of multiple contradictions, and the boundaries between them are fluid.

In Ulefoss, the local politician is at the centre of a wide range of communication channels, expectations and demands which cannot be handled except by a sophisticated manoeuvring through different statuses and contexts where ideas of legitimacy vary greatly. Among neighbours, friends, colleagues and co-workers, the legitimacy of the politician is often dependent on his or her ability to appear trustworthy at a personal level, that is as a whole social person, while in the formal context of the municipal council, legitimacy more often depends on his or her ability to perform a clearly defined role and act in an instrumental or, alternatively, a performative fashion.

In the Norwegian political tradition in general, the flow of legitimacy between the people and the system has been managed efficiently by very strong political parties. The Labour Party in particular has been a powerful mediator between arenas of power and the grass roots. Although it is clear that its national govern-

mental responsibility has contributed to some internal bureaucratization, the ideological power and the informal sector of the party
have remained strong. It seems reasonable to hypothesize that this
ideological force is closely related to the party's ability to maintain a
relatively unitary and undifferentiated moral community within its
own ranks. My focus in the following discussion is on the relationship between the moral economy of this relatively undifferentiated
community, on the one hand, and the effects on bureaucratic pressure and professionalization, on the other. The new system of
governmentality introduced by *Eldreplanen* threatened the moral
community because it changed the formal role of the politician as
well as the idea of politics.

The social organization of the Norwegian Labour Party has
produced strong leadership, yet it would be misguided to interpret
the Labour Party ideology of solidarity and equality as manipulation from above. The idea of equality can be seen as an extension of
norms of reciprocity and social control in working-class culture.
Such norms have limited the power of leaders, not only through
formal control, but perhaps primarily by means of a culturally
homogeneous and tight social organization. The potential for
control within a social group sharing a moral universe lies in the
multiplicity of their social relations. Moral control is hard to maintain if, say, leaders are known to their followers in a specialized and
public capacity only. Therefore, the efficiency of moral control
depends on drawing on broad fields of relevance in social relations,
so that, for instance, private matters may be made relevant in the
evaluation of leadership performance.

In order to grasp the moral economy of the Labour Party, we
may explore *the sense of tradition* among its members, and ask to
what extent the party serves as an objectified reservoir of meaning
and legitimacy. My material from Ulefoss clearly indicates that not
only do many members look upon the party as a meaningful objec-
tivation, as a thing, they also project into it a sense of *moral and
historical agency* (Vike 1991).Thus, the history of the Labour Party
or the nation is not only a matter of registered facts; it is first and
foremost an expression of collective, heroic struggle for equality and
welfare. In this sense, history is invested with a moral force on its
own. The power of this moral force is drawn from the way members
construct a link of identity between the heroes of the past and the
here-and-now – a link which objectifies a *transcendental* aspect of
the identity of Labour Party members. Thus, a common feature in

party meetings, jubilees, etc. is the systematic de-emphasis of individuality. As a moral community, the Labour Party illustrates how the Norwegian political tradition has been able to combine an extreme degree of bureaucratic institutionalization with relatively broad participation and popular support. In a sense, the party has been able to serve as a de-institutionalized buffer against the system. The political scientist William Lafferty argues that in the Labour Party traditional and modern forms of community meet.

> The Norwegian Labour movement has thus functioned as a massive mediation mechanism between traditional and modern forms of a specific, Norwegian community. By 'translating' the traditional values to a functionalist and up-to-date model of government, the social democracy has provided a rare achievement in conservative adjustment.
>
> (Lafferty 1986: 33; HV's translation)

Lafferty's hypothesis is reasonable, yet I doubt that it is fruitful to regard the Labour Party political community as traditional. As my case study indicates, the moral community is more than a cultural trait that has survived. It is genuinely contemporary in the sense that it is actively reproduced and transformed in the present. The moral community serves as a device for political resistance and leadership control and, in this sense, it is reproduced by what Lafferty identifies as modern forms of community.

This study shows that different forms of political activity, which all seem equally 'modern', become deeply antagonistic because they influence the organization of politically relevant knowledge in very different ways. The organization of knowledge can be described on the basis of three important variables: sharedness, rules of relevance and overall goals. How available is the type of knowledge considered relevant to a particular issue, and how is knowledge related to identity? How are the boundaries between different sectors of knowledge defined, and who guards them? To what extent is knowledge made to serve instrumental goals, and how does this feed back on sharedness, rules of relevance and the possibility for reproducing the political community itself?

Below, I discuss the way opposing views on the organization of knowledge stirred opposition and political resistance among those who claimed to be ordinary members of the Labour Party in Ulefoss. Political resistance, in order to present itself as a *moral alternative* to the administratively dominated discourse, took the form of an attempt to break down the formal aspects of political discourse. This involved introducing experiences and actions which by some were seen as vulgar, irrelevant and destructive. This may be seen as a way of reproducing, strengthening and taking control of the moral economy of the party and – in part – the larger community. Let me first discuss the problem of differentiation.

MARX AND WEBER ON MODERNITY

The recent history of Ulefoss is far less dramatic than in many communities in other parts of the world, for instance in rural Malaysia. However, it is an example of the great transformation commonly known as modernization, of which European industrialization, social democracy, as well as the post-war green revolution in South-East Asia, are but different instances. I refer to this process as the growth and diffusion of a set of institutions rooted in the transformation of the economy by means of technology (Berger et al. 1974: 9), and the corresponding progressive economic and administrative rationalization and differentiation of the social world (Featherstone 1991: 3).

Underlying the academic debate on modernity is a widely-shared assumption that it promotes individualization. In the words of Derek Sayer:

> Bound up with capitalism are novel and distinctive forms of sociation, and embedded in these are new kinds of individual subjectivity.
>
> (Sayer 1991: 2)

According to Marx, certain distinctive forms of social relations form the very core of capitalist production, namely, private ownership of the means of production, division of labour (and the corresponding processes of social differentiation), and generalized commodity production. The primary form of this new type of social relation is *abstractness*. The idea of the abstract individual is a logical outcome of the general rationalization of capitalist culture, its primary carriers being the non-possessing worker (as universalized human capacity), capital, commodities, and universal means of exchange (all-purpose money). This goes logically together with increasing the autonomy of both activities and individuals or, more correctly, social capacities (social statuses).

The idea of the economy illustrates Marx's perspective on the differentiation of social activities. From previously having been subordinated to other human concerns, and indeed integrated as but one element in social practice, in capitalist societies it takes on an autonomous form and is made impersonal. Consequently, it is removed from the actors' own control, or to phrase it differently, the economy is externalized and made subject to its own laws. The process of specialization complements differentiation and reinforces it. In the present discussion, I will indicate that, because politics is made subject to these transformative powers, it constitutes an important source of controversy and resistance in Ulefoss.

The activity which is seen as reintegrating these various elements illustrates both the property of universality (or abstractness) attributed to them, as well as the prototypical way in which the autonomous, modern individual is continually reaffirmed as such in social relationships. This activity is exchange, of which the pure form is the market transaction. Here, individuals – ideally (or ideologically) free and equal – negotiate and transfer ownership of quantifiable items by means of privately owned, universal means of exchange. Hence the act of exchange must not only be seen as a confirmation of exchange value as such, but also as ways of constructing subjects as exchangers. This idea can be pursued further, and need not be limited to economy alone. What Marx described in his analysis of capitalism was indeed a cultural revolution (Corrigan and Sayer 1985) in a broad sense. Thus, one is justified in treating the model described above as a model for analysing not only the economy, but also the processes whereby new modes of social interaction are generated. Reification is a key mechanism in this process, and social capacities (statuses and roles) and social experience are heavily influenced by this aspect of modernization.[3]

This perspective may offer a bridge to the work of Max Weber, which is often thought of as presenting a very different perspective on modernization to Marx. I do not share such a view, although it is correct that Weber's iron cage vision of rationalization differs from Marx in that the former sees the rationalization process not as arising directly from the production process, but as a sub-system in its own right (Habermas 1987: 144). Weber's basic focus is on the transposition of cultural rationalization into social rationalization (Habermas 1987: 168). The main danger represented by rationalization, as Weber sees it, is the increasing reification of social relationships, i.e. the subordination of social relationships to the expanding, calculating means–ends orientation. This threatens the moral–practical basis of social action, he insists. For my purposes it is also interesting to note that the very concept of rationality – as the calculated pursuit of specific ends, i.e. profit, and forever renewed profit (Weber 1974: 17), and the emphasis on a methodological conduct of life, presupposes an unprecedented emphasis on individuality. Non-rational, collectively-held moral conventions are (more often than not) obstacles to the functioning of rational profit-seeking, as well as value maximization in the more general sense.

In short, modernization involves a specific type of rationality, which, according to both Marx and Weber, develops new forms of governability that require social relations to be properly differentiated and reified. This makes them appear as things and subject to specialized, expert knowledge and control. The *Eldreplanen* controversy in Ulefoss may be seen as a political conflict over the right to define the nature of political problems – that is, whether or not the power generated by processes of differentiation and reification is legitimate, and indeed whether or not it is possible and desirable to do something to guard oneself against it. The plan constructed the political field in a new way. Both the subject matter of the politicians as well as the social relations between the participants in local politics were transformed in ways which made the process of policy-making appear to many people as alienating. The political problem – how to make elderly care better and more efficient – was defined on the basis of a metaphorical construction of the political field as various kinds of units (clients, money, beds, units of service, etc.) and flows (resources and expenses), and the social relations between the political participants were largely seen merely as a function of the formal division of political labour, the guiding principle of which was the division between those who control the relevant knowledge and those who do not.

POLITICAL RESISTANCE

The *Eldreplanen* controversy took the form of a heated conflict between the municipal bureaucracy and the leading politicians (of most parties, except the Conservative Party) on the one hand, and on the other hand, the grass roots of the Labour Party, most of the elderly and many others who usually were not active in political work and discussions.

The controversy did not start as a discussion, but as a presentation. The plan document served as a reference point throughout the process, and because it was presented basically as a finished product, it contributed strongly to the effect that participants' roles had become redefined. The reformers presented themselves as producers/performers/experts, while the opponents had little choice but to act as customers/audience/laymen. Since the plan was based on an attempt to eliminate the discontinuity between political debate, decisions and administrative action, little room was left to incorporate considerations and experiences which were not directly relevant to the economic perspective as defined by the reformers. The administration considered this economic construction of the 'elderly problem' to be beyond discussion because of its status as a superior tool for precise analysis and action.

Three key elements of this controversy mobilized by the popular opposition will be analysed: first, the rejection of key symbolic and procedural aspects of administrative discourse; second, the development of counter strategies related to the generation of popular, political opinion in alternative arenas; and, third, the rejection of substantial elements of the technology of government.

The first, the rejection of key symbolic and procedural aspects of administrative discourse, contained the following elements:

• Interruption and breaking up of lines of argument.
• Leaving meetings.
• Stirring up emotional reactions.
• Rejecting the hegemony of the sophisticated style of speech.

These activities made public meetings increasingly unattractive among the reformers. In fact, these tactics were primarily pursued by older people whose rebellious attitude made a strong impression on many local, elected politicians as well as on others who witnessed it. Information meetings – the most frequently used mode of communication during the controversy, both within and outside the party context – always started with the presentation of the background to the plan and of a thorough explanation of its content by a central person from the health and welfare department. After that, the meetings often turned into more or less unstructured quarrels where the basic premises of the discussion were rejected. Sentiments and strong feelings were mobilized, and the professional, sophisticated style of the administrative, pseudo-scientific discourse was translated into everyday, 'vulgar' language and often made unrecognizable. In Bourdieu's terms (in Thompson 1984: 47), the authorized language, which tends to make those deemed incompetent exclude themselves from the right to speak, lost its legitimacy in these meetings, simply due to the sheer collective and emotional strength of the opposition.

Another typical feature of the information meetings was that the agenda changed from a discussion of procedural details in the plan to a question of why old people were being 'thrown into exile'. The participants moreover openly questioned the intentions of the reformers and accused them of lying about the quality of the existing elderly care. They did this by:

- Constructing unfavourable reputations.
- Strengthening alternative arenas.
- Insisting on informality and the relevance of the moral community.

Primarily performed outside the arenas of direct confrontation, these strategies were complementary to the former set. They were carried out within a variety of backstage political contexts in the community – informal coffee parties, breaks in party meetings, and discussions at the shopping centre – and were attempts to strengthen the social, moral and informal aspects of political opinion-making.

Constructing unfavourable reputations was a very strong weapon in the hands of those who had a place within this thriving informal network in the grass roots of the Labour Party. During the controversy, intimate knowledge of persons in power was conspicuously spread and directed toward a reduction – or total destruction – of their prestige. The credibility of some of the leading politicians, for instance, was put to the test by a rumour that they failed to take proper care of their own, elderly parents. For the administration, the consequences of unfavourable reputations were less serious, at least on a short-term basis. The most active administrators had chosen not to live in Ulefoss. Instead, they commuted from the neighbouring municipality and were thus less available for moral sanctioning.

Finally, there were those strategies which attacked the underlying rationality of the plan itself. These included the following:

- Rejecting the temporal image promoted by the plan.
- Developing alternative criteria of evaluation.
- Rejecting the idea of politics as an administrative process.
- Avoiding responsibility for solving the 'elderly problem'.
- Rejecting universalism.

With regard to the first, the opponents insisted throughout the controversy that the long-term perspective and the administrators' corresponding projections were of no decisive importance to the political strategy in the contemporary context. The prognoses were not considered reliable, and the whole perspective was seen as deeply immoral. They insisted that the core question was the situation for today's elderly, and moreover that the plan treated them not as living persons but rather as not-yet-dead. What the plan really tried to achieve, they argued, was to limit the scope of political choice.

The heavy stress on projections and economic predictability involved in the long-term perspective was challenged by the view that many of the variables involved in the plan could not be made subject to quantification at all. The most obvious and potent example was the issue of the old people's home in Ulefoss. The focus upon the tragic fate of old and sick people among the residents was so heavily foregrounded by the opponents that the argument that the home seized 25 per cent of the total welfare budget never became a legitimate part of the discourse. Especially revealing was disagreement about the meaning of security for the elderly. In order to undermine the claim that old people's ideas and feelings about security were primarily about efficient administration of economic resources, the opponents continually mobilized counter-expertise in public meetings – personal, practical experiences of how elderly care actually worked.

The opponents 'avoided responsibility' by consistently manoeuvring to avoid being turned into responsible politicians by the reformers. They rejected the requirement to present an alternative financial programme, while the opponents' action was guided by the overall principle of recreating what they regarded as genuine politics, which meant emphasizing popular participation and common sense; in contrast, they insisted that financial planning was the business of administrators. This strategy was only partially successful, since the opponents' leading spokespeople were caught in a double bind. As members of the Municipal Assembly several opponents in fact felt unable to vote against the plan, because they fell short of an alternative solution to the overall financial problems in the municipality. A substantial number of the Labour Party members responded to this double bind by being conspicuously absent from several of the meetings where the decisions were made.

Finally, the opponents rejected universalism by creating a normative environment (Scott 1985: 305) which mobilized whole identities in the discourse as opposed to the specialized role model promoted by the reformers. Breaking down the agenda and introducing instead stories from their own personal lives was but one element in this activity. In other words, the opponents rejected the idea that the plan as a whole related only to abstract aspects of their life, and that formal, rational discourse was the only acceptable mode of articulating one's point of view. This normative environment, actively created through collective political resistance, was made into an effective buffer against the individualizing power of rational discourse. In the information meetings, it became impossible for the reformers to accuse individual opponents of having the facts wrong. The normative environment penetrated the social power of the reformers by the opponents rejecting the representation of this power as individual competence and substituting the facts with what appeared reasonable to the opponents. From this we see that the opponents' category of *politikk* (as opposed to *administrasjon*) contained a fundamental criticism of the decision-making process as a whole. Instead of accepting the idea of *politikk* as an institutionalized, strictly formal and largely autonomous activity, they insisted on making their own experiences relevant.

CONCLUSIONS

This material from Ulefoss throws light on some aspects of political resistance in contemporary Norwegian society. The case has shown that loyalty to the idea of party tradition served as a legitimation of collective resistance against alienation and accumulation of power. Basically, this ideological practice involved an attempt to reproduce a moral universe within which the actions of those in power were kept within limits and controlled from below. This strategy was relatively efficient despite the fact that – characteristically, perhaps – the opponents were unable to recreate this normative environment in the most formal context, the Municipal Assembly, where the final decisions were made. Although some of the most radical among the elderly showed up there and demonstrated their bitterness by crying openly, and although many representatives were demonstratively absent, the mobilization did not prevent the plan from being supported by the Assembly, albeit in a modified form. As the first test of a new form of governance, *Eldreplanen* opened a new path for administrative influence and instrumental policy-making in the municipality.

Knowledge was a central factor in this struggle for control and influence. The criticism directed against the reformers was the argument that their strategy served as a means for de-qualifying ordinary people as participants in local politics. The mobilization of the moral community, however, challenged the idea that political activity was a strictly formal, autonomous sphere of interaction dominated by a series of individual transactions between producers and consumers of politics. In the same vein, this mobilization opposed the premise that it was the quality of the products, not the process of production, which was to be regarded as the vital factor in the political process.

If we regard the rationalized version of contemporary politics as an attempt to introduce a universal standard of political transaction, we may again draw on Marx's critique of modernity and his insistence that the idea that universal autonomy thus created is a potentially alienating ideological construction (Sayer 1991: 58–73). The underlying logic of this construction is the same as that which generates commodification, a logic which makes power appear as sets of universally exchangeable items to be accumulated, possessed, and presented by individuals.[4]

In our case it appears that the ability to make political judgements parallels what Marx in *Capital* (1979) labelled *commodity fetishism*. In other words, knowledge appears as a thing, the apparent autonomy and objectivity of which serves to hide its social nature. In contrast to the world of commodities proper, the item to be accumulated within this context is individual competence. Given the status of the information provided by *Eldreplanen* as facts, the ability to understand and deal with them depended more on whether or not one was a learned person than on one's sensitivity to other people's views concerning what is reasonable and what is not. Knowledge fetishism makes knowledge appear as something to be possessed by competent individuals.

The expertise model of knowledge, as we may call it, was predicated upon a separate epistemology as well as a distinct type of social organization. First, it was constructed upon a set of formally-defined universalist principles. Second, it implied, as pointed out above, that knowledge was accumulated individually as competence. Third, competence seemed to lend itself more easily to exchange than discourse, and hence it appeared as an object to be presented. Fourth, knowledge-as-competence seemed more easily adapted to instrumental purposes than did discursive knowledge. In short, expertise involved a reification of experience in the sense that it put priority on what was formally instrumental at the cost of the social reproduction of a political community of participants whose experiences were differently positioned.

NOTES

1 Fieldwork was carried out in Ulefoss in 1989–90 as part of my Master's Degree at Department of Social Anthropology, University of Oslo. I thank my adviser, Professor Eduardo Archetti for stimulating discussions and good advice. The research was in part funded by Norges forskningsråd.

  The text was first presented in the EASA workshop 'The Art of Government and the Morality of Policy' in Oslo in 1994. I am grateful for the comments I received there. I also thank colleagues at the University of Newcastle-upon-Tyne and at the University of Sussex, where a revised version of the EASA paper was presented later the same year. The chairpersons of the EASA workshop, Cris Shore and Susan Wright, have commented extensively on the manuscript and have contributed greatly to its improvement.

2 Thus, the tenant would ask the landowner for help when he was in need of land to farm, and the landowner would turn to his tenants and ask for help when there was transplanting, harvesting, or repairing jobs to be done, even if the 'help' involved paid work. As the material basis for this egalitarian ideology eroded, so did the poor peoples' ability to appeal to morality as a means for maintaining their own relative status. Nevertheless, increased moral pressure may reduce the scope and speed of such changes. From several villages in Malaysia, researchers report that landowners, presumably as a result of moral pressure from neighbours and kin, hire more labourers for higher wages than they actually need (Scott 1985: 192). From this, it is easy to see that norms may serve as a resource in social processes.

3 This point was made by Marx in *The German Ideology* (1846) and convincingly discussed by Derek Sayer (1991). Although Marx focuses on the consequences of the differentiation of the economy, the process he describes is general. The notion that this leads to a new way of conceptualizing social relations is paramount here, especially the increasing significance of things as mediators of social relations. And since things may be individually accumulated, this also enhances the importance of individuality as well as the possibility of legitimating power (e.g. concealed as competence, see below).

4 People appear to be independent of one another because their mutual dependency assumes the unrecognizable form of relations between commodities (Sayer 1991: 64). I am not arguing here that political competence and commodities are identical phenomena, only that they seem to be generated by the same set of processes and that they seem to be related to modern individuality in much the same way.

REFERENCES

Archetti, E. (1991) 'Argentinean tango: male sexual ideology and morality' in R. Gronhaug, G. Haaland and G. Henriksen (eds) *The Ecology of Choice and Symbol. Essays in Honour of Fredrik Barth*, Bergen: Alma Mater.

Berger, B., Berger, H. and Kellner, H. (1974) *The Homeless Mind*, New York: Vintage Books.

Corrigan, P. and Sayer, D. (1985) *The Great Arch. English State Formation as Cultural Revolution*, Oxford/New York: Basil Blackwell.

Featherstone, M. (1991) *Consumer Culture and Postmodernism*, London: Sage Publications.

Habermas, J. (1987) *The Theory of Communicative Action* (Vols 1 and 2), Boston: Beacon Press.

Lafferty, W. (1986) 'Den sosialdemokratiske stat', *Nytt Norsk Tidsskrift* No.1.

Lukes, S. (1981) *Emile Durkheim*, Harmondsworth: Penguin.

Marx, K. (1979) [1867] *Capital* (Vol. 1), Harmondsworth: Penguin.

—— (1970) [1932] *Fra den tyske ideologi* (Verker i utvalg 2), Oslo: Pax forlag.

Rowlands, M. and Warnier, J. P. (1988) 'Sorcery, power and the modern state in Cameroon', *Man* 23 (1): 118–32.

Sayer, D. (1991) *Capitalism and Modernity. An Excursus on Marx and Weber*, London: Routledge and Kegan Paul.

Scott, J. (1985) *Weapons of the Weak. Everyday Forms of Peasant Resistance*, New Haven/London: Yale University Press.

Thompson, J. B. (1984) *Studies in the Theory of Ideology*, Cambridge: Polity Press.

Vike, H. (1991) *Contested Signs. Political Discourse in a Norwegian Industrial Community* (unpublished thesis), Department of Anthropology, University of Oslo.

Weber, M. (1974) *The Protestant Ethic and the Spirit of Capitalism*, London: Allen and Unwin.

Chapter 9

Poverty in a 'post-welfare' landscape

Tenant management policies, self-governance and the democratization of knowledge in Great Britain

Susan Brin Hyatt

FROM GOVERNMENT *OF* THE POOR TO GOVERNMENT *BY* THE POOR[1]

The slogan, 'power to the people!' once firmly rooted in the oppositional leftist movements of the 1960s, has undergone a
transformation. That call for certain functions to be transferred
from government bureaucracies directly into the hands of 'the
people' has now become emblematic of a number of contemporary
social policies, particularly those currently being advocated by the
Conservative New Right in democracies throughout the West.

One arena within which this surprising turn of events can be
clearly charted and examined is through the analysis of policies
pertaining to the management of state-subsidized housing in
Britain. Since 1979, a series of policies devised by the ruling
Conservatives has increasingly targeted the tenants, themselves, as
the agents best qualified to rescue their communities from an accel-
erated spiral of deterioration and decline which, by the mid-1980s,
was widely recognized to have rendered most British public sector
housing estates virtually unliveable.

A parliamentary white paper produced in 1987, for example,
argued that:

> *In the public sector the emphasis must be on greater consumer
> choice and more say for tenants.* This can be achieved by offering
> a variety of forms of ownership and management; this will help
> to break down the monolithic nature of large estates. There
> should also be physical improvements to the housing and the
> general environment on these estates; greater involvement of
> private sector resources; and encouragement of local enterprise

and employment *so that residents can themselves improve their quality of life.*

(HMSO 1987: 1; SBH's emphasis)

Embodied in this statement is the conviction that once left to their own devices, it will be the *tenants* themselves, rather than trained professionals, who ultimately possess the requisite skills and relevant knowledge essential for improving 'their quality of life'. Such a formulation, which transforms categories of people – like public sector tenants – from their previous role as the *objects* of policy into a new-found prominence as the *practitioners* of policy, represents a significant cultural shift in our notions about the function of government in relation to poverty. 'Modern' governments once acted to reconfigure poor individuals and their communities from 'the top down'. In contrast, the policies of the New Right strive to create the optimal conditions within which the poor's *own* fullest potentialities for self-governance are presumed most likely to flourish, thereby supposedly enabling them to renew their own communities from 'the ground up'.

Encouraging tenants to take on management of their own housing estates, the idea for which partially originated in the tenant activism of the 1970s (see Hague 1990), has now become the cornerstone of the Conservative government's policies for reforming that housing whose ownership remains in the public sector.[2] Through special Section 16 grants, administered by the Department of the Environment (DoE: the agency in Britain responsible for housing policy) and designated for training sessions and courses, tenants of public sector housing are being encouraged to form Tenant Management Organizations (TMOs) in order to take on responsibility for those functions usually carried out by their local councils. These include such tasks as: collecting rents, 'organising repairs and maintenance; and making sure buildings are kept clean and tidy' (DoE 1994a).

The goal of this chapter is not to evaluate the efficacy of such housing policies nor is it to examine in any great detail their material outcome; it is, rather, to uncover the ways in which tenant management policies represent one technology constitutive of a new mode of governance that Nikolas Rose has described as 'advanced liberalism'. As he explains:

Whilst welfare sought to govern *through* society, advanced liberalism asks whether it is possible to govern without governing *society*, that is to say, to govern through the regulated and accountable choices of autonomous agents – citizens, consumers, parents, employees, investors.

(Rose 1993: 298; emphasis as in the original)

Whereas 'advanced liberal' rule now relies on the conviction that government can instil a capacity for *self*-regulation in people, liberal governance, in contrast, had once been effected largely by means of strategic interventions undertaken by 'experts', whose access to specialized knowledge authorized them to govern others, particularly the poor. Again, as Rose explains:

Persons and activities were to be governed *through* society, that is to say, through acting upon them in relation to a *social* norm, and constituting their experiences and evaluations in a *social* form . . . political rule would not itself set out the norms of individual conduct, but would install and empower a variety of 'professionals' who would, investing them with authority to act as experts in the devices of social rule.

(Rose 1993: 285; emphasis as in the original)

Advanced liberal policies, with their emphasis on values such as 'freedom' and 'individual choice', might also be conceptualized as post-welfare in nature in that they unbalance that delicate equilibrium between the 'authority of expertise' essential for the establishment of social norms on one hand and the job of governing on the other.

Rather than building the sorts of communities intrinsic to the 'liberal' nature of the welfare state, designed to facilitate the collective governance *of* the poor, the current trend is toward fashioning environments intended to foster self-government *by* the poor. As such, advanced liberal policies make manifest a new understanding of 'the problem of poverty' by privileging the value of the local knowledge held by public sector tenants and poor people while simultaneously diminishing the importance of that professional knowledge which had once been deployed by 'experts'.

In the current climate of advanced liberalism, poverty is represented not as a social problem but as a new possibility for poor individuals to experience 'empowerment' through the actualization of self-management. As will be seen in later sections of this chapter, however, from the point of view of the tenants, what they are being asked to do is not only to take on the sizeable chore of *managing* their own communities; they are also being put in the somewhat more precarious position of being asked to *police* them.

SUBSIDIZED HOUSING AND THE RISE OF 'THE SOCIAL' IN GREAT BRITAIN

The history of public housing in Britain offers a particularly vivid illustration of the contrast between those 'social' (or liberal) models for government once characteristic of the welfare state and emergent 'post-welfare' (or advanced liberal) strategies. Built mostly during the inter-war and post-war periods, large-scale public sector housing developments, generally known as 'council estates', were one of the great experiments of high modernity. The purpose of creating such communities was not only to increase the physical well-being of the working classes; they were also intended to bring about a *moral* improvement as well. Like colonialism, campaigns for better housing conditions undertaken in the earlier part of the twentieth century were civilizing missions, aimed at reforming the urban poor who made up Britain's own domestic 'dark continent'.[3]

In 1907, for example, representatives of a number of local authorities in northern England met in Bradford to consider the problem of workers' living conditions in rented lodgings. Welcoming the delegates to this conference, the then Mayor of Bradford, Alderman J. A. Goodwin, remarked:

> We can speak here in Bradford for facts which we know, that there are in this city a number of those houses let in lodgings, and that in them, particularly those let in single rooms, there is carried on a vicious kind of life which is very detrimental to the moral welfare of the community.
>
> (Houses Let in Lodgings 1907: 3; SBH's emphasis)

In reading through the proceedings of this conference, it becomes clear that what concerned the delegates was not only the notion that poverty compelled families to live in conditions unfit for human habitation. What worried them just as much was their shared perception that poor housing conditions posed a *moral* threat to the overall well-being of the populace and needed to be tackled not in the interest of social justice but towards minimizing the risks of criminality and disorder perceived to emanate from poor communities (see Horn 1994: Ch. 2).

During the inter-war period, most British public housing took the form of suburban or peripheral estates owned and managed by local municipal councils. They were comprised primarily of semi-detached 'cottages', arranged along grassy cul-de-sacs and each with its own garden (Burnett 1991: 234).

Though they lacked a number of amenities, such 'villages' were constructed to replace the squalor and depravity associated with slum life by a completely new *milieu* (Rabinow 1989) intended to mimic an idealized vision of English country life. Standards for personal conduct in these communities were rigidly imposed and maintained. In his record of urban poverty in the 1930s, for example, George Orwell made the following observation about life in the new council estates:

> Give people a decent house and they will soon learn to keep it decent. Moreover, with a smart-looking house to live up to they improve in self-respect and cleanliness, and their children start life with better chances. Nevertheless, in a Corporation estate there is an uncomfortable, almost prison-like atmosphere, and the people who live there are well-aware of it.
>
> (Orwell 1965 [1937]: 71)

Similarly, a woman's history project on one estate in Bradford Metropolitan District recorded the following recollections of council estate life prior to the 1960s:

> Tenants had to get permission to do anything to their houses. In the eyes of the tenants, the rent man was the council spy. 'Everybody had to do their garden. They used to come round periodically and look to see. If you hadn't done it you were warned and then they evicted you.' Another comments, 'They used to collect your rent [door-to-door] at that time. You had to ask permission to do anything . . . the rent man would report anything that wasn't authorised.'
>
> (Lower Grange Women's History Project 1989: 16)

The idea that it was possible to engineer and administer a particular environment in such a way so as to 'produce' a specific sort of person was intrinsic to modernity and to the rise of 'the social'. Replacing an earlier view, in which social order appeared both arbitrary and inevitable, the 'modern' outlook was that society was rather more like a laboratory, amenable to intervention through the applications of such new technologies as urban planning, hygiene, and public health. As such, 'the social' constituted a domain which could be purposively planned, regulated and governed (Horn 1988, 1994; Rabinow 1989).

At the time of Margaret Thatcher's first election in 1979, 30 per cent of the British population still lived on council estates. The presence of those 'authorities' who had once enforced the collective forms of social control that had characterized council estate life during the inter-war and immediate post-war periods, such as 'housing visitors', door-to-door rent collectors and resident caretakers, had gradually declined due to a number of factors, not the least of which was their enormous cost to the public sector (see Power 1987: 66–90; Kemp and Williams 1991: 137). Therefore, the deteriorating council estate represented *the* perfect medium within which the Conservatives could experiment with cultivating colonies made up of a new kind of poor person – a poor person who, rather than being dependent on professionals employed through the largesse of the state, was now actively encouraged to be self-governing. Such a reform programme would contrast markedly with the qualities they attributed to the Labourite forms of municipal socialism, qualities which they claimed were particularly endemic within the sphere of public housing management: expense, inefficiency, paternalism and overblown bureaucracy.[4]

By the late 1980s, putting the responsibility for housing management in the hands of the tenants had emerged as the 'new frontier' for a distinctively Conservative housing policy. In the parliamentary debate leading up to the passage of the 1988 Housing Act, Thatcher's then Secretary of State for the Environment, Nicholas Ridley, argued in favour of giving more autonomy to tenants stating that:

> While many local councils have an undeniably good record as landlords, a significant number do not. They have managed properties inefficiently and with little respect for tenants' wishes and have provided a poor service. Such failings characterize a monopoly, where the spur of competition is absent and the consumer is unable to take his business elsewhere.
>
> (Hansard 1987: 628)

References to 'the spur of competition' and to 'consumers' reinforced the sense that the post-war consensus in support of a publicly-funded welfare state in Britain had ruptured decisively. The production of this new image of council tenants as consumers, who were now being given rein to exercise their rights of free choice in an unfettered market place, required that tenants also be regarded as independent beings, fully capable of making responsible choices for themselves, rather than as 'clients' who were passive recipients of welfare provision.

Under the regimes of the welfare state, government *of* the poor had taken place through the mediations of an array of 'experts', including social workers, health visitors, and, as we have seen above, rent collectors and housing officers. Now, the interventions of those same experts, who were expensive and whose intermediary role was portrayed as interfering with the freedom of the poor to act as consumers, needed to be curtailed if not eliminated entirely. It thus became necessary to transfer that mantle of authority to tenants by regarding their indigenous 'expertise' as equal, if not superior, to that of trained professionals or 'outsiders'. A consultation paper produced by Britain's Department of the Environment (DoE) in 1992, for example, averred that:

> *Local services are best monitored by those who receive the services directly.* The Government is therefore committed to the further diversification of local authority housing management, and to an increasing role for tenants in deciding the level of service they want, selecting the organisation which is best able to deliver that service within the resources available, and monitoring its performance.
>
> (DoE 1992: 5; SBH's emphasis)

This requirement that public sector housing providers now needed to be accountable to their tenants compelled local authorities to sponsor a certain number of educational activities designed to equip tenants to take on their new supervisory role. As a 'guidance note' issued by the Department of the Environment stated in no uncertain terms:

> Tenants will be best served by the provision of clear advice and information backed up with the opportunity to inspect full contract documents at local centres or by attendance at local meetings. Written material should always be in plain language, with summaries and guides where necessary. In some instances tenants may benefit from training – for example, where they are involved in detailed consideration of contract documents – and authorities should consider whether or not this needs to be provided.
>
> (DoE 1994b: 4)

For the first time, information about costs, repairs, letting policies and other management matters were opened up for discussion
between housing professionals and tenants, bespeaking at least the
symbolic creation of a new kind of parity previously unknown to
working class and poor citizens of the welfare state. It is thus to a
consideration of the implications of this process of democratizing
knowledge in relation to the constitution of a 'post-welfare' system
of governance, and to its implications for the policing of poor
communities, that we will now turn our attention.

DEMOCRATIZING KNOWLEDGE AND THE POLICING OF COMMUNITIES

Implicit within those post-welfare policies characteristic of
'advanced liberalism' is the presupposition that 'expertise' can be
regarded as a readily transferable commodity which, once bestowed
upon groups like council tenants, will automatically render them
capable of significantly altering their own environments without
interference from outside.

The metamorphosis of council tenants and other poor people,
from subjects once dependent on the expert guidance of others into
autonomous beings already possessed of their own expertise, is part
of a broader movement usually referred to more generally as
'empowerment'. In an incisive article on the War on Poverty in the
United States, and on the role of what she terms, 'the will to
empower', Barbara Cruikshank makes the following point:

> What specifically must be explored is the degree to which these
> technologies of citizenship – methods for constituting active and
> participatory citizens, such as those aimed at empowering the
> poor – link the subjectivity of citizens to their subjection, and
> link activism to discipline.
>
> (Cruikshank 1994: 29)

The experience of one group of tenants in Bradford, who
attempted to take over the management of their own estate, offers a
cautionary tale illustrative of precisely such a link between activism
and discipline (see also Hyatt 1994).[5]

Lower Grange is a council estate built in the mid-1920s and
located on the western periphery of Bradford, one of the most
economically ravaged metropolitan districts in northern England.
Over the years, the quality of the housing had failed to keep pace with

the times and by the mid-1980s an article published in Bradford's daily newspaper described conditions on the estate as follows:

> Deprivation and squalor is something the residents of Bradford's massive Lower Grange estate have had to live with. Most of the 771 homes on the city's oldest council estate still have outside toilets. Damp permeates virtually all of the houses, leaving a trail of black mould and peeling wallpaper.
>
> (Stott 1985)

A group of activist tenants on Lower Grange, most of them women, initiated a campaign calling on Bradford Council to implement a long-overdue programme of modernization. One such activist was quoted in the same newspaper article, saying, 'We don't want to be moved away, we want decent homes on Lower Grange estate' (ibid.). New central government policies intended to diminish the role of councils in providing subsidized housing, however, meant that local councils like Bradford's had very few capital resources at their disposal for substantial rehabilitation of ailing housing stock and almost no funds for new construction. Eventually, all of the parties involved accepted the fact that there was very little possibility of redeveloping the estate without the involvement of private developers and housing associations.

Housing Associations, which are voluntary sector, quasi-governmental organizations,[6] had become central government's preferred providers of new low-income housing for rent, supplanting municipal landlordism. Faced with this situation, the Lower Grange tenants decided to make use of two basic tenets of central government policy in order to try and enter into the redevelopment process as players to be reckoned with and as part of their attempt to remain together as a community in the face of massive upheaval.

First, they decided to make use of a measure called 'Tenants' Choice', a provision of the 1988 Housing Act. Tenants' Choice had originally been devised by central government in order to further encourage the privatization of municipal housing by permitting tenants to vote for alternative landlords to take over the management of their estates. Much to the government's surprise, most local authority tenants, and those living on Lower Grange were no exception, would have preferred to remain under the purview of their local councils.[7] As an early flyer produced by the Lower Grange tenants during their initial campaign for redevelopment stated:

Some Councillors have suggested that we talk to Housing
Associations or Private Developers . . . However, we have talked
to almost everybody on the estate and everybody wants to keep
the Council as Landlord and keep out private developers. '*The
Council must save our community*'.

(emphasis as in the original)

When it became clear that the council lacked sufficient resources to
'save their community', the tenants implemented the second part of
their strategy, concocted in order to prevent 'outsiders' from taking
over the estate: they voted that their alternative landlord would be,
in fact, themselves, in the form of a particular configuration
favoured by central government, a housing association. As one
community activist later commented:

And what we used as well was the government's own philosophy
of enterprise and helping yourself. You know, the Tenants'
Choice Bill was supposedly to give people more choice in
housing. So, we stabbed them in the back with their own legislation! You can't say, well, you want tenants to have a choice then
say, 'No, you can't have it. It's for everybody else but not for
Lower Grange'.

The group received a grant from a charitable trust to help them
hire a housing consultant and they embarked on a course of action
directed toward the goal of becoming fully certified as the Lower
Grange Housing Association. There was no funding, however, for
the group to sponsor the construction of new homes to replace the
third of the houses on the estate judged by the council to be struc-
turally defective and consigned to demolition. Ultimately, they
agreed to work with a large national housing association, 'British
Isles',[8] which had already been brought into the overall redevelopment plan. British Isles would finance the building of a number of
new homes for rent, including a smaller development-within-the-
development designated for the twenty-two households who
remained committed to joining the Lower Grange Housing
Association. Forty other households, who had originally signed on
to the Tenants' Choice plan, ultimately lost faith in the process and
finally agreed to take Bradford Council up on its offers to rehouse
them elsewhere.

With only twenty-two households now remaining in the scheme, it
became increasingly evident that the tenants were not going to be able

to marshal adequate resources to allow them to act as their own land-lord. As the leader of the campaign, Margaret Chapman, later told me:

We used the Tenants' Choice Act to get what we wanted – we used it to get the [new] houses where we wanted them. No way could we have taken on managing those houses, ourselves. You've got to have a degree in mathematics, to be honest, you'd need a few degrees between you! The ordinary person couldn't take on that sort of responsibility. And, saying that again, it was an unpaid job. Who in their right mind is going to commit themselves to that kind of life-long responsibility?

In all of the governmental rhetoric about tenant participation and self-management, the reality, that most remaining council tenants had limited education and literacy skills, and that they were expected to take on enormous amounts of work without any mone-tary compensation, was lost. In fact, for the duration of its two-year lifespan, the Lower Grange Housing Association's office was, for all intents and purposes, Margaret Chapman's house. People called in at all times of day and night to ask about the allocation of the new homes for rent and about the status of the redevelopment plans in general. All of this activity was taking place in the midst of a community that had literally become a construction zone.

In the autumn of 1991, members of the Lower Grange Housing Association finally moved into their new houses, which had been built and were still being managed by the British Isles Housing Association. Another tenant, Linda Kenny, who had been serving as secretary of the housing action group, described to me what happened next:

After we moved into the new houses, everyone seemed to drop off . . . I couldn't put any time into attending the training sessions because I had started college . . . But, we just didn't have the expertise to [manage the houses.] At the last meeting, at the Community Centre, there was quite a good turnout, but I think everyone was relieved to [vote to] have British Isles take over.

I have to say, I wouldn't have liked to collect the rent from others . . . I don't really want to know nobody's business around here and I don't really want them to know mine . . . We did hear things about certain people knowing things they shouldn't be knowing – that's a breach of confidentiality, isn't it?

Without adequate training or ongoing support for their efforts, the tenants of Lower Grange were unable to take on all of the tasks involved in acting as their own landlords. They had none of the resources or amenities associated with management or administration – no office space, photocopier, secretarial assistance or telephones, save Margaret Chapman's own. They were expected to use their living rooms and kitchens as workspaces and to cobble together whatever other resources they needed as best they could.

Most problematically, the tenants of Lower Grange realized that managing their own houses essentially meant *policing* one another. Linda Kenny described to me what transpired when she attended a meeting organized by British Isles shortly after the new homes had been built. The meeting was convened to discuss how tenants could become more actively involved in managing the estate. Most of the problems raised by the community residents who were present on that occasion pertained to such matters as rowdy neighbours, messy gardens and noisy children. As Linda remarked:

> People wanted to know what British Isles would do about it. Well, British Isles wanted *us* to set up these committees [to address such problems], but then you could create a situation where it's 'us' and 'them' right within your own little community. And, they wanted one person from each committee to go around the estate, and to be in charge, and to say to the other tenants, like to the mother who's got an unruly kid, 'Look – you've got to stop it'. I don't think that should be anybody in the community's job – it should be solely British Isles' job. Because otherwise, you could cause complete chaos.

In being asked to monitor one another's behaviour, the tenants of Lower Grange quickly discovered that their participation in such schemes for 'empowerment' could foster an even greater breakdown of the social order in their communities than that which was already being fomented by the crises of structural unemployment and increasing impoverishment. Tenants who became involved in tenant management schemes on other estates confronted similar conflicts between their activism and the expectation that they should police their fellow residents. Another leading tenant-activist from a different estate in Bradford described to me how she saw the role of the Tenant Management Organization in her community:

> So we're trying to make [the other] tenants accept responsibility for everything – rubbish, their children, other people who come

into the building. If we can just build up their sense of responsibility, make them into more responsible people, we might upgrade the behaviour patterns of the people living on the premises. If not, they might feel so uncomfortable that they want to move. We'll wave them good-bye if that's the case. Once we can actually get in on the allocation process, we can stipulate all of the do's and don'ts before they actually come in, and if they know that it's going to be quite a stringent operation, where you're going to be watched and monitored for the first few months you live here, they may not be so keen on moving in if they're that kind of tenant. People who don't have anything to worry about won't feel intimidated by it.

Despite the arduousness of taking on such responsibilities, given their new-found access to formerly privileged information, many tenants who enter into the self-management process do begin to construct a new sense of their own authority. Several of them have turned their homes into veritable offices replete with computers, filing cabinets and a host of certificates and diplomas displayed on their walls attesting to their mastery over that knowledge which was once the exclusive property of employees of the welfare state.[9] The paid welfare professionals who had once 'ruled' poor communities are now being replaced by unpaid 'local experts', the tenants, themselves. As one tenant-activist told me,

When I'm at home, I'm just another woman stuck in a council house. Inside the house, I feel as if I'm in a rut and everything's caving in on me. But, once I leave that house, I'm a different person . . . Something in my life has got to be perfect. And, when I come out of my house and go to the tenants' group, that's the perfect part of my life. That's what makes me just as good as anybody else.

In keeping with this spirit of promoting parity with the experts, Bradford Metropolitan Council's Department of Housing, like many other local authorities, has recently produced a folder for its tenants which it calls, 'Up and Running: A Starter Pack for Tenant Participation' (City of Bradford Metropolitan Council n.d.). The cover illustration shows a carefully composed multi-ethnic and mixed gender group of people, collectively engaged in constructing an edifice out of building blocks labelled 'consulting', 'negotiating', 'planning', 'training', and the like.

These are the privileged skills being offered to tenants in their brave new world of self-management. A letter to tenants from the City Housing Officer introduces the material in the pack, and part of it reads as follows:

> The Directorate of Housing and Environmental Protection is committed to achieving effective consultation and participation with its tenants.
>
> We recognize that the relationship we build with our tenants must be based on a foundation of openness and trust. To manage a progressive housing service we must move forward together to develop these relationships and I feel this can be secured by:
>
> • *Providing you with information on our performance in housing management and other service areas.*
>
> • *Taking time to talk and listen to each others [sic] ideas and expectations.*
>
> • *Encouraging you to become actively involved in decisions that affect you, your home and environment.*
>
> (City of Bradford Metropolitan Council n.d.;
emphasis as in the original)

For council tenants, the idea that they would be privy to this sort of dialogue with housing managers contrasted sharply with their previous experiences of interaction with the council. As one tenant who had begun lobbying for improved living conditions on her estate in the 1980s told me, 'The Council didn't like people to wake up – they liked people to be passive and just live with their problems'. Another older woman, a pensioner, reminisced, 'You used to bow and scrape to the Council. You daren't say owt [anything] for fear of being chucked out of your house!' The new spirit of 'openness and trust' between tenants and their housing directorate may have seemed like a break with past practice. A number of tenant-activists, however, were sceptical that it was accompanied by any actual change in power relations. As one activist remarked:

> I think that in terms of dealing with tenants, the Council has had a change of mind about its approach, and now it's grasped this consultation and involvement. Its had to because it is under threat from . . . changing legislation. Having said that, in reality, although there's a willingness to listen and to talk, to include

people, they've not had a change of heart. It's still very much the Council in control. They want your views, they want you to get involved but at the end of the day, they want to be the ones to determine the outcome.

Such doubts notwithstanding, examining the implications of measures designed to cast tenants into a role as 'partners' with their local authorities and housing departments is crucial for understanding the nature of post-welfare rule and its attendant philosophy of advanced liberalism. It is through the adoption of just such measures, intended to undermine the role of 'trained' professionals and experts, that the entire notion of 'the social' as a sphere of human activity amenable to governance through strategic interventions is being reconfigured, creating chaos and confusion within those communities already most battered by the disabling repercussions of de-industrialization and economic decline.

HOUSING POLICY AND POVERTY UNDER THE REGIMES OF ADVANCED LIBERALISM

It is the inscription of tenants' abilities to act upon their own environments through the modality of 'self-help' that constitutes 'empowerment' within the texts of post-welfare policies. As Cruikshank has noted:

> 'Self-help' did not mean that autonomous selves got together to help one another. Rather, self-help meant that the government intervened to create relations of help between selves . . . The poor were to indicate their own needs and the causes of their impoverishment; in doing so, it was hoped they would enlist themselves in meeting those needs.
>
> (Cruikshank 1994: 44)

The institutionalization of this ethos of 'self-help', through policies like tenant self-management, is the critical step that makes possible a new discursive strategy for the exercise of government. Rather than extending the modern project of seeing the poor as a 'defective' population, in need of professional guidance and discipline from the outside, the public sector tenant is now, as Miller and Rose (1990: 22) have written of the worker, linked 'into the social order as a democratic citizen with rights and responsibilities'. The 'self-managing tenant' has therefore become one of the heroes of

New Right ideology, the poor citizen who is self-reliant rather than dependent, self-governing rather than governed, empowered rather than powerless.

Post-welfare policies, like tenant self-management, are thus imbued with the promise that they are able to change 'welfare dependants' into active citizens thereby enfranchising public sector tenants into the world of productive and entrepreneurial activity without any need to invest significant public resources. Such an alchemy has transmuted public housing from a site of deprivation into a place for opportunity, where poverty and enterprise can co-exist happily side-by-side rather than in stark contrast to one another. Any discussion of poverty as inequality or disadvantage has been effaced from the discourse on housing reform all together, leaving the formidable tasks of governance and policing in the hands of the besieged and overburdened tenants, themselves.

However 'empowered' the new tenant managers may be – and they are precious few and far between[10] – they, along with their fellow public sector tenants, remain among the most impoverished members of the population in the UK. The sheer amount of voluntary labour required on the part of these activist tenants, most of them women, means that tenant management is highly unlikely to become the norm in the vast majority of communities. As one tenant-activist pointed out in a speech she delivered in Bradford City Hall:

> Ten years ago, [our] estate . . . was recognized as a hard-to-let area, an embarrassment to the Council and embarrassing for the tenants who lived there. Today the same estate is regarded as a success story, a model of tenant participation with a waiting list of prospective tenants.
>
> But, as the founder of the Tenants Association in 1983, I have invested an estimated 4000 hours of my time – free. The Tenant Management Cooperative is currently being staffed by committee members until a housing officer can be appointed. This has two members working 4 hours a day since 1993 – a total of 1,840 hours of free labour.

Despite its many impracticalities as a strategy for effecting broadly-based public housing reform, tenant management policies are initiatives deserving of serious analysis. They have received a disproportionate share of funding from a rapidly dwindling pot of public resources, and have spawned an entirely new industry in

Britain consisting of tenant-participation trainers and consultants, publications, 'how to' manuals, courses and awards. While one 'class of experts', employees of the welfare state bureaucracy – such as housing officers, rent collectors and social workers – are being discredited and gradually eliminated in the move toward 'advanced liberalism', a whole new group of *paid* professionals has been created to work alongside the mostly volunteer tenant-activists. These new professionals are experts in the arts of empowerment and self-help, whose job it is to inculcate within tenants a sense of their own autonomy and agency by encouraging them to take on challenges such as self-management (see Baistow 1994/5; Cruikshank 1994: 49–51).

Certainly very few of us would advocate a return to those days when the atmosphere of public housing estates was, as George Orwell put it, 'prison-like'. It seems almost ludicrous in retrospect to consider that, up until the 1970s, tenants were unlikely to get permission to make any sort of alteration in their homes no matter how cosmetic or trivial (see D. Miller 1988: 357). Even with these restrictions, however, government *of* the poor, onerous as it was, still invoked the prospect of social and moral betterment and enforced 'standards' for communal living that many tenants now long for in the midst of circumstances which feel to them increasingly out of control, and, hence, *ungovernable* by any means available to them.

And, what does government *by* the poor promise in exchange for its 'freedoms'? Behind that embrace of advanced liberal rule, which valorizes the authenticity of indigenous knowledge, celebrates the self-determination of individual communities and swaps the modernist notion of 'experts as mediators' for a new concept of 'experts as enablers', lurks the spectre of hopelessness.

Essential to the construction of 'the social' and to its enactment through the mobilization of particular policies was the assumption that, in the end, problems could be identified and known, difficulties measured and quantified, solutions devised and implemented. However 'acted upon' the poor were within such a liberal system of governance, however restrictive and narrow was its vision of morality, its ultimate project was one of bringing forth progress through creating a 'better' society.

Now, advanced liberal rule has shifted the emphasis from that project of *social improvement* to a therapeutic model of *self-improvement* (Rose 1992; Cruikshank 1993), even when many of those selves might be consigned to live in communities abandoned to the ravages of deteriorating physical conditions, crime, drugs, isolation and despair. When so many of the causes behind the exponential growth in poverty throughout the post-industrial West are the result of decisions being made every day in London and New York, Singapore and Tokyo, the 'new knowledge' that tenants are being offered through training programmes in housing management begins to take on the chimerical quality of a devalued currency.

Foucault has reminded us that through 'the arts of government' power is always in play, contouring both the nature of our experiences of the world in which we live and our ability to make sense of them. As he has written, 'The problem is not changing people's consciousness – or what's in their minds – but the political, economic, institutional regime of the production of truth' (Foucault 1980: 133). Those policies characteristic of advanced liberal rule, like tenant self-management, have set as their 'problem' precisely that goal: the changing of poor people's consciousness. And, while the consequences of that project to refashion the public sector tenant into a different kind of subject – one who is self-governing and granted the 'authority of expertise' – are likely to be varied and often unanticipated, the most profound of all 'truths', that poverty has once again become an acceptable and taken-for-granted feature of our late twentieth-century urban landscapes, is cunningly cloaked beneath the 'liberatory' rhetoric of this post-welfare era.

NOTES

1 I would like to thank all of the tenant-activists, and Margaret Chapman, Anna Frater, Linda Kenny and Gina Thompson in particular, for sharing their thoughts and experiences with me. My mentors Jacqueline Urla and Barbara Cruikshank spent many hours helping me to develop and refine my arguments. I am indebted to Sue Wright for her thoughtful comments on an earlier version of this chapter and for her generous interest in and ongoing support for my work. Naturally, I take full responsibility for the way in which I have represented and interpreted the events recounted in this chapter. Fieldwork for this project was undertaken with grants provided by the Social Science Research Council and the National Science Foundation (Dissertation Improvement grant DBS-9223510) in the USA; writing up was funded by a grant from the Charlotte Newcombe Dissertation Fellowship. This article was written during my one-year tenure as a

Visiting Research Fellow in the Department of Anthropology at the University of Durham, and I thank Professor Michael Carrithers and the other members of the department for their collegiality and for providing such a fine environment in which to think and write.

2 Some Conservative housing policies were intended to remove housing from the public sector all together. One of the more successful of these policies was called 'Right to Buy', which offered sitting tenants considerable discounts as an incentive to purchase their homes from their local councils. Over one million of the best council properties were sold to tenants through this scheme (see Cole and Furbey 1994: Ch. 7). By the time tenant management came on line as a formal policy initiative, not only had most of the best housing stock been sold off but the remaining tenants were also likely to be among the most impoverished, with those in work having taken advantage of the chance for home-ownership (ibid.).

3 The parallels between Victorian efforts at poor relief and housing reform, and the language of colonialism are striking. For a discussion of the ways in which the discourses of both colonial exploration abroad and campaigns for social reform in Britain each reflected and helped to construct the other, see J. and J. Comaroff (1992).

4 For an anthropological analysis of municipal socialism in Britain, see Wright (1993).

5 My account of the campaign to establish the Lower Grange Housing Association is based on interviews with key participants, on my own fieldwork in Bradford, and on written materials collected by community worker David Jenkins and compiled in an unpublished collection entitled, 'Tenants' Choice: A Tactical Solution? Campaign for the Lower Grange Housing Association, Bradford'. I thank David for his generosity in making this material available to me. Lower Grange is the real name of this community and the tenants quoted above have requested that I identify them with their real names. In other cases, tenants' names have been omitted.

6 Housing associations were first established during the Victorian era as charitable organizations, run mostly by middle-class reformers bent on improving the living conditions of the working classes (see White 1992). In their zeal to replace councils with alternative landlords, the Department of the Environment elevated housing associations to a new-found prominence by providing them with direct grants to finance the construction of new housing for the moderate and low-income rental markets, while simultaneously eliminating the ability of local authorities to raise funds for such construction (see *Inquiry into British Housing* 1991: 80–4). For an analysis of some of the problems now emerging in the new 'housing association estates', see Page (1993).

7 For two very interesting accounts of tenant resistance to the proposed transfer of management of their estates away from their local authorities and to quasi-governmental bodies known as Housing Action Trusts (HATS), see Shaughnessy (1989) and Woodward (1991).

8 The name of the housing association involved on Lower Grange has been altered.
9 The motives of tenants who enter into these training schemes are varied. Local authorities often encourage tenants' groups to take on management training because funding from central government for physical improvements on council estates usually hinges upon some demonstrable evidence of 'tenant participation'. There are a variety of consultancies offering training to tenants which they usually pay for with the help of Section 16 grants. The two largest, both of which are heavily funded by the Department of the Environment, are the Tenants Participatory Advisory Service (TPAS) and the Priority Estates Project (PEP).
10 In Bradford, as of this writing, no tenants' association has successfully taken over management of its own estate. Despite the hours of training and the genuine dedication of groups of core activists, the administrative tasks involved have proven to be too overwhelming. Many activists have also reported to me that being asked to take on the responsibility for policing their communities has contributed to their experiences of 'burn-out', as excessive demands were made on their time and/or they were accused by their neighbours of being 'informers' for the police, social services or other agencies.

REFERENCES

Baistow, Karen (1994/5) 'Liberation and regulation? Some paradoxes of empowerment', *Critical Social Policy* 42: 34–46.
Burnett, John (1991) [1978] *A Social History of Housing 1815–1985*, London: Routledge.
City of Bradford Metropolitan Council (n.d.) *Up and Running: A Starter Pack for Tenant Participation*, Bradford: Department of Housing and Environmental Protection.
Cole, Ian and Furbey, Robert (1994) *The Eclipse of Council Housing*, London: Routledge.
Comaroff, Jean and Comaroff, John (1992) 'Homemade hegemony', in *Ethnography and the Historical Imagination*, Boulder: Westview Press.
Cruikshank, Barbara (1993) 'Revolutions within: self-government and self-esteem', *Economy and Society* 22: 327–44.
—— (1994) 'The will to empower: technologies of citizenship and the War on Poverty', *Socialist Review* 23: 29–55.
DoE (1992) 'Tenant involvement and the right to manage', London: Department of the Environment and Welsh Office, December.
—— (1994a) 'A better deal for tenants: your new right to manage', London: Department of the Environment and Welsh Office, March.
—— (1994b) 'Tenant involvement in housing management: a guidance note by the department of the environment', London: Department of the Environment, March.
Foucault, Michel (1980) 'Truth and power', in C. Gordon (ed.) *Power/Knowledge: Selected Interviews 1972–1977*, New York: Pantheon

Books.

Hague, Cliff (1990) 'The development and politics of tenant participation in British public housing', *Housing Studies* 5: 242–56.

Hansard Parliamentary Record (1987) *Debate on the Housing Bill*, cols 619–736, 30 November 1987.

Horn, David (1988) 'Welfare, the social and the individual in interwar Italy', *Cultural Anthropology* 13: 189–98.

—— (1994) *Social Bodies: Science, Reproduction, and Italian Modernity*, Princeton NJ: Princeton University Press.

'Houses let in lodgings: Conference of North of England Local Authorities (1907)', Proceedings of a conference held at Bradford Town Hall, 4 July 1907.

HMSO (1987) *Housing: The Government's Proposals*, London: HMSO.

Hyatt, Susan Brin (1994) 'Tenants' choice or Hobson's Choice? Housing the poor in the enterprise culture', paper presented at the biannual meeting of the European Association of Social Anthropologists, Oslo University, 25 June.

Inquiry into British Housing (1991) York: Joseph Rowntree Foundation.

Kemp, Peter and Williams, Peter (1991) 'Housing management: an historical perspective,' in S. Lowe and D. Hughes (eds) *A New Century of Social Housing*, Leicester: Leicester University Press.

Lower Grange Women's History Project (1989) *'Some day we'll build a home on a hilltop high': A women's history of Lower Grange*, unpublished booklet.

Miller, Daniel (1988) 'Appropriating the state on the council estate', *Man* 23: 353–72.

Miller, Peter and Rose, Nikolas (1990) 'Governing economic life', *Economy and Society* 19: 1–31.

Orwell, George (1965) [1937] *The Road to Wigan Pier*, London: Heinemann.

Page, David (1993) *Building for Communities: A Study of New Housing Association Estates*, York: Joseph Rowntree Foundation.

Power, Anne (1987) *Property Before People: The Management of Twentieth-Century Council Housing*, London: Allen and Unwin.

Rabinow, Paul (1989) *French Modern: Norms and Forms of the Social Environment*, Cambridge MA: MIT Press.

Rose, Nikolas (1992) 'Governing the enterprising self', in P. Heelas and P. Morris (eds) *The Values of the Enterprise Culture: The Moral Debate*, London: Routledge.

—— (1993) 'Government, authority and expertise in advanced liberalism', *Economy and Society* 22: 283–99.

Shaughnessy, Haydn (1989) 'Housing action trusts and communications structures: a study of state-tenant negotiations in a Manchester housing estate', *International Journal of Urban and Regional Research* 13 (2): 339–54.

Stott, Gordon (1985) 'A living hell of dirt and disease', *Bradford Telegraph and Argus*, 4 May.

White, Jerry (1992) 'Business out of charity,' in C. Grant (ed.) *Built to Last? Reflections on British Housing Policy*, London: ROOF Magazine.

Woodward, Rachel (1991) 'Mobilising opposition: the campaign against Housing Action Trusts in Tower Hamlets', *Housing Studies* 6: 44–56.

Wright, Susan (1993) ' "Working class" versus "ordinary people": contested ideas of local socialism in England', in C. Hann (ed.) *Socialism: Ideals, Ideologies and Local Practices*, London: Routledge.

Chapter 10

Managing Americans
Policy and changes in the meanings of work and the self

Emily Martin

The historical roots of the word 'policy' now support two related branches of meaning. In the first branch, 'policy' flows from its Greek and Latin origin into associations with civil administration and government, and in the second branch policy flows into associations (via Latin *poltus*) with the polished, refined, cultivated and polite (OED). Both branches of the word's meanings are concerned with social order, but they focus on order at very different levels: at the level of large institutions in the first branch and at the level of individual persons in the second.

In this chapter, I move toward an ethnographic analysis of contemporary forms of civil administration in the US that are being achieved through 'policies' that encourage a conflation of these two levels: individual persons have begun to manage themselves in such a way that they will continuously change and improve. In the domains of work and health especially, self-management devoted to continuous improvement is becoming the clarion call through which, it increasingly comes to seem, survival of the nation, the corporation and the person will be accomplished as we approach the next millennium. As Nikolas Rose put it for 'enterprise culture':

> The well-being of both political and social existence is to be ensured not by centralised planning and bureaucracy, but through the enterprising activities and choices of autonomous entities – businesses, organisations, persons – each striving to maximise its own advantage by inventing and promoting new projects by means of individual and local calculations of strategies and tactics, costs and benefits . . . Enterprise forges a link between the ways we are governed by others and the ways we should govern ourselves.
>
> (Rose 1992: 145–6)

It has often been pointed out that policy decisions contain more leeway, freedom of choice and flexibility than judicial decisions (Gould and Kolb 1964: 501–11). Policy is a guide to action, a translation of general goals into an overall plan, that may lack the concrete, material coercion of the law and the police. Policies can be set by governmental bodies, all kinds of institutions, from courts to kindergartens; they can be set by informal clubs, grass-roots organizations, families, or even a single person. It makes sense for a college student to say she has a policy of no smoking in her dormitory room. Policies may come with instructions as to how to handle infractions, but, on the other hand, they may not, leaving that decision to whatever consensus might emerge in the moment of need. Whatever power might back up a policy is highly variable from one kind of group to another and within any group over time. It ranges from what might be called 'Policy with teeth', which performs much like legal edicts, to policies without, which are hopeful encouragements toward a desired goal. The very flexibility in the meaning of the term 'policy' means that policies are a central means by which the new flexible, continuously changing, self-managed person is being constituted.

For example, in my ethnographic research with human resource managers, the experts in US corporations who have taken over the old functions of 'personnel departments' and who are instrumental in helping workers become self-managed, I have learned that producing written policies for the corporation is one of their most important jobs.

> HR [human resource] policies are guides to management's thinking, and they help management achieve the organization's HR objectives. Policies also help define acceptable and unacceptable behavior and establish the organization's position on an issue.
>
> (Carrell et al. 1995: 15–16)

Grouped under the heading 'human resource policies' will be a mixed bundle of things, some policies operating with a law-like force (entitlements and expectations surrounding termination of employment), some occupying a middle ground that could be relied on if legal measures were pursued (statements about the unacceptableness of sexual harassment), and some policies stating goals that HR hopes everyone expects to work toward (continuous improvement of work design through employee input).

The challenge of understanding policies of self-management is apparent when we consider their relationship to various forms of power. For example, the 'polish' within the notion of policy can obviously be imposed by definitive power from the outside as when we hold an apple and polish it or cause a military cadet to polish his or her shoes on threat of punishment; but how can an apple polish itself? Why would cadets keep their shoes polished if there were no threatening sanctions in play? In self-management the manager somehow gets internalized: externally imposed control becomes internally generated motivation.

KINDS OF POWER

To go further we need to consider the various sorts of power that might operate in relation to policies. In the Classical age, as Foucault describes it, power was exerted by the sovereign through repressive legal codes and the force of the state apparatus. Punishment was wrought on the very body of the criminal, as in the opening scenes of *Discipline and Punish* where a prisoner's body is slowly pulled to pieces by teams of horses (Foucault 1979). In contrast, with the coming of modern power, gossamer micro-controls that hold the body in time and space arise in a multitude of contexts: prisons, hospitals, schools, the military, the factory. Docile bodies are produced through the gaze of the prison managers in the Panopticon, or the disciplinary gaze and questions of the therapist, doctor, sociologist or demographer.

Modern power, bio-politics, arose together with, or as Foucault puts it, consubstantial with, changes in the economy and polity involved in the rise of the self-affirmation of the bourgeoisie. As the bourgeoisie came into its own, its self-definition was based in part on knowledge of the populations of the nation states of which it was the core: their size, rate of growth, health, composition. The inherited 'pure' blood of the aristocracy of the classical era gave way to the 'normal' healthy blood, body, brains and brawn of the bourgeoisie (Foucault 1980a: 125–6).

The process of normalization lies at the heart of how modern power operates: the 'normalizing gaze . . . establishes over individuals a visibility through which one differentiates them and judges them' (Foucault 1979: 184).

Our norms are always on the move as if their goal was to bring every aspect of our practices together into a coherent whole. To this end various experiences are identified and annexed as appropriate domains for theoretical study and intervention. Within all these domains, the norms do not rest but, at least in principle, are endlessly ramified down to the finest details of the micropractices, so no action that counts as important and real falls outside the grid of normality. In addition, as in normal science, the normalising practices of bio-power define the normal in advance and then proceed to isolate and deal with anomalies given that definition.

(Dreyfus and Rabinow 1982: 258)

Foucault is at pains to explain why it is so hard for us to see the nature of modern power, especially why we continue to think of power as if it were repressive, in the Classical mode, what he calls its 'emaciated form' (1980a: 86), rather than 'productive' as it is in its modern form. The reason, he ventures, is that 'power is tolerable only on condition that it mask a substantial part of itself. Its success is proportional to its ability to hide its own mechanisms' (ibid.).

If Foucault's suggestion for why we fail to recognize the nature of modern power is at all plausible, then another question immediately presents itself: might there be ways, from the vantage point of the 1990s instead of the 1970s when Foucault wrote these analyses, why we now, having learned our Foucauldian lesson, think of everything as if it were an instance of modern power when, within it another quite different form of power is arising?

This thought is given force by Foucault's notion that kinds of power arise consubstantially with important shifts in the nature of the economy and the polity. In an interview with Jean-Pierre Barou and Michelle Perrot, Perrot says to Foucault: 'You are opposed to the idea of power as a super-structure, but not to the idea that power is in some sense consubstantial with the development of forces of production, that it forms part of them.' Foucault replies:

Absolutely. And power is constantly being transformed along with them. The Panopticon was at once a programme and a utopia, but the theme of a spatialising, observing, immobilising, in a word disciplinary power was in fact already in Bentham's day being transcended by other and much more subtle mechanisms for the regulation of phenomena of population, controlling their fluctuations and compensating their irregularities.

(Foucault 1980b: 159–60)

Many political economists are trying to describe a major shift in the forces of production which was beginning to take place at the time of the publication of Foucault's work. This shift, associated with late capitalism, is often termed flexible accumulation (Harvey 1989: 155). The hallmarks of flexible accumulation are technological innovation, specificity, and rapid, flexible change. It entails:

flexible system production with [an] emphasis upon problem solving, rapid and often highly specialized responses, and adaptability of skills to special purposes; an increasing capacity to manufacture a variety of goods cheaply in small batches.

... an acceleration in the pace of product innovation together with the exploration of highly specialised and small-scale market niches ... and new organisational forms (such as the 'just-in-time' inventory-flows delivery system, which cuts down radically on stocks required to keep production flow going).

(Harvey 1989: 155–6)

Labourers experience a speed-up in the processes of labour and an intensification in the de-skilling and re-skilling that is constantly required. New technologies in production reduce turnover time dramatically and this entails similar accelerations in exchange and consumption. 'Improved systems of communication and information flow, coupled with rationalizations in techniques of distribution (packaging, inventory control, container-ization, market feed-back, etc.) make it possible to circulate commodities through the market system with greater speed' (ibid.: 285). Time and space compression occur, as time horizons of decision-making shrink and instantaneous communications and cheaper transport costs allow decisions to be effected over a global space (ibid.: 147). Multinational capital operates in a globally integrated environment: ideally, capital flows unimpeded across all borders, all points are connected by instantaneous communications, and products are made as needed for the momentary and continuously changing market.

What Foucault says about a 'consubstantial' relationship between forms of power and forms of the forces of production leaves undetermined the meaning of 'consubstantial'. Other writers, for example, Jameson (1984) and Harvey (1989), have suggested a variety of ways of understanding how the social formation of late capitalism can relate to 'culture' – such things as architecture, art or literature. According to Jameson, postmodern forms reveal the 'cultural logic' of late capitalism; they are the 'internal and super-structural expression of a whole new wave of American military and economic domination throughout the world' (Jameson 1984: 57); they instantiate a 'cultural dominant', a 'new systemic cultural norm', a 'dominant cultural logic or hegemonic norm' (ibid.: 57). They are a 'figuration of . . . the whole world system of present-day multinational capitalism' (ibid.: 79). They are an approach to a representation of a new reality, a peculiar new form of realism, a kind of mimesis of reality (ibid.: 88). For Harvey these forms are also mimetic, 'In the last instance' they are produced by the experience of time–space compression, itself the product of processes in flexible accumulation (ibid.: 344).

In this chapter, I make no assumption that the economic realm is so simply determinant of cultural forms. Without being able to solve in this context the precise causal nature of their connection, I simply want to raise the question: what might be the next step in the historical development of the body and kinds of powers regulating it that would come into existence along with a dramatic shift in political economic organization, such as that being brought about by flexible accumulation? What changes in our bodies might be necessary for such a shift to occur? Perhaps docile bodies held in minutely controlled time and space by the disciplinary gaze have more to do with the dominance of total institutions and mass production systems characteristic of the early to mid-twentieth century. One might well ask, what will be next? Does the emergence of policies that encourage self-management depend on a kind of power that goes beyond docile bodies?

WORK AND LIFE

Flexible accumulation has already brought swiftly changing relations between the domain of work and the domains of home and leisure outside of work. The rapid increase in 'home work', ever greater provision of domestically-related benefits for those still employed in corporate workplaces, the sustained effort to reveal and harness the inner feelings and emotions of managers as well as workers, all hint at seismic shifts in the boundaries between categories that were once separated in a different way. These changes are an aspect of what Donzelot (1991) calls 'changing people's attitudes toward change'. In the society that is being forged (in the French case Donzelot describes, it is through the legal right of every worker to 'continued retraining' (*formation permanente*)) people are thought to require an active attitude toward change:

> *Formation permanente* must therefore literally be a continuous process of retraining, from the cradle to the grave, designed to provide the individual with a feeling of autonomy in relation to work, and at work. It has to break down the split within the subject between a world of work, which is disagreeable but [is valued and] confers an identity and rights, and that other world external to work, which is protected by the law and yet has no real value in itself, serving merely as a costly and futile compensation.
>
> (Donzelot 1991: 273)

Areas of life once putatively separate from the valued world of work (childhood, reproduction, family, sex, leisure, retirement, home, play) come to have real value as laboratories of human development, revealing human capacities for change and growth. Correspondingly, the realm of work itself becomes another realm where social needs will be satisfied (ibid.: 253).

PERSONS, GROUPS AND THEIR INTERFACES

Arguing from the French case, Donzelot suggests a profound shift is occurring in the relation between the position of the subject and society:

> What is actually at issue is the production of something altogether different from a discourse – a transformation, a point of coalescence of the position of the subject and the order of social relations of production. It does not signify the mechanical subordination of the one to the other, but rather the act of placing both terms on one and the same footing of truth.
>
> (Donzelot 1991: 275)

The truth will reside neither in the subject, made up of inner memory, childhood, a singular history, nor will it be made up of Marxism's forces that bear down on subjects from outside. Instead:

> the subject subsists only in his capacities, that he is a potential to be realized, not a truth to be deciphered; and that history is a myth since reality lies only in the environment that surrounds us, in the organized forms of our social relations which it is for us to

modify according to the capacity change offers us to realize ourselves more fully.

(Donzelot 1991: 276)

It is important to see the difference between this 'changing attitude toward change' and normalizing practices suited to panoptical power. Change, of a kind, is pervasive in panoptical power. In Foucault's account of discipline, for example:

> the elements are interchangeable, since each is defined by the place it occupies in a series, and by the gap that separates it from the others. The unit is, therefore, neither the territory (unit of domination), nor the place (unit of residence), but the rank: the place one occupies in a classification, the point at which a line and a column intersect, the interval in a series of intervals that one may traverse one after the other. Discipline is an art of rank, a technique for the transformation of arrangements. It individualizes bodies by a location that does not give them a fixed position, but distributes them and circulates them in a network of relations.

(Foucault 1979: 145–6)

So, in particular contexts such as schools or the military, individuals continuously circulate within this grid:

> Each pupil, according to his age, his performance, his behaviour, occupies sometimes one rank, sometimes another; he moves constantly over a series of compartments . . . it is a perpetual movement in which individuals replace one another in a space marked off by aligned intervals.

(ibid.: 147)

Not only do individuals shift among the points on the grid, the lines and columns that make up the parameters of the grid also undergo change over time, sometimes as a result of effects produced by the grid itself. As Ian Hacking describes the practices of counting deviants to produce official statistics in England in the nineteenth century:

> New slots were created in which to fit and enumerate people. Even national and provincial censuses amazingly show that the categories into which people fall change every ten years. Social change creates new categories of people, but the counting is no mere report of developments. It elaborately, often philanthropi-

cally, creates new ways for people to be.

(Hacking 1986: 223)

In contrast, according to Donzelot, a different set of constitutive conditions often applies today. It is not just that individuals circulate among the points on a grid, nor just that the parameters defining the axes of a grid change over time. It is, in addition, that (as it comes more and more to seem) there could be no grid or set of grids which could completely describe any individual, since the categories in terms of which each individual faces the world will be the result of processes the individual has manifested from within his own course of development. The individual comes to consist of potentials to be realized and capacities to be fulfilled. Since these potentials and capacities take their shape in relation to the requirements of a continuously changing environment, their content, and even the terms in which they are understood, are also in constant change.

New technicians will emerge wielding new techniques (policy and policies important among them) that 'posit an intermediate plane of resolution through action designed to overturn the statutory position of the subject, that sort of juridical shelter for the reign of imagination'. The subject will be extroverted 'towards a world of possibilities that exhaust imagination' (Donzelot 1991: 276). This world is neither inside the subject nor outside, but in the interface zone between the subject and its environment. In some ways, the line between the person and the world becomes less sharp and certain: inner self shades into interface which is already partly of the self and partly of the world.

This world 'that exhausts imagination' represents something like a new continent for the production of knowledge, the operations of power and the reaping of profit. The interface between subject and environment represents an endless frontier, an eternally receding horizon for exploration and development. Because that zone, a field of constant response, is in continuous change, it is endlessly varied and the possibilities for developing it are also endless.

The new continent calls forth above all else, the need for management. In the sense meant by Stephen Ball in 'Management as moral technology: a Luddite analysis', management as a concept and practice in Western cultures is certainly not new.

Management is a theoretical and practical technology of rationality geared to efficiency, practicality, and control. It is a means to an end and its participants are also means . . . [It is a view] which contends that social life can be mastered scientifically and can be understood and organized according to law-like generalizations.

(Ball 1990: 157)

As Miller and Rose said in 'Governing economic life' (1990), before management can take place, a set of processes and relationships have to be conceptualized as an economy which is amenable to management. What is new is that a new site of management has come into view, and new entities have emerged to do the management. In the next part of the chapter, I examine a series of contexts in the US where we can observe management going on at this interface.

CORPORATE SELVES

I begin with an example that shows the absence of management across an interface. In Robert Jackall's *Moral Mazes* – based on ethnography done in manufacturing corporations in 1980–1 – managers strive for a smooth, seamless appearance, an impenetrable inner self hidden behind a perfectly contrived appearance. This is a world where:

appearances – in the broadest sense – mean everything . . . The wise and ambitious manager learns to cultivate assiduously the proper, prescribed modes of appearing. He dispassionately takes stock of himself, treating himself as an object, as a commodity. He analyses his strengths and weaknesses and decides what he needs to change in order to survive and flourish in his organization. And then he systematically undertakes a program to reconstruct his image, his publicly avowed attitudes or ideas, or whatever else in his self-presentation that might need adjustment. Such self-regulation requires simultaneously great discipline and 'flexibility' since one must continually adjust oneself to meet the ever-changing demands of different career stages and, of more immediate consequence, the expectations of crucial social circles in ever-changing organisational milieux.

(Jackall 1988: 59)

As one manager said, 'I don't have the responsibility for a salesman's job in this company, but I sell everybody every day. What I sell is me – myself' (ibid.: 61).

Jackall uses Karl Mannheim's conception of 'self-rationalization' or self-streamlining to convey the sense of this experience. For Mannheim, 'self-rationalization' means 'the individual's systematic control of his impulses . . . so that every action is guided by principle and is directed towards the goal he has in mind' (ibid.: 55). The highest stage of this kind of rationalization involves self-observation: this 'aims primarily at an inner self-transformation . . . for the sake of remoulding or transforming himself more radically . . . persons who are confronted more frequently with situations in which they cannot act habitually and without thinking and in which they must always organize themselves anew' will have more occasion to do this (ibid.: 57).

This account relies heavily on Erving Goffman's analysis of the self, which uses the metaphor of an actor back stage or on stage to describe how people make different presentations of the self in different situations. In Jackall's description, as in Goffman's, the speaking parts inside the person are all occupied by parts of the same self. The 'rational' part of the self keeps the back stage roles back stage and manages the presentation of the front stage roles, according to the situation. Goffman's book perhaps should have been called 'The SELF Presentation of the Self in Everyday Life'! In other words, all the management takes place inside, and the finished product is shown on the person's outside surface. This is an edge, not an interface. In contrast, and moving toward management of interface zones, look at what is going on in the high-tech corporation (called by the pseudonym 'Tech' in the book) studied more recently by Gideon Kunda and described in *Engineering Culture*. Management in this company might be called a kind of applied Foucault rather than applied Goffman. Instead of parts of the self all residing inside a person, with some parts managing others, there is an 'other' inside managing many parts of the self. Many who work at Tech report 'being a Techie'. An engineering manager put it this way:

> You know, I like Tech. I don't think of leaving. People might say the culture swallowed me, but there really is a feeling of loyalty I have. We have a lot of that in the culture. We like working for Tech. It is a positive company. You get really involved. I get a real charge when Tech gets a good press [or offended when other companies dump on Tech].
>
> (Kunda 1992: 170)

Kunda summarizes the pervasive sentiment that person and company can become one: employees use 'the imagery of immersion, incorporation, psychological maturity, and religion'. The organizational self is presented as tightly coupled with the company: the 'mature' self is bound by ties of belief, strong emotions, and even religious fervour, all of which, members seem to imply, are quite authentic. At the extreme, self-definitions merge (at least temporarily) with the shared definitions of the culture, suggesting the collapse of the boundaries between self and organization (ibid.: 177).

In this collapse, the person appears to gain, not lose, agency and initiative. An engineering supervisor speaks about his struggle to accept one of the fundamental principles of Tech's culture, 'individual responsibility and ownership':

> *I'm a slow cultural learner.* It took me two years to learn mainly that 'it is your own ownership'. You can do anything you want, but you have to push. The idea is that you are a professional and responsible. You gotta feel the ownership. Don't sit and wait. You're a grown-up. The onus is placed on you to live up to expectations. Don't bitch about problems; go do something about it. I buy that. You know, I'm trying to get my son into Tech – that should tell you something.
>
> (ibid.: 171; EM's emphasis)

This employee and many others seem to see the interface between the person or group and its environment as managed through corporate culture. The way 'culture' is described by businesses often makes explicit its use as an interface with the environment. As it is explained in one business management book:

> Culture gives form and meaning to human values . . . Because culture is a phase in natural evolution and because culture has adaptive functions, it extrudes values that reflect human experience in coping with an environment that either sustains or diminishes life . . . Value structures order perceptions of one's environment. Those patterned perceptions become the experiential basis for understanding environmental forces.
>
> (Frederick 1995: 84)

Another example:

What organizational culture does is to solve the group's basic problems of:

1 survival in and adaptation to the external environment and

2 integration of its internal processes to ensure the capacity to continue to survive and adapt.

(Schein 1985, quoted in Frederick 1995: 85)

Culture as an interface is nothing deep, nothing arising from inside, nothing that connects to the past. It is a thin and slippery conception of culture that best provides a way of managing the intermediary zone, in the flat, horizontal interactional zone between the corporation and its environment. As an anthropologist, I often find myself cringing at the way corporations use culture – it seems so superficial! But nothing more than an almost transparent membrane, so it appears, would serve as well.

It is not that Tech employees do not feel ambivalence or distance from some aspects of the company, as well as scepticism about the uniqueness of their 'culture' (Kunda 1992: 181). But the extent to which people speak passionately of immersion, incorporation and loyalty to the death, indicates that at Tech the 'culture' has to some extent got inside the self where it plays a part in 'self-management'. So it is possible that, instead of self-presentation of self, here we have culture as inner manager of the self. The self becomes something different – an entity intermediate between the old self and non-self, operating in an interface zone.

As corporate culture takes up residence inside worker's selves, they are meant to become better able to work in organizations that, in the words of an organizational development training firm, are 'flexible and cost effective while continuously improving service and quality. Accomplishing more with fewer people will require skilled employees who can work in teams, problem solve, make decisions and use technology.' The result hoped for is flat, non-hierarchical, fluid, mobile groups linked across interfaces to a myriad of other similar groups and guided by flexible corporate policies about achieving a flexible corporate culture.

SANE AND INSANE SELVES: ATTENTION DEFICIT DISORDER

A health bill was recently unanimously passed by the largely Republican Senate. Although the main portion of the bill contained measures to smooth the way for workers to change jobs without losing their health insurance because of 'pre-existing conditions', an amendment was added which requires insurers to provide 'coverage for mental illnesses that is equivalent to the coverage provided for other conditions like heart disease, diabetes and cancer'. The amendment, which may or may not end up in the final bill approved by both houses of government, is being hailed by mental health professionals as a 'monumental development, an event of extraordinary magnitude for all people who suffer from psychiatric illness' (Pear 1996). It is condemned as strongly by business organizations and insurers because it will raise costs. Its supporters, such as Paul Wellstone, defend it because, given the current understanding of mental disorders as derived from biochemical processes, 'mental illness could be treated as effectively as heart disease or diabetes' (ibid.). Mental illnesses become chronic biomedical problems that can be 'managed' with the proper dose and timing of the correct biochemical agents.

Such a 'Policy' in the making rests on innumerable prior policies, which are part and parcel of a broad and complex cultural setting. Focusing as an example on one sort of mental illness called attention deficit disorder (ADD) may help us understand such a context in relation to the forms of power and kinds of selves introduced above. In the US, accounts of ADD have recently been flooding the press, the best-seller list, and the airwaves. ADD has recently made the cover of *Time*, an editorial in the *New York Times*, and a PBS episode of the Merrow report aired widely in the fall of 1995. What is of compelling interest about this condition is that it is in the process of redefinition from being a disability to being a strength. In ADD, the exact qualities praised fit perfectly with the kind of emergent self Donzelot described: always changing, scanning the environment, dealing with all aspects of the interface with the outside in creative and innovative ways. In ADD, this is happening through the books, newsletter and Internet organizing of Thomas Hartmann, himself a person with adult ADD, who has a son diagnosed as ADD. Hartmann argues that in human evolution there were two main types of cultures, based around hunters and farmers respectively. Hunters constantly monitor their environment, they notice everything and continuously scan the landscape. They are 'flexible, capable of changing strategy at a moment's notice', bored by routine tasks, and easily frustrated. But they 'take risks', facing danger that 'normal' individuals would avoid (Hartmann 1993: 14–16). Hartmann puts 'normal' in scare quotes, and this is a hint of what comes next. In a chapter entitled ' "Normal" people: the origins of agriculture', we learn that farmers are slow and steady, see the long-range picture, are not easily bored, are team players – cautious and patient (ibid.: 20–1).

The picture is that neither farmer nor hunter should be taken as the paradigm of the normal. The abilities of both are necessary to the common good (ibid.: 23). Both are genetically determined traits that, on the model of sickle cell anaemia or Tay Sachs, represent evolutionary survival strategies in certain circumstances (ibid.: 13). ADD people are the genetic descendants of people in hunter cultures. In order to 'Turn a "disorder" back into a skill' (another chapter title) one tactic is for hunters to find jobs suited to their skills – inventor, politician, policeman, trial lawyer, writer, explorer, surgeon, for example. The literature on ADD is filled with examples of the 'Edison trait': individuals who had an important impact on the course of history and manifested many of the traits of ADD.

Business is the contemporary domain where those with ADD can flourish. One of Hartmann's books on ADD called *Focus Your Energy: Hunting for Success in Business with Attention Deficit Disorder* is usually shelved with the business books. Hunters' 'strong sense of individualism, high creativity, and the ability to be a self-starter' (Hartmann 1994: 56) make them far more likely to start their own companies than non-ADD people.

ADD is said to entail a 'distorted' sense of time and space: In ADD, 'distortions of time-sense' mean time is not experienced as a 'fairly consistent and linear flow' as it is in others (Hartmann 1993: 3). ADD individuals 'have an exaggerated sense of urgency when they're on a task, and an exaggerated sense of boredom when they feel they have nothing to do' (ibid.: 3). For them time is fluid and elastic (ibid.: 14, 72); it flashes by one moment and becomes hopelessly mired the next.

As rapidly as it is described, however, these distortions become assets. In an environment which is in many ways stretching, cramming, speeding, warping and looping poor old linear time and space, these perceptual abilities quickly can seem to be talents in accord with new realities instead of irrational delusions. ADD is itself cited as an exemplar of a complex, non-linear phenomenon, one with multiple causes, no clear boundaries, or sharp delineations. In science generally, future trends involve developing a new model of the complex, 'organizing the chaotic mix of seemingly unrelated simplistic elements into a more integrated and comprehensive framework of understanding, approaching a clearer picture of complexity' (Ratey 1995: xii). Those with ADD are instantiations of complex systems in a constantly changing environment, and their special characteristics are best managed across the interface to the environment – 'managing their environment to serve their quirky brains' (ibid.: xiii).

A diagnosis of ADD comes with a readily available – indeed, often mandated – internal manager, of the sort that operated in Kunda's Tech. For ADD, the manager is 'Ritalin' and, although the reasons are certainly more complex than I can indicate here, it is still striking that this 'manager' is regarded in highly ambivalent ways by patients themselves, as well as their families and other advocates. 'Ritalin' is called a 'benign medication which assists millions of children' in a bi-partisan petition to remove it from the DEA's tightly controlled drug list. Thom Hartmann urges caution in its use, and John Merrow points out that the Ciba–Geigy company, which manufactures 'Ritalin', has been funding the national support group (which is in favour of relaxing access to 'Ritilan') for ADD since 1988 to the tune of over a million dollars.

Are people who have ADD 'normal'? Hartmann asserts that ADD belongs in the ranks of the normal because its associated genes are important to the evolutionary strategies of our species. Others argue the opposite: ADD is caused by abnormal brain chemistry, itself caused by an abnormal gene (Maugh 1996). Only drug therapy can compensate for this physiological handicap and return the ADD child or adult to normal functioning.

A more telling way in which other accounts embrace ADD within the 'normal' is by stressing that conceptions of the nature of human development itself are changing in such a way that continuous change and shifts are not only expectable, they are desirable. For example, a textbook about ADD in children and adults contains the following description of child development, which is widely representative of current thinking in the US:

The human brain and certainly the 'mind' must be seen . . . As an interactive and interdependent collection of subsystems. This requires us as professionals or even parents to marvel at the development of a child and to see him, from the moment of birth, as a complex individual constantly evolving, always becoming . . . The child of yesterday is always changed tomorrow and in a moment we can but glance at a dynamic process and not a static individual . . . we must always be inferring where a child has been, where he is heading, and what barriers or opportunities are presently encumbering or freeing him.

(Fadely and Hosler 1992: 147–8)

Such a world view of the nature of the developing person lies behind the formulation of a myriad policies of all kinds, some with teeth, some with none, that appear in educational institutions. The following example from a K-12 private school, is taken from their 'Drug and Alcohol Policy' which is designed to:

create opportunities for moral and social growth and allow each student to acquire internalized [words missing] engage and ener-gize the school community – students, teachers, and parents – to interact powerfully with students to shape and nurture produc-tive behavior and self-discipline. This energized and involved community thus provides powerful supports for complex human growth.

(Postscript 1996: 3)

People with ADD – mercurial of mood, always in motion, scan-ning the interface, eyes flickering – may well come to be regarded as normal even when they refuse their medications. If rationality itself is changing in such contexts as work, life and value, making room for personal growth at work, value at home, and demanding restless change and development of the person in all realms, then ADD might readily come to be regarded as normal – even ideal – for the human condition under these historically specific circumstances. This would be very intriguing, and it would provide a good place to explore what I have only made a small start on: what would happen when 'norms' in the Foucauldian sense could no longer be specified because any possible point of reference would not stay still long enough? As a management consultant told me 'Things aren't going to return to "normal" because there is no "normal" to go back to'.

In conclusion, we can see how 'Policies with teeth', with legal or other coercive backing, are often preceded by a myriad of policies, with no teeth, but plenty of links to prevailing cultural ideas about the nature of the person and society. The evidently wide appeal of the model of mental health in the bill proposed by the Senate speaks to the way this bill, which may well become a 'Policy', rests on much that has happened in the realm of policies beforehand. Both 'Policy' and policies are inextricably connected to the sea of culture on which they float, a sea whose condition seems to have inescapably become turbulent waters in a constant state of change. The flexibility and variety inherent in the range and type of social forms we know as 'Policy'/policies means that they are likely to become more important than ever before for students of culture to notice and analyse.

REFERENCES

Ball, Stephen J. (1990) 'Management as moral technology', in S. J. Ball (ed.) *Foucault and Education: Disciplines and Knowledge*, London: Routledge.

Carrell, Michael R., Elbert, Norbert F. and Hatfield, Robert D. (1995) *Human Resource Management: Global Strategies for Managing a Diverse Work Force*, Englewood Cliffs NJ: Prentice Hall.

Donzelot, Jacques (1991) 'Pleasure in work', in G. Burchell, C. Gordon and P. Miller (eds) *The Foucault Effect*, Hemel Hempstead: Harvester Wheatsheaf.

Dreyfus, Hubert and Rabinow, Paul (1982) *Michael Foucault: Beyond Structuralism and Hermeneutics*, Brighton: Harvester Press.

Fadely, Jack and Hosler, Virginia (1992) *Attentional Deficit Disorder in Children and Adults*, Springfield IL: Charles C. Thomas.

Foster, Judy (1988) 'In your mind's eye: incredible, but true, you can visualize your tennis success', *World Tennis* 35 (8): 22–5.

Foucault, Michel (1979) *Discipline and Punish*, New York: Vintage.

—— (1980a) *The History of Sexuality,* Vol. 1, New York: Vintage.

—— (1980b) *Power/Knowledge: Selected Interviews and Other Writings, 1972–1977*, New York: Pantheon.

Frederick, William (1995) *Values, Nature, and Culture in the American Corporation*, New York: Oxford University Press.

Goffman, Irving (1959) *The Presentation of Self in Everyday Life*, New York: Anchor.

Gould, Julius and Kolb, William (1964) *A Dictionary of the Social Sciences*, London: Tavistock.

Hacking, Ian (1986) 'Making up people', in Thomas Heller, Morton Sosna and David Wellbery (eds) *Autonomy, Individuality and the Self in Western Thought*, Stanford CA: Stanford University Press.

Hartmann, Thom (1993) *Attention Deficit Disorder: A Different Perception*, California: Underwood Books.

—— (1994) *Focus Your Energy: Hunting for Success in Business With Attention Deficit Disorder*, New York: Pocket Books.

Harvey, David (1989) *The Condition of Postmodernity: An Enquiry into the Origins of Social Change*, Oxford: Basil Blackwell.

Jackall, Robert (1988) *Moral Mazes: The World of Corporate Managers*, New York: Oxford University Press.

Jameson, Fredric (1984) 'Postmodernism, or the cultural logic of late capitalism', *New Left Review* 146: 52–92.

Kunda, Gideon (1992) *Engineering Culture: Control and Commitment in a High-Tech Corporation*, Philadelphia: Temple University Press.

Mannheim, Karl (1940) *Man and Society in an Age of Reconstruction*, London: Kegan, Trench, Trubner.

Maugh, Thomas H. (1996) 'UCI scientists link attention deficit to gene', *Los Angeles Times*, A (2) 1 May: 1, 17.

Merrow, John (1995) *Attention Deficit Disorder – a Dubious Diagnosis?* (VHS Video), Columbia SC: South Carolina ETV.

Miller, Peter and Rose, Nikolas (1990) 'Governing economic life', *Economy and Society* 19 (1): 1–31.

Nohria, Nitin and Berkely, James (1994) 'The virtual organization. Bureaucracy, technology and the imposition of control', in Charles Heckscher and Anne Donnellon (eds) *The Post-Bureaucratic Organization: New Perspectives on Organizational Change*, Thousand Oaks CA: Sage.

Pear, Robert (1996) 'Mental health a big winner in Senate Bill', *New York Times*, A (5) 24 April 1996: 1, C22.

Postscript (1996) 'The New Park School drug and alcohol policy', *Postcript*, Baltimore MD: The Park School.

Ratey, John (1995) 'Foreward', in Thom Hartman *ADD Success Stories: A Guide to Fulfillment for Families With Attention Deficit Disorder*, Grass Valley CA: Underwood Books.

Rose, Nikolas (1989) *Governing the Soul: The Shaping of the Private Self*, London: Routledge.

—— (1992) 'Governing the enterprising self', in P. Heelas and P. Morris (eds) *The Values of Enterprise Culture*, London: Routledge.

Schein, Edgar H. (1985) *Organizational Culture and Leadership*, San Francisco: Jossey-Bass.

Epilogue

Chapter 11

Anthropology and policy research
The view from Northern Ireland

Hastings Donnan and Graham McFarlane

POLICY-ORIENTATED ANTHROPOLOGY SEEN FROM ABOVE AND BELOW

As everyone in anglophone anthropology (at least) is aware, anthropologists in the academy periodically feel obliged to account for themselves across the boundaries which are erected vis-à-vis the worlds occupied by those concerned with formulating, implementing and evaluating public policy. Such accounting was prevalent in the 1980s, and is still with us, perhaps inevitably, given the now sedimented bureaucratization and professionalization of the discipline in the academy, given the culture of enhancement which is being allowed to run rampant there and given the many other voices (within and without the academy) claiming expertise in providing descriptive and prescriptive models for the social world in which we live (Grimshaw and Hart 1994). For the audience within the academy, meantime, heavier doses of 'direct policy relevance' and 'engagement with real issues', ideally worked out in conjunction with other disciplines, are often presented as elements in the prescription for lifting anthropology out of its supposed states of theoretical malaise and ongoing crisis (e.g. Firth 1992; Rappaport 1993).

Of course, it is no surprise that this 'engagement' rhetoric gains its greatest approval, among anthropologists at least, when it is produced by those securely ensconced within the academy, and especially when it is produced by the big names in the discipline. For the large numbers of trained anthropologists carving out an all too precarious niche for themselves outside the academy, largely in policy-related research environments, such comments may at times be heartening, in the sense that the rhetoric confirms aspects of their own self-image. However, there are problems with this kind of discourse, especially, but not exclusively, among those outside the comparatively safe haven of the academy.

For one thing, the comments can appear patronizing, even if the élite's rhetoric is genuinely motivated by a desire to signal solidarity with this reserve army of labour. Those anthropologists working outside the academy seem to resent those inside, somewhat belatedly, or only periodically, voicing recognition of their work, while continuing, it seems, to find it difficult to find places in the mainstream journals for their writings, or to find academic posts for them. Those in the academy cannot be really serious about their support. (Paul Bohannan noted more than ten years ago how sceptical he was about the genuineness of the support for policy-related research, quoting, among others Lévi-Strauss (see Bohannan 1980)). Another source of worry seems to lie in the vision, or at least the version, of anthropology which is presented by those in the academy as being part of the needed 'engagement'.

This vision is of an anthropology willing to engage with other disciplines, but which is certain of its disciplinary core and unwilling to compromise its central questions and ways of answering them. This anthropology is globally comparative, concerned with worlds of meaning as they are constructed by people; is fundamentally humanistic and reflexive in its attempt to deconstruct or analyse these worlds of meaning and the social action connected to them; and is ever rethinking how to use its concepts, especially its central concepts like society, sociality and culture. This anthropology is not simply definable by its research 'methodologies' and research 'techniques', since despite the mystique still attached to 'fieldwork' in some quarters, everyone within the discipline is aware that fieldwork is a gloss for a promiscuous blend of all sorts of quantitative and qualitative research styles, none of which are the exclusive property of anthropology. (Different versions of 'ethnography' have become very popular in many social science disciplines.) This anthropology is not definable by a Third World subject matter either, since it is concerned with the thinkings and doings of all people everywhere.

Seen from the perspective of those who are engaged with the world of social policy, this vision of anthropology would seem to be, at first glance, liberating. And it is not surprising, given this apparently liberating vision of anthropology and the rhetoric of engagement, that some of those in the academy should have turned their attention to the analysis of the world views, practices and ideologies of policy makers and other policy 'professionals', as an adjunct to the many studies of the localized effects of their policy initiatives (see Herzfeld 1992, and the contributions to this volume). Out of this will hopefully come a genuine 'anthropology *of* public policy': comparative studies of the policy field which focus on the social practices of policy formulation, delivery and evaluation, together with the ideological groundings of these processes. However, despite the rhetoric about what anthropology should be about, those engaged with the policy arena can feel that their practice falls short of the ideal of providing this '*anthropology* of public policy'. In other words, studies in the policy field can appear as seriously compromised versions of the anthropological vision.

This chapter deals with an at least partially negative case for the construction of the 'anthropology of public policy' and a local manifestation of the general issues outlined above. Despite those aspects of life in Northern Ireland which would be conducive to the development of the anthropology of public policy, despite the impressive track record of anthropologists involved in policy fields, especially in the field of policy evaluation, and despite the fact that everyone involved in this research can give voice to the vision of anthropology which we have described, the research on which we reflect here falls short of the ideal in various ways. Our consideration of these shortcomings begins by looking briefly at the context within which policy research in Northern Ireland has developed and is carried out.

THE CONTEXT FOR POLICY RESEARCH IN NORTHERN IRELAND

Northern Ireland is a small place, both demographically and territorially, and it has what some have considered to be a unique set of social, economic and demographic problems relative to the rest of the United Kingdom. The most reported and most visible of these problems has obviously been the overt sectarian violence, known locally as 'the Troubles', which has riven the area for at least the last twenty-seven years and which has contributed to the fact that the social topography of the north-east of Ireland has emerged as one of the most researched in western Europe. Certainly it has been violent conflict which has preoccupied many of the local and international scholars researching in Northern Ireland, and in heady local and international debates, they have used the region as a testing ground for general theories on, for instance, nationalism, ethnicity, identity and conflict. Reviewing this mountain of research in the 1980s, and while acknowledging its generally high quality, Whyte (1990) lamented its comparative lack of practical impact in finding 'solutions' to the problem, pointing out that nothing much seemed to have changed as a result of all the effort.

In retrospect, part of the problem in identifying policy relevance in this work was the existence of a scholarly culture in which there seemed to be an ideological separation between, on the one hand, research on the politics of division, and debates about its causes and consequences, and, on the other hand, social research dealing more directly with policy issues affecting nation states throughout the industrialized world, research in which the local sectarian/ethnic division was treated as a backdrop. For a long time, these two research trajectories were kept more or less distinct, something which state research funding in the 1980s tended to solidify by encouraging grant applications for research projects not focused solely on the analysis of division (see Jenkins 1989).

Most researchers knew that all policy-related arenas and issues in Northern Ireland were affected to different degrees by the local 'Troubles', but they knew how to play the game of obtaining grants by being less explicit about this fact. However, a change occurred in the late 1980s. Researchers in Northern Ireland began to be more explicit about the inadequacy of compartmentalizing sectarianism from other areas of social life. Their rhetoric rejected the artificial division between conflict research and research into other aspects of local society and culture. As one writer argued, the province's distinctiveness within the United Kingdom lay not 'simply in the Troubles, nor in the nature of communal division, but in the way [these] interact with "normal" social issues' (O'Dowd 1989: 15). This view has permitted a more realistic purchase on policy issues, since it demands productive comparison of similarities and differences between the policy fields of Northern Ireland and those relating to the rest of western Europe and beyond.

Anthropologists have been involved in all these debates, as one kind of voice among many. There have been numerous overviews of the strengths and weaknesses of anthropological research in Ireland, north and south (see, for instance, Donnan and McFarlane 1983, 1986; Curtin et al. 1993; Wilson 1994). As we suggested in a volume dealing explicitly with policy-related research (Donnan and

McFarlane 1989), anthropologists working in Northern Ireland have been drawn to policy research by the same factors which have influenced the entry of anthropologists to this field elsewhere: partly out of a sense of personal commitment and a genuine desire to contribute to debates of practical concern and, more cynically, partly because this has often been where jobs could be had, especially for those recently graduated in the discipline. However, specific local factors also encourage participation in policy research in Northern Ireland. The small scale and dense networks of Northern Irish intellectual and political life seemed to hold out reasonable hope that the academic voice would be heard in positions of power. At the level of rhetoric at least, those in the corridors of power have proclaimed themselves open to academic advice on social affairs, whether this advice is based on quantitative and supposedly representative surveys of attitudes and opinions, or on more qualitative research methodologies. Indeed, over the last decade, social scientific research has provided the intellectual rationale for various policy initiatives which have resulted in the setting up of a Central Community Relations Council and the Opsahl Commission (looking for paths to resolving the conflict), and has contributed to the introduction and refinement of Fair Employment and Equal Opportunities legislation (see, for instance, Cormack and Osborne 1983; Crozier 1989, 1990).

The influence of the small scale and density of the network of academic researchers and policy professionals is manifest in how discussions within this network are framed. At a 1995 conference in Belfast, which brought together state 'customers' and social scientists in receipt of ESRC and other research funding, there was the usual talk about the different problems facing policy professionals and academic researchers, about the need to understand each others' needs and about the problems of communication and dissemination of research findings. However, it was also clear from events at this conference that the 'public transcript' (Scott 1990) describing relations between researchers and state customers is one of useful dialogue, and of constructing 'a world run by compromises', as one state official put it.

Of course, there was much 'hidden' talk (gossip!) at play at this conference as well, talk which had to do with predictable issues like academic obscurantism, ideological smoke screens and the broad issue of the ethics of doing policy-related research for state bodies. However, the dense network of personal relationships among all those present made it difficult for anyone to frame their talk by relating individual researchers and policy professionals to broad categories like 'typical representatives of the state' or 'typical academic researchers'. It was the virtues and foibles of individuals known 'in the round' which explicitly framed the talk. We do not claim that such typifications were not operating by implication in relation to given individuals, but we would argue that a clear 'them' and 'us' boundary was difficult to discern in the pattern of gossip. Characteristics like clear-headedness, ideological duplicity, ethical robustness and careerism were attributed to individual researchers and individual state representatives alike. We think that it would be too glib to argue for the existence of a fundamental boundary between academic researchers and state representatives in the policy arena in Northern Ireland.

The social context for policy research in Northern Ireland differs from that in Britain in other ways too. Stimulated by a limited regional focus, there has been an increasing degree of interdisciplinary collaboration in policy research in Northern Ireland. Just as social scientists working in the policy field often know personally those who may sponsor their research, so they also know – and meet regularly at conferences, seminars and in less formal settings – academics from other disciplines with similar research interests as themselves. In these settings, there does seem to be an openness to the viewpoints of social scientists and at least the potential of anthropological research. Anthropologists researching in the policy arena in Northern Ireland have thus to some extent been able to operate in an environment in which their voice might be heard, both by academic colleagues and by those who have the power to employ them or commission research. It was against this apparently positive and welcoming background that anthropologists in Northern Ireland began to engage with the policy arena. Although one early policy-related study by an anthropologist was carried out in the 1940s (Mogey 1947), much of this work began in the 1980s, as we discuss below.

ANTHROPOLOGISTS AND POLICY-RELATED RESEARCH IN NORTHERN IRELAND

Although this section focuses only on a selection of examples, it may be helpful first to sketch out the range and extent of anthropological involvement in the policy field in Northern Ireland. These are summarized in Table 1, which also indicates that anthropological contributions to policy research in the province are of recent origin. Few of these projects have been initiated by the researchers themselves, and where researchers have not been approached directly to do such research, their involvement in this area has usually been in response to newspaper advertisements or invitations to tender.

Despite those features, mentioned above, which make the practical aspects of policy involvement in Northern Ireland somewhat distinct, researchers working there have been preoccupied with similar policy issues as researchers throughout the United Kingdom. Since the 1980s, many social scientists in Northern Ireland – including social anthropologists – have been involved in evaluating the various processes of delivery of recent governmental policy initiatives. This suggests that anthropology, like other social sciences and the penumbra of state sponsored agencies in Northern Ireland, is involved, in a real sense, with governmentality (see Wright 1995: 88). As Table 1 indicates, policy research in Northern Ireland tends to have been dominated by projects focusing on aspects of economic restructuring, unemployment, gender and ethnic discrimination in the workplace, housing and education. As suggested above, these studies do take on a local flavour, one inevitably sensitive to – and often arising out of – the wider sectarian division which pervades Northern Irish life. Thus one study (Irwin 1991) evaluated the role of education in promoting social integration between Catholic and Protestant, while a study of the impact of state capitalization on the fishing industry demonstrated how government grants for improving the quality of the fishing fleet reinforced sectarian segregation and increased the chances of Protestants acquiring modern vessels (Dilley 1989).

However, it is the complex *interplay* between local factors, such as sectarianism, and other factors including unemployment or gender, which constitutes the foci of several other studies. In a series of publications, Howe (1989b, 1990, 1994) examined the experience of unemployment in two Belfast housing estates, one Catholic the other Protestant, showing how the daily realities of being unemployed are shaped not so much by the cultural preconceptions of Catholics and Protestants *per se* as by the structure of state economic development policy, and its inevitably localized consequences for the sectarian geography of the north. Stepping back from essentialist arguments about cultural differences between

Table 1 Policy-related research by anthropologists in Northern Ireland

Researcher(s)	Date	Topic	Location	Publications
Blacking et al.	1985–7	Unemployment	Larne	Blacking et al. 1989
Butler	1980–3	Travellers	Derry, Tyrone	Butler 1985
Byron and Dilley	1983–5	Fishing	Down	Byron and Dilley 1988a, 1988b; Dilley 1989
Cecil et al.	1983–5	Community care	Derry	Cecil et al. 1985, 1987; Cecil 1989
Dawson et al.	1990–2	Farming	Down Fermanagh	Dawson 1997 Macaulay 1997
Donnan and McFarlane	1987–8	Unemployment	Belfast	Donnan and McFarlane 1988
Howe	1982–5	Unemployment	Belfast	Howe 1985, 1988, 1989a, 1989b, 1990
Hughes	1992–3	Community relations evaluation	NI	Knox et al. 1992
Irwin	1987–9, 1990–1	Education	Belfast	Irwin 1991
McLaughlin	1982–6	Unemployment	Derry	McLaughlin 1989; Davies and McLaughlin 1991
McLaughlin and Ingram	1988–90	Clothing industry	NI	McLaughlin and Ingram 1991
Milton	1987–	Environment	NI	Milton 1990, 1991, 1993a, 1993b
Mogey	1940s	Rural economy	NI	Mogey 1947
Ogle	1986–9	Housing	Belfast	Ogle 1989
Wilson	1991–2	Tourism	NI	Wilson 1993

Catholics and Protestants, Howe (1985, 1990) also examined the bureaucratic administration of welfare benefits and their delivery at the cultural boundary between those responsible for enacting policy and their 'clients'. He documented how the widely held distinction between 'deserving' and 'undeserving' claimants is confirmed and reproduced in everyday practice in social security offices. This interface between client and policy professional, especially at those points where there is correspondence or disjunction in cultural assumptions, was a central theme in Donnan and McFarlane's (1988) research on counselling provision for the long-term unemployed in a socially heterogeneous area of Belfast. This research did not identify any serious differences in the ideal models of what constitutes 'counselling' held by professionals and clients nor, indeed, any sharp disagreement between Catholics and Protestants. However, it did indicate that there are cultural barriers to the take-up, delivery and perceived relevance or usefulness of 'counselling' services, located in both organizational and client world views. The somewhat parochial view of Northern Ireland was again challenged in a report commissioned by the Northern Ireland Equal Opportunities Commission, which argued that it is a more global cultural construction of 'training', and associated cultural constructions of 'skill', which underlie and explain the relatively disadvantaged position of women in the Northern Ireland clothing industry. Arguing against the parochial 'victimology' practised by members of the two main ethnie in the north, this report stressed that gender inequality at work may well be greater than inequalities based on ethnic or sectarian identity in Northern Ireland (McLaughlin and Ingram 1991; see also, Davies and McLaughlin 1991). The issue of ethnicity is mainly irrelevant in Milton's work on rural and urban planning policy (see Milton 1990, 1993a, 1993b).

While inevitably sensitive to issues of sectarian or ethnic division, much of the policy research carried out in Northern Ireland shows that it is not sufficient to treat Northern Ireland as unique, simply because it is divided along sectarian lines. Northern Ireland has been affected by the same problems as the rest of Europe, and social anthropologists have made a contribution to the understanding of the consequences of these problems.

However, if circumstances in Northern Ireland seem favourable for the production of effective policy research, anthropology has apparently not always fulfilled its potential. For amidst all the bustling research and interdisciplinary communication, anthropology has usually been the quiet voice, which, while recognized by both policy makers and other social scientists as having something *potentially* important to contribute, is one that has somehow been unable to deliver the goods in a manner which is anthropological in the pure sense, in the eyes of some disciplinary colleagues at least.

In order to unravel the issues involved here, we provide a brief case study. In this context it is little more than an apt illustration of the fate of policy-related anthropological research in a seemingly favourable research environment.

GETTING TO KNOW NORTHERN IRISH FARM HOUSEHOLDS: ANTHROPOLOGY MARGINALIZED

From 1990 until 1992, a small team of social anthropologists (Andrew Dawson, Iain Macaulay as fieldworkers and Graham McFarlane as coordinator) was involved in a research project investigating the changing economic strategies of Northern Irish farm households as they were confronted by shifts in international policies for agriculture and for the rural economy generally ('Changing farm economies and their environmental relationships', ESRC Joint Agriculture and Environment Programme, Award W103 25 1009). In the 1990s version of European policies for rural areas, the fundamental assumption was that the interests of agricultural producers were no longer to be considered necessarily paramount, but were to be assessed relative to issues like the protection of the environment, the reduction of food surpluses and rural development generally. The project investigating Northern Irish farm households' awareness and responses to this changing world was multi-disciplinary, involving agricultural economists, political scientists, rural sociologists and ecologists as well as the anthropologists. As one would expect, the project adopted a blend of different research techniques, the backbone of which were a large-scale interview questionnaire survey of 1,200 farm household heads across Northern Ireland, and further detailed surveys in three 'case study' areas. These surveys were accompanied by detailed interviews with individuals who were identified as occupying élite positions in the agricultural sector – politicians and government officers at all levels, members of statutory and voluntary organizations which mediate relations between the state, the European Union, and individual farm households. The surveys were also to be preceded and accompanied by residential fieldwork in selected locations.

As is common in such collaborative endeavours, there was much talk at the planning stages about the triangulation of research findings, about the difficulties and the opportunities involved with all attempts at reaching general conclusions from different perspectives and with different research tools. Apparent throughout, at least in rhetoric, was a desire to break out of what McLaughlin (1991) has called the 'oppositional poverty' of confronting quantitative with qualitative research methods, of defining the two sets of methods as if the two were irreconcilable, being inextricably anchored in two different social scientific world views. Linked to this was an openness to the potential of the anthropological blend of research techniques and its centrepiece of close involvement with people. This is probably not a surprising attitude in relation to the rural sociologists and political scientists involved in the team, since when one looks across the academic boundaries towards rural sociology and political science, it would seem that over the last decade or so abstract empiricism has been displaced from the centre of those disciplines by sophisticated theoretical and methodological projects focusing on the central question of how to connect studies of creative agency with studies of large scale, encompassing structuring processes. In trying to answer this question, more narrowly defined studies of people's activities, carried out in the context of their complex networks of relationships, have become *de rigeur* in both rural sociology and political science. So, too, has an awareness of the mediating significance of something called 'culture'. The anthropologists involved with the team were not marginalized because of their espousal of their approach, even if they did have to provide introductory courses on the kinds of questions which anthropologists set themselves and the kinds of research techniques which they wanted to adopt (*pace* Okely (1987), for whom such courses were experienced as demoralizing).

The apparently positive environment in which this group of anthropologists was able to carry out its work is again emphasized by the overall team's agreement about the aims which the anthropologists set themselves as contributors to the project. These were set out explicitly in one of the many internal memos and progress reports, as well as at meetings of the scientific team. One formulation of this is set out below:

> The aims of the ethnographic ['ethnographic' was the term used by the project directors in all its dealings with the ESRC] component of the project have been to analyse the inter-relationships between socio-cultural factors and the economic strategies of different kinds of farm households. Farm households are seen as generating strategies to maintain or advance themselves in the context of features both internal and external to the household, features which operate both as constraints and opportunities for them. We would stress that 'socio-cultural' factors do not constitute a residual category when other kinds of constraints are sifted out. Rather, the ethnographers emphasize the social and cultural mediation of all the factors which impinge on the farm

household. The strategies generated by households are seen as
the outcome of decisions negotiated between different members
of the farm household, negotiations where age and gender differences play key roles. Economic strategies are decision outcomes
about livelihood in its broadest sense (in agriculture; in
agriculturally-related activities; in non-agricultural work; on-
farm and off-farm; in the domestic and extra-domestic domains;
in the 'formal' and 'informal' economic sectors).

The ethnography has two main functions in the overall
project. First, the ethnography is capturing some of the detail
and complexity in how households are negotiating change.
Second, and equally important, the ethnography will help the
team to interpret, illustrate or, at times, modify some of the
statistically based findings of the land user survey.

This is not the place to present the 'findings' of the project.
Neither is it the place to attempt a detailed analysis of the complex
social processes out of which the project's initial 'deliverables' (e.g.
interim and final reports to sponsors, public meetings, academic
conferences) emerged or were created. The project, like all projects,
provided arenas in which personal career strategies and academic
interests were worked out in complex ways, and where shifting
power relations were evident. What is germane here are some more
modest reflections on what became of the anthropological elements
outlined in the above quotation as the project progressed to the final
report stage. The story is a somewhat familiar one.

The fieldworkers, especially, provided input into the development
of the interview schedules to be used in the large-scale surveys, both
with regards to the range of topics to be addressed and to the ways
in which questions were formulated. The fieldwork was already
under way at this stage, but there was no sense of the ethnographic
fieldwork being seen as a pilot study for the surveys, since there was
a huge body of background knowledge and personal experience of
surveys among the rest of the team which enabled the team to
generate the main body of the interview schedules. At the same
time, the fieldworkers (and those involved with the élite interviews)
provided interim reports on their work which were discussed in
detail at team meetings. At these meetings, ethnographic 'findings'
were constantly played off against the background knowledge and
everyday understandings of rural life in Northern Ireland held by
team members, most of whom had lived in the region for much of

their lives. The fieldworkers were quizzed on a vast range of topics of interest to the non-anthropologist team members, and encouraged to find out more about everything from attitudes towards politicians to local people's opinions about environmental issues, from relationships between the genders in the households to plans for succession. This was all very flattering.

However, this process seemed to reflect some hidden assumptions. Often the initial generalizations and conclusions in the fieldwork reports provoked nods of agreement and recognition among the rest of the team, but just as often they were challenged as being odd, idiosyncratic, or somehow 'unrepresentative' in the light of the general background knowledge of agriculture in Northern Ireland held by other team members. There were warning signs here: the talk of representativeness was in fact signalling a deep-seated adherence to a view in which one can grasp the world through quantitative analysis of representative survey responses, which is an aspect of that hankering 'for a "real" positivist hold on a world of slippery intangibles' identified by, among others, Wright (1994: 3). The constant demands for more information about an array of issues reflected not so much serious acceptance of the theoretical assumption that everything is culturally mediated and open to being 'caught unawares' by anthropologists, but rather a less refined assumption that the qualitative approach adopted as one strand in the research was simply a way to get at some complex or sensitive issues. Anthropology was being constructed as a methodology or, even worse, as a kind of research technique.

The anthropologists on the team noted the warnings and inevitably fought their corner, but out of the struggles for pre-eminence within the teams (in which, on more than one occasion, the anthropologists were jocularly described as 'academic imperialists'), and faced with deadlines to meet, the final report of the project (a fairly brief affair) was produced. This seems to replicate how many reports incorporate anthropological insights and findings. At times, fieldwork 'findings' are drawn upon to help explain some correlations in the survey data; at other times, the correlations seem to be interpreted in an apparently ad hoc fashion, or at least interpreted in relation to the common-sense, extra-project knowledge held by the team members. The ideal of triangulation was severely compromised, especially where survey findings did not square neatly with the ethnographic material, an area for fruitful rethinking of questions and methodologies according to some writers (see Trend 1978). Much of the ethnographic material is featured in a section dealing with socio-cultural constraints, a kind of residual category of 'other' issues, issues which are not obviously 'economic', 'ecological' or 'political'.

We are not arguing that these outcomes were simply the result of the fact that the anthropologists involved in the project were somehow subject to more powerful academics, that they were somehow naive victims in the academic politics of the project. This is not another tale of how the hapless anthropologists were stung in their involvement in interdisciplinary and policy work. There are certainly many such tales in the literature, mostly blaming the policy professionals, but occasionally (and perhaps more honestly) putting the blame on the inadequacy of the discipline in the context of the world as defined for policy (see Fuller 1982). The anthropologists here may have been the weaker actors in the academic politics of the project, but they did ultimately cooperate in the confabulation of the report, like the others in the team, fully aware of the writing constraints involved and the need to communicate a message clearly to the sponsors. In so doing, despite the rhetoric used in team meetings, the final report reflected a somewhat truncated version of 'anthropology', a version which we feel is typical of much policy-related anthropological work in Northern Ireland. When purveyed, usually by default, this truncated version of anthropology is potentially detrimental both for the contribution which anthropology might make to policy debates, and for the standing of 'policy research' within the discipline more generally.

'TRUNCATED' ANTHROPOLOGY AND POLICY RESEARCH IN NORTHERN IRELAND

We would argue that the final product of the research described above is but one instance of a more general trend in anthropological writing about policy concerns in Northern Ireland. Faced with sponsors – and, in multidisciplinary teams, colleagues – who want to get what they think is usable knowledge, presented in a way which is readable and on time, anthropologists have adapted pragmatically by compromising theoretical concepts, epistemological principles and methodological rigours which they would otherwise take for granted in more academic arenas.

The environment in which anthropologists find themselves working is one where there is, perhaps inevitably, a skewed vision of what anthropology is 'about' among policy professionals and members of other disciplines. In this environment, certain key words form part of a shared vocabulary, but the meanings attached to these words diverge radically between the different parties involved. As any anthropologist would expect, a term for which there are multiple meanings is 'culture'. For the policy professionals, and members of other disciplines, anthropologists are experts on 'culture', but for the non-anthropologists who use and think about the term, 'culture' still has the definitional attributes which anthropologists have been calling into question since at least the 1960s. For the non-anthropologists, 'culture' seems to be thought of as a relatively discrete collection of essential or fundamental beliefs, values, assumptions and behavioural traits, passed on like a tradition from generation to generation, in an only slowly changing form. This 'culture' is attached to, or belongs to, identifiable categories of people; and in Northern Ireland there are many possible sub-cultures based upon ethnicity, class or occupation, locality and gender, all nesting in complex ways within the larger weave of Northern Irish society and, for the less parochial, in networks of relationships beyond Northern Ireland.

Anthropologists working in Northern Ireland are aware of the ongoing debates about the concept 'culture' within the discipline, and the deconstructionist, anti-essentialist trend within these debates. Indeed, most anthropologists working in the policy field would question the version of culture expounded by the non-specialists with whom they are involved, in discussion with colleagues. Furthermore, the ethnography of the ethnic conflict in Northern Ireland, for all its shortcomings, has consistently argued that it is much too simplistic to understand the ethnic conflict simply in terms of a competition between discrete ethnic blocs, each holding discrete cultures or traditions (for one of the latest statements, see Buckley and Kenney 1995). Since serious anthropological interest in the ethnic conflict developed in the 1970s, terms like 'Catholic' and 'Protestant' have been used in analysis, but they are used as generalizations to be unpacked and deconstructed in pursuit of complex particularity. Indeed, this deconstructionist thrust in anthropological work on the ethnic division has provided the basis for a thoroughgoing critique of the state-sponsored Community Relations/Cultural Traditions initiatives, which see at least partial solutions to the Northern Ireland 'problem' to lie in the establishment of greater mutual understanding and contact between the two major ethnic blocs (this is very similar to the anthropological critique of 'multi-culturalism' in the United States; see Segal and Handler 1995).

However, when anthropologists (often the same anthropologists) are working in the policy field, much of this theoretical understanding tends to get set aside. The idea of culture can appear as little more than a gloss for the various spoken and unspoken attitudes and world views held by 'the unemployed', 'counsellors', 'farmers' wives', and 'fishermen' about the policy issues and domains in which they are involved, or even, more generally, as a gloss for some more undifferentiated collectivity's attitudes and perceptions towards issues like being 'a good neighbour'. The use of 'culture' in this way provides a kind of contextual flavour to the discussion of more real 'structural' (usually economic or political) processes. In short, it becomes a residual category, as was experienced in the farming study discussed above.

In the policy environment in Northern Ireland, since the central anthropological concept of culture can end up being thought about, and indeed written about, by all parties involved with projects in much the same way (as local flavour and as a gloss for people's attitudes and perceptions), it is hardly surprising that anthropology has come to be seen less as a discipline with its own distinctive theoretical concepts, concerns and questions, and more as a collection of research techniques, essentially qualitative in nature. For some, both within and outside anthropologists' networks, anthropology seems close to a kind of journalism (especially whenever residential fieldwork is not possible). We do not see any real problems with this association between journalism and anthropology, especially when the association is made between anthropology and *good* journalism (indeed, in Northern Ireland some of the best writing about the ethnic division and social problems has been produced by journalists). However, for others concerned with the maintenance of academic boundaries and for the reputation of anthropology, this is very worrying. Anthropology, as we like to think of it in seminars and elsewhere, seems to dissolve away.

Indeed, in such a context where academic boundaries appear dissolvable, and in the context of a labour market where the number of academic posts in anthropology is still limited, it would seem sensible for some trained anthropologists working in the policy field to market aspects of their training in anthropological research techniques in order to switch disciplines. In other words, some researchers now work in sociology or social policy departments, on problems largely driven by sociological agendas, adding a qualitative spin to data mainly collected by survey, though they began their academic lives by writing doctoral dissertations based on qualitative material collected during long-term residential field research.

ANTHROPOLOGY, POLICY AND THE MUTUAL SUSPENSION OF DISBELIEF

This switching of disciplines is, of course, the most obvious sign that anthropology can become compromised as it confronts the world of policy professionals (and members of other disciplines working there). However, parachuting into other disciplinary domains is perfectly rational given the limited career opportunities open to graduates in anthropology. Much more general among anthropologists, both inside and outside the academy, is the kind of compromise which we discussed above. On the one hand, when they talk among themselves, there *is* a general agreement about what anthropology should be about in the field of policy, and a general acceptance that anthropology is defined not by its methods but by the questions it sets itself, and that these questions revolve around 'culture'. On the other hand, there is an acquiescence to the view of the world established by people from other disciplines and by policy professionals, a view where 'culture' is the word used to gloss vague, residual, attitudinal elements.

This latter conceptualization of 'culture' is implicit in most initial publications and final reports on the projects carried out by anthropologists in Northern Ireland. Granted, when they have had time to reflect on the material, usually when safely ensconced in the academy, some of the same writers have engaged more fully with central anthropological debates about 'culture', whether in relation to discourse analysis (see Milton 1993a, 1993b), ideology (see Howe 1990, 1994) or identity (see Dawson 1997). However, it is the more simplistic version of 'culture' which prevails in the project literature. Elements in the Northern Irish context may exaggerate this tendency.

From many conversations with policy professionals it is obvious to us that those who work in statutory and non-statutory agencies in Northern Ireland know as well as anthropologists that the world is a complex place, with no single issue reducible to a set of key variables which can be manipulated to produce 'true' accounts. But since these people's jobs entail identifying just such variables (in pursuit of approximate truths or a plausible account in the light of their common-sense knowledge of what people are like), of necessity they too must engage in a compromise: they must suspend their disbelief that the world can be understood in fairly simple positivistic ways. Anthropologists must also suspend their disbelief if they want their reports to be read (and indeed if they wish to be employed again), and, to signal their suspension of disbelief, they must produce research summaries which generalize a way through the 'slippery intangibles' and complexity. The non-theorized version of 'culture' which pervades project literature helps to provide summarizable and generalized accounts of the complex reality with which we all have to deal. The pressure to engage in this mutual suspension of disbelief in the Northern Ireland context could derive, ironically, from one of the very factors which could be seen as being conducive to letting anthropology's more reflective and perhaps louder voice be heard. It is the existence of a world of close personal relationships which pull together academics and policy professionals which may make it difficult (not least for career reasons) for anthropologists to question loudly the vision of the world which they have been involved in reproducing.

REFERENCES

Blacking, J., Byrne, K. and Ingram, K. (1989) 'Looking for work in Larne: a social anthropological study', in H. Donnan and G. McFarlane (eds) *Social Anthropology and Public Policy in Northern Ireland,* Aldershot: Avebury.

Bohannan, P. (1980) 'You can't do nothing', *American Anthropologist* 82: 508–24.

Buckley, A. D. and Kenney M. C. (1995) *Negotiating Identity: Rhetoric, Metaphor and Social Drama in Northern Ireland,* Washington: Smithsonian Institution.

Butler, C. (1985) *Travelling People in Derry and Tyrone,* Londonderry: World Development Group.

Byron, R. and Dilley, R. (1988a) *Ulster Fishermen: A Study in Social Organisation and Fisheries Policy,* Belfast: Policy Research Institute.

—— (1988b) 'Social and micro-economic processes in the Northern Ireland fishing industry', in R. Jenkins (ed.) *Northern Ireland: Studies in Social and Economic Life,* Aldershot: Avebury (in association with the Economic and Social Research Council).

Cecil, R. (1989) 'Care and the community in a Northern Irish town', in H. Donnan and G. McFarlane (eds) *Social Anthropology and Public Policy in Northern Ireland,* Aldershot: Avebury.

Cecil, R., Offer, J. and St Leger, F. (1985) *Informal Welfare in a Small Town in Northern Ireland: A Report to the Department of Health and Social Services, Northern Ireland*, Coleraine: University of Ulster.

—— (1987) *Informal Welfare: A Sociological Study of Care in Northern Ireland*, Aldershot: Gower.

Cormack, R. J. and Osborne, R. D. (eds) (1983) *Religion, Education and Employment*, Belfast: Appletree Press.

Crozier, M. (ed.) (1989) *Varieties of Irishness*, Belfast: Institute of Irish Studies.

—— (1990) *Varieties of Britishness*, Belfast: Institute of Irish Studies.

Curtin, C., Donnan, H. and Wilson, T. M. (eds) (1993) *Irish Urban Cultures*, Belfast: Institute of Irish Studies.

Davies, C. and McLaughlin, E. (eds) (1991) *Women, Employment and Social Policy in Northern Ireland: A Problem Postponed?* Belfast: Policy Research Institute.

Dawson, A. (1997) 'Identity and strategy in post-productionist agriculture: a case study from Northern Ireland', in H. Donnan and G. McFarlane (eds) *Culture and Policy in Northern Ireland*, Belfast: Institute of Irish Studies.

Dilley, R. (1989) 'Boat owners, patrons and state policy in the Northern Ireland fishing industry', in H. Donnan and G. McFarlane (eds) *Social Anthropology and Public Policy in Northern Ireland*, Aldershot: Avebury.

Donnan, H. and McFarlane, G. (1983) 'Informal social organisation', in J. Darby (ed.) *Northern Ireland: The Background to the Conflict*, Belfast: Appletree Press/Syracuse University Press.

—— (1986) ' "You get on better with your own": social continuity and change in rural Northern Ireland', in P. Clancy, S. Drudy, K. Lynch and L. O'Dowd (eds) *Ireland: A Sociological Profile*, Dublin: Institute of Public Administration.

—— (1988) *Counselling and the Unemployed in Belfast*, Belfast: Policy Planning and Research Unit.

—— (eds) (1989) *Social Anthropology and Public Policy in Northern Ireland*, Aldershot: Avebury.

Firth, R. (1992) 'A future for anthropology?' in S. Wallman (ed.) *Contemporary Futures: Perspectives from Social Anthropology* (ASA 30), London: Routledge.

Fuller, C. J. (1982) 'Is anthropology special?', *Royal Anthropological Institute Newsletter* 48: 16–17.

Grimshaw, A. and Hart, K. (1994) 'Anthropology and the crisis of the intellectuals', *Critique of Anthropology* 14: 227–61.

Herzfeld, M. (1992) *The Social Production of Indifference: Exploring the Symbolic Roots of Western Democracy*, Oxford: Berg.

Howe, L. (1985) 'The "deserving" and the "undeserving": practice in an urban, local social security office', *Journal of Social Policy* 14: 49–72.

—— (1988) 'Doing the double: wages, jobs and benefits in Belfast', in R. Jenkins (ed.) *Northern Ireland: Studies in Social and Economic Life*, Aldershot: Avebury (in association with the Economic and Social Research Council).

—— (1989a) 'Social anthropology and public policy: aspects of unemployment and social security in Northern Ireland', in H. Donnan and G. McFarlane (eds) *Social Anthropology and Public Policy in Northern Ireland*, Aldershot: Avebury.

—— (1989b) 'Unemployment, doing the double and labour markets in Belfast', in C. Curtin and T. M. Wilson (eds) *Ireland From Below: Social Change and Local Communities*, Galway: Galway University Press.

—— (1990) *Being Unemployed in Northern Ireland: An Ethnographic Study*, Cambridge: Cambridge University Press.

—— (1994) 'Ideology, domination and unemployment', *Sociological Review* 42 (2): 315–40.

Irwin, C. (1991) *Education and the Development of Social Integration in Divided Societies*, Belfast: Policy Planning and Research Unit.

Jenkins, R. (ed.) (1989) *Northern Ireland: Studies in Social and Economic Life*, Aldershot: Avebury (in association with the Economic and Social Research Council).

Knox, C., Hughes, J., Birrell, D. and McCready, S. (1992) *Evaluation of District Council Community Relations Programme: Report to the Liaison Committee*, Coleraine: Centre for Study of Conflict.

Macaulay, I. (1997) 'Inside the citadel: rural development policy in practice', in H. Donnan and G. McFarlane (eds) *Culture and Policy in Northern Ireland*, Belfast : Institute of Irish Studies.

McLaughlin, E. (1989) 'In search of the female breadwinner: gender and unemployment in Derry city', in H. Donnan and G. McFarlane (eds) *Social Anthropology and Public Policy in Northern Ireland*, Aldershot: Avebury.

—— (1991) 'Oppositional poverty: the quantitative/qualitative divide and other dichotomies', *Sociological Review* 39: 292–308.

McLaughlin, E. and Ingram, K. (1991) *All Stitched Up: Sex Segregation in the Northern Ireland Clothing Industry*, Belfast: Equal Opportunities Commission for Northern Ireland.

Milton, K. (1990) *Our Countryside, Our Concern: The Policy and Practice of Conservation in Northern Ireland*, Belfast: Northern Ireland Environment Link.

—— (1991) 'Interpreting environmental policy: a social scientific approach', in R. Churchill, L. Warren and J. Gibson (eds) *Law, Policy and the Environment*, Oxford: Blackwell.

—— (1993a) 'Belfast: whose city?', in C. Curtin, H. Donnan and T. M. Wilson (eds) *Irish Urban Cultures*, Belfast: Institute of Irish Studies.

—— (1993b) 'Land or landscape – rural planning policy and the symbolic construction of the countryside', in M. Murray and J. Greer (eds) *Rural Development in Ireland: A Challenge for the 1990s*, Aldershot: Avebury.

Mogey, J. M. (1947) *Rural Life in Northern Ireland*, Oxford: Oxford University Press.

O'Dowd, L. (1989) 'Ignoring the communal divide: the implications for social research', in R. Jenkins (ed.) *Northern Ireland: Studies in Social and Economic Life*, Aldershot: Avebury (in association with the Economic and Social Research Council).

Ogle, S. (1989) 'Housing estate improvements: an assessment of strategies for tenant participation', in H. Donnan and G. McFarlane (eds) *Social*

Anthropology and Public Policy in Northern Ireland, Aldershot: Avebury.

Okely, J. (1987) 'Fieldwork up the M1: policy and political aspects', in A. Jackson (ed.) *Anthropology at Home* (ASA 25), London: Tavistock.

Rappaport, R. (1993) 'The anthropology of trouble', *American Anthropologist* 95: 295–303.

Scott, J. C. (1990) *Domination and the Art of Resistance: Hidden Transcripts*, New Haven: Yale University Press.

Segal, D. A. and Handler, R. (1995) 'US multiculturalism and the concept of culture', *Identities* 1: 391–407.

Trend, M. G. (1978) 'On the reconciliation of qualitative and quantitative analysis: a case study', *Human Organization* 37: 345–54.

Whyte, J. (1990) *Interpreting Northern Ireland*, Oxford: Oxford University Press.

Wilson, D. (1993) 'Tourism, public policy and the image of Northern Ireland since the troubles', in B. O'Connor and M. Cronin (eds) *Tourism in Ireland: A Critical Analysis*, Cork: Cork University Press.

Wilson, T. M. (1994) 'A question of identity', in T. M. Wilson (ed.) *The Unheard Voice: Social Anthropology in Ireland*, Belfast: Fortnight (supplement 324).

Wright, S. (1994) 'Culture in anthropology and organizational studies', in S. Wright (ed.) *Anthropology of Organizations*, London: Routledge.

—— (1995) 'Anthropology: still the uncomfortable discipline?', in A. S. Ahmed and C. Shore (eds) *The Future of Anthropology: Its Relevance to the Contemporary World*, London: Athlone.

Index

Abu-Lughod, L. 13, 145
academy: and European culture
  176; policy-orientated
  anthropology in 261–3; and
  sexual equality in Sweden
  116–26
ACT UP 62
administration: reform in Norway
  31–2, 195–215
Adonnino, P. 173
Africa, HIV/AIDS in 15, 22–3,
  59–80
alienation 3, 5, 209, 213, 214
Althusser, L. 13, 29, 166
Anderson, B. 137, 145, 157, 166,
  167, 177
Andrews, G. 20
Ang, I. 180
Anthropology in Action 4
anthropology of policy 3–10,
  261–3; methodological
  implications 14–18
Appadurai, A. 7
Apthorpe, R. 18, 20–1, 35n1
Archetti, E. 198
Ardener, Edwin 185
Armstrong, D. 101
Armstrong, S. 70
Arnold, T. 54
attention deficit disorder (ADD) 34,
  251–5
audiovisual policy of European
  Union 26–7, 165–89

Baget-Bozzo, G. 175

Bailey, F.G. 13
Baistow, K. 233
Bakhtin, M. 78
Balkanization (Mestrovic) 167
Ball, S.J. 16, 247–8
Balladur, Edouard 179, 189n12
Barou, Jean-Pierre 242
Barth, F. 13
Barzanti, R. 175
BASAPP 4
Bashevin, S.B. 140
Bassett, C. 62, 71
Bateson, G. 23, 89, 92
Bateson, M. 92
Baumann, G. 45
Baxter, P.W.T. 43
Baylies, C. 68
Berer, M. 62
Berger, B. 207
Berger, H. 207
Berri, Claude 181
Beveridge Report 31
Bhabha, H. 167
bilingualism, Canada 138, 139
bio-politics 241
Bisseret-Moreau, N. 64
Björk, N. 123
Black, A. 166
Blacking, J. 268
Bloch, M. 12, 60
body, bodies: hospital setting
  88–103; and power/management
  241, 244
Bohannan, P. 262
Botswana 72

Bourdieu, P. 20, 23, 88–9, 92, 210
Bowman, G. 167
Bradford, housing *see* housing
　policies
Breton, R. 139
British Association for Social
　Anthropology in Policy and
　Practice 4
Brock, G. 184
Buchan, D. 181, 183
Buckley, A.D. 7, 275
Bujra, J. 68
Bumsted, J.M. 138
Burchell, G. 6, 9, 17, 32
bureaucracy 5; *see also*
　administration, governance,
　government, local politics
bureaucratization 204, 206
Burgelman, J.-C. 169, 172, 175, 182
Burnett, J. 221
Butler, C. 268
Byron, R. 268

Cabral, A.J. 66
Cairns, Alan C. 140
Caldwell, J.C. 74
Caldwell, P. 73
Canada, cultural politics of
　populism and national identity
　25–6, 136–61
Canada 125 Corporation/
　celebrations 25, 137–60 *passim*
Canetti, E. 43
Cannell, F. 6
capitalism 207, 243–4
Capitan, C. 59
Caplan, P. 14
Carael, M. 62
Carovano, K. 66, 76
Carrell, M.R. 240
Cecil, R. 268
Certeau, M. de 13
Cerullo, M. 62
Chambers, E. 7
Chapman, Malcolm 165
Chapman, Margaret 226–7, 228
Chatterjee, P. 136, 144, 160
Chikinkata, of Zambia 75

Chimera-Dam, J. 70
citizen, policy and 3, 6, 19, 24
citizenship, concepts of 27, 136,
　160, 175
civil administration in United States
　see management policies, in US
civil society 28; Canada 25, 143–5,
　155, 156, 160
class 60, 132
Cliff, S.A. 78
closure techniques, in Swedish
　education 121–2
clothing industry, Northern Ireland
　268, 269
Colebunders, R. 70
Coleman, R. 70, 75
Collignon, R. 60
Collins, R. 170, 171, 175, 178, 183,
　188n3
colonialism 235n3; and HIV/AIDS
　in Africa 22, 62, 63, 71
Columbus celebrations 139, 140
commercialization 175
commodification of knowledge 214
communication policy, European
　26–7, 165–89
community 13, 20; in Canada
　150–9, 160; and development
　language 53–4; *see also*
　resistance
conflict research, Northern Ireland
　264, 265, 275
Connolly, B. 187
Conservative Party: British 19, 160
　(European audiovisual policy
　186–7, housing policies 32–3,
　217–36); Canadian 25, 137,
　139–60; *see also* New Right
containment, policy of 8
Cook, J. 71
Cormack, R.J. 265
corporate culture 250–1
corporate nationalism, in Canada
　148–9
Corrigan, P. 208
Côte d'Ivoire, effects of culturalist
　interpretation of HIV/AIDS
　60–1, 73–7

Crawford, A. 72
critical social sciences 61
critical sociology 29
Crozier, M. 265
Cruikshank, Barbara 224, 231, 233
Crystal, D. 55
cultural agent, policy as 24–9;
    cultural politics of populism and
    Canadian national identity
    136–61; European Union
    audiovisual policy and politics
    of identity 165–89; gender
    equality policy in post-welfare
    Sweden 107–34
cultural imperialism, European fear
    of 27, 171, 175, 180, 181
cultural pan-nationalism 167, 170,
    177, 178, 185
cultural policy, European
    Commission 26–7, 165–89
culturalist discourse 22–3, 59, 60,
    71–3, 79; effects in Côte d'Ivoire
    73–7
culture 88; changes in meaning of
    18–19; conceptualization in
    policy literature 35, 271, 275–6,
    277, 278; and policy 255–6; and
    style of governance 27, 28
Curtin, C. 264
Czarniawska-Joerges, B. 16

D'Andrade, R. 17
Darwin, Charles 11
Davies, C. 268, 269
Davis, H. 170
Davy, D. 55
Dawson, A. 268, 270, 277
De Bruyn, M. 63
De Certeau, M. 13
De Clercq, W. 173
De Cock, K. 63
De Koning, K. 68
deconstructionism 275
Delacourt, S. 149, 150, 159
Delors, Jacques 170, 182, 187,
    188n7, 189n9
Denenberg, R. 62

Denmark 109, 111; oncology ward
    23–4, 88–103
Depardieu, Gerard 181
Department of Environment 218,
    223, 235n6, 236n9
Desclaux, A. 76
Deutsch, K. 166, 177
development groups, and
    HIV/AIDS 66–7
development: policy research 18,
    43–57; case study 21, 46–53;
    discourses of 66–71
Dewalt, B. 7
difference 26–31; politics of, in
    Canada 147, 151, 153–4, 157–8,
    160; see also national identity
Dilley, R. 267, 268
dirigisme, and European
    audiovisual policy 26–7, 171,
    172, 178, 186, 187
discipline 246
discourse analysis 277
Discourse and Society 80n3
discourse: of policy 18–24; of
    power in Denmark 23–4,
    88–103; differences in 99–101;
    HIV/AIDS policy in Africa see
    HIV/AIDS; see also closure
    techniques, containment,
    language
disempowerment 60, 66, 68, 70,
    197–8, 230–1
Dodwell, D. 182
Donnan, H. 17, 34, 188, 264,
    265, 268
Donzelot, J. 244–5, 247, 252
Dreyfus, H. 8, 9, 242
dualism 13
Duke, M.S. 53
Durkheim, E. 29–30, 198

economic policy in Northern
    Ireland 267
Economist 182, 183
Edouards, M. 114, 115, 118
education policy: Great Britain 16;
    Northern Ireland 267, 268;
    Sweden 26, 107–8, 114, 116–19

(effects of 131–3, government bill for increased sexual equality 119–23, report on teacher training colleges 117, 130, state-commissioned report on research 123–6, *We are all Different* report on schools 126–9)

Edwards, J. 7

elderly, care for, in Norway 31–2, 195–215; context of industrial community 202–4; decision-making and Labour Party ideology 204–7; modernization exemplified by Ulefoss 207–9; moral economy and policy 197–9; political resistance 209–13; the reform plan 199–202

Elgqvist-Salzman, I. 117

Elias, C. 71

elites 25, 131, 166; Canada 149; European, and culture 172–5, 182, 183; *see also* academy; expert knowledge

empowerment discourse 68; and housing policy 219, 224, 228, 231, 232, 233, 241–4; *see also* disempowerment

encapsulation 13

Engels, F. 11, 13, 29

enterprise culture 28, 32, 232, 239

equal opportunities, in Sweden 26, 107–34

Escobar, A. 60, 68

ethnic cleansing 167

ethnic minorities, Canada 25

ethnicity 59, 165; in Northern Ireland 264, 267, 269, 275–6; in Sweden 132

ethnography 262

European Association of Social Anthropologists 5

European Community/Union: Declaration on the European Identity (1979) 176; Directive on Television Broadcasting (1989) 27, 171, 183, 184, 188n6; Hahn Report 188n3; People's Europe

campaign 173; and sexual discrimination/equality in Sweden 113, 115, 133; Sweden and 133n11; *Television Without Frontiers* Green Paper 169–71, 173, 188n3

European federalism 27, 167, 168, 172, 185, 189n14

European identity 26–7, 165–89; anthropology, identity and politics of communication 165–7; audiovisual policy and European integration 167–9; audiovisual policy and supranationalism 177–9; flaws in EU strategy for promoting 180–5; politics of media policy 172–7; television without frontiers 169–72

Evian, C.R. 63, 78

expert knowledge 9; British housing policy 33, 219, 223, 233; resistance to, in Norway 31–2, 195–215; Sweden 118, 124; *see also* academy; elites

Fadely, J. 255

Fairclough, N. 62

family, and government 30

Fardon, F. 43

farming research 41–9; in Northern Ireland 268 (case study 270–4); *see also* development policy research

Featherstone, M. 207

Feaver, G. 140

Fegan, Brian 57n3

feminism 60, 80n3, 112, 121, 124, 131

Feminist Issues 80n3

field (Bourdieu) 20, 23, 88–9, 90, 92–3, 102

field, the/fieldwork 262; reconceptualizing 14–18, 88

'fields' of political activity (Schwartz and Turner) 13

film *see* audiovisual policy of European Union

Finland 111
Firth, R. 261
Fischer, M. 15
fishing industry, Northern Ireland
    267, 268
Flew, A. 11
flexible accumulation 243, 244
Florin, C. 116, 117, 121
Fog Olwig, K. 88
folk society 13
folkhemmet 110–11
Fontaine, P. 173
Foster, R.J. 137
Fotheringham, A. 161n7
Foucault, M. 4, 5, 8, 17, 18, 19, 20,
    25, 29, 30, 31, 34, 44, 60, 89, 144,
    153, 234, 241, 242, 243, 246,
    249, 255
Fox, R. 16
France, and European media policy
    171, 172, 173, 175, 178–87
    passim
Francis, D. 138
Frankenberg, F. 61
Frederick, W. 250, 251
freedom 9–10, 27, 28, 219; of the
    poor 223
Freirian philosophy 68
Friedman, Milton 28
Fuller, C.J. 274
functionalism 174

Gaddis, J.L. 8
Gallie, W.B. 19
Gardner, D. 183
GATT talks on world trade 171,
    172, 180–3
Gavin, B. 170
gaze (Foucault) 21, 44, 241
Gellner, E. 166, 167, 175, 177
Gemeinschaft 13, 150, 153, 157, 158
gender 59, 60; and HIV/AIDS in
    Africa 62, 63 (*see also* gender
    and development discourse);
    Northern Ireland 267, 269
gender and development discourse
    22–3, 59, 66–71
gender equality policy in Sweden

26, 107–34; effects of sex
    equality policy in education
    131–3; policies of equality
    between men and women
    111–15; policies of sexual
    equality and issues of gender in
    higher education 116–19;
    reactions to a government bill
    for increased sex equality
    119–23; report on teacher
    training colleges 117, 130; state-
    commissioned report on
    research 123–6; *We are all
    different* report on schools
    126–9; welfare state 109–11
genre, policy writing as 43–4
George, S. 168
Gilmour, E. 70
Global 2 46
global/local 13
globalization 28, 175, 176
Gluckman, M. 13
Goffman, E. 249
Gollner, A.B. 140
Goodwin, J.A. 220
Gordon, C. 6, 144
Gordon, G. 66
Gordon, I. 15
Gore, Charles 57n5
Gould, J. 240
governance 4, 5–6, 12, 14, 16, 17,
    24, 186; culture as model of 187;
    definition of 17; and nation state
    27–9; *see also* neo-liberalism;
    power; rational governance/
    government; social democratic
    model
government: anthropology and art
    of 10–12, 14, 103; and national
    identity 24–9; policy and 5, 9; *see
    also* rational governance/
    government
governmentality 29–35, 144, 267
Grace, V.M. 68, 77
Gramsci, A. 13, 29
Grant, C. 187
Great Britain: and European
    identity 178, 179, 186–7;

education policy 16; governance
31; housing policies 31, 32–3,
217–36; medical science 6; neo-
liberalism and individual 19–20
Green, B.S. 43, 44
Green, E.C. 72
Green Revolution, case study 21,
46–53
Greenfeld, L. 136
Grillo, R. 18, 60, 166
Grimshaw, A. 261
Guillaumin, C. 79
Gwyn, R. 150

Habermas, J. 208
Hacking, I. 246–7
Hadden, B. 66, 68, 70
Hague, C. 218
Hall, S. 136, 137, 144
Handler, R. 143, 276
Hannerz, U. 54
Hansen, H.P. 23–4
Harney, R.F. 138
Harris, Mike 160
Hart, K. 54, 261
Hartmann, Thomas 252–3, 254
Harvey, D. 243, 244
Harvey, P. 139
Hastrup, K. 88
Hayek, Friedrich von 28
health care *see* elderly, care for;
    HIV/AIDS in Africa; hospital
Hedlund, E. 111, 112
Heelas, P. 6
Heise, L.L. 71, 79
Held, D. 136, 137
Hernes, H.M. 112, 114
Hervik, P. 88
Herzfeld, M. 263
Heyward, W.L. 69
Hills, Carla 182
Hirdman, Y. 110, 111
HIV/AIDS in Africa 15, 22–3,
59–80; culturalist discourse
71–3; effects of culturalist
discourse in Côte d'Ivoire 73–7;
gender and development
discourse 66–71;

medical/epidemiological
discourse 22, 59, 61–6; policy
implications of discourses 77–9;
theoretical frameworks 60–4
Hobsbawm, E. 137, 166
homosexuality 20; and national
identity in Canada 147, 153
Horn, D. 220, 221
Hosler, V. 255
hospital, patients' bodies and
discourses of power in Denmark
23–4, 88–103; clinical praxis
91–3, 102; daily round and its
interpretation 93–8, 102;
different discourses 99–101;
ethnographic examples 95–8;
hospital as negotiated order 90;
policy 88–90, 102; policy
documents 90–1, 92, 93, 102
Houses Let in Lodgings 220
housing, research in Northern
Ireland 267, 268
Housing (White Paper) 217–18
Housing Act (1988) 225
housing policies in Great Britain 31,
32–3, 217–36; democratizing
knowledge and policing of
communities 224–31; from
government *of* the poor to
government *by* the poor 217–20,
233; history of subsidized
housing 220–4; and poverty
under advanced liberalism
231–4; 'Right to Buy' 235n2
Howe, L. 267–8, 277
Huber, P.C.J. 62
Hughes, J. 268
Human Embryology and
Fertilisation Bill (1990) 6
human resource policies 240–1
Hyatt, S.B. 19, 31, 32–3, 160, 224

identity 3; research in Northern
Ireland 264, 277; *see also*
European identity; national
identity
identity formation, anthropology
and 137, 165–7

identity politics 136
ideology 24, 35, 186, 277
India 136, 160
individual 4, 19–20, 29; abstract, of
    modernity 207–9
individualism 28; *see also* enterprise
    culture; neo-liberalism
industry 13
Ingram, K. 268, 269
intellectuals 25, 166; *see also*
    academy; expert knowledge
intergovernmentalism 178, 186
international money markets 27
International Rice Research
    Institute (IRRI) 21, 48–53
Irish famine 11
Irwin, C. 267, 268
Ivory Coast *see* Côte d'Ivoire

Jackall, Robert 248, 249
Jameson, F. 243–4
Jämsides 114
Jämställdhet 26, 107–34
Janks, H. 67
Japan, European audiovisual policy
    and 27, 169, 171
Jay, A. 10
Jeffrey, B. 149
Jenkins, David 235n5
Jenkins, R. 264
Johansson, U. 116, 117, 121

Kabeer, N. 66
Kanstrup, C. 66
Karin, Q.A. 65, 67, 70
Kellner, H. 207
Kemp, P. 222
Kenney, M.C. 275
Kenny, Linda 227, 228
King, D. 28
Kisekka, M.N. 64
KIT 66, 67
Klugman, B. 66
knowledge, democratization of, and
    housing policy 224–31, 233–4
Knox, C. 268
Knudsen, A. 94
Koestler, A. 5

Kolb, W. 240
Kunda, G. 249–50, 251, 254
Kuper, A. 35n1

Labour Party: British 19–20;
    Norway 195, 197, 199, 203–7,
    209, 211, 212
Lafferty, W. 206
laissez-faire society/economics 26,
    28, 186–7
Lang, Jack 183
language: and disease 60, 74–6;
    policy as 12, 18–24; discourses of
    HIV/AIDS in Africa 59–79;
    discourses of power and
    patients' bodies 88–103; and
    national identity in France 169,
    172, 177–8, 179, 180–5; political,
    in traditional societies 12;
    writing development policy
    43–57
Le Palec, A. 70
legal profession 6
legitimacy 3, 11–12, 24, 27, 141,
    145, 159–60, 204
Lévi-Strauss, C. 262
Levin, C. 62, 66
levirate 71, 73, 74
Levy, C. 170
Lewycky, L. 139
liberalism 9–10, 136, 160; *see also*
    neo-liberalism
Liep, J. 88
Linköping University 114, 120,
    125, 129
Lipsky, M. 5
Lloyd-Jones, D. 12
local/global 13
local politics, and reform and
    resistance in Norway 31–2,
    195–215
locality, and nation 154–9; *see also*
    community
Lock, M. 89–90, 99, 100, 102
Locke, John 144
Lorenzco, E.T. 49
Lower Grange Housing Association
    224–32, 235n5

Lower Grange Women's History Project 221
Lukács, G. 50
Lukes, S. 9, 198
Lupton, D. 89, 90, 94
Lynn, J. 10

Maastricht Treaty 168, 170, 173, 174, 178
Macaulay, I. 268, 270
McBride, S. 140
McCarthyism 8
McCoy, D. 70, 75
McFarlane, G. 17, 34, 188, 264, 265, 268, 270
McHugh, P. 52, 55
MacIntyre, A. 52
Mackey, E. 25–6, 138, 139, 141, 142, 149, 150, 151
McLaughlin, E. 268, 269, 270
macro/micro 13, 102
Malaysia 198, 207
Malinowski, B. 7
Malthus, Thomas 11
management policies, in US 34, 239–56; corporate selves 248–56; kinds of power 241–4; persons/groups 245–8; work and life 244–5
Mannheim, Karl 249
Maranan, R.G. 49
Marcus, G. 15
Marcus, J. 15
Marcus, T. 64
market 6, 20, 28, 29, 32, 131, 140, 208
Martin, E. 19, 34, 101
Martin, M. 68
Marx, Karl 13, 29, 207–9, 214, 215n3
Marxism 66, 245
Marxist anthropology 13, 94
mass communication policy, European see audiovisual policy of European Union
Maugh, T.H. 254
Mauss, M. 7
Mbali, C. 72

media policy see audiovisual policy of European Union
medical discourse, in hospital 61–4; 100–1
medical science 6
medico-moral discourse of HIV/AIDS 22–3, 59, 61–6
Mercer, M.A. 72
Mercouri, Melina 184
Merrow, John 254
Merson, M. 62
Mestrovic, S. 167
methodology 14–18
Mhloyi, M. 62, 71
Michard, C. 60
Miller, D. 233
Miller, P. 9, 231, 248
Milne, D. 140
Milton, K. 268, 269, 277
Mintz, S.W. 13
missionaries, and HIV/AIDS 63
mobilizing metaphors (Wright) 20
modernity: and housing policy 220, 221; Marx and Weber's critique 207–9, 214
Mogey, J.M. 266, 268
monetarism 28
Monnet, Jean 188n4
Moodley, K. 139
morality: and housing policy 220–1; and policy 10–11; and resistance in Norway 195, 196, 197–9, 205, 206, 207, 212, 213, 214
Morley, D. 175, 180
Motsei, M. 70
Msaky, H.I. 70
Mulroney, Brian 140, 159
multi-site ethnography 14, 25, 93, 138–9
multiculturalism: Canada 25, 26, 138–41, 147–8, 150–1, 157, 158; US 276

NACOSA 78
Nader, L. 14
Nairn, T. 137, 166
Nash, J. 13
nation 59; vs. state 143–5

nation states 27, 166, 167, 177, 178
National AIDS Convention of
    South Africa 78
national culture 27, 28, 177
national identity 24–9, 136, 137, 166
national identity, Canadian 25,
    136–61; Charlottetown Accord
    and constitutional change 140,
    148–50, 151, 159–60;
    construction of 24–8, 165–7; key
    aspects of celebratory policy
    141–5; legitimacy and common
    sense 159–60; multiculturalism,
    constitutional crisis and
    celebrations 138–41; naturalizing
    imagery, celebratory taboos and
    invented symbols 145–54, 155–6,
    157; 'the people' at Wallaceford
    Pumpkin Festival 150–4;
    populism and locality at
    Brookside Raise-the-Flag Day
    154–9; Swedish 107, 132–3
nationalism 137, 139, 165, 166, 175,
    177, 179, 186; research in
    Northern Ireland 264
Nelson, N. 65
neo-liberalism 4, 9–10, 19–20, 28–9,
    30, 32–4; European Union 171,
    178, 186; and HIV/AIDS 77;
    housing policy and poverty
    under regimes of advanced
    liberalism 32–3, 217–36
New Right 20, 28, 33, 60, 136, 159,
    160, 186; see also Conservative
    Party
new social movements 60, 68
Nochlin, Linda 49, 52
normalization 30
North Atlantic Free Trade
    Association 27
Northern Ireland, policy research
    34–5, 261–78; anthropology,
    policy and mutual suspension of
    disbelief 277–8; context 263–6;
    examples of anthropological
    policy-related research 266–9;
    marginalization of anthropology
    270–4; policy-orientated

anthropology 261–3; 'truncated'
    anthropology in case study
    274–7
Norway 109; policy for care of the
    elderly 31–2, 195–215
Ntuli, N. 76
Nxumalo, Z. 75

O'Dowd, L. 264
Of course we are different! 129
Ogle, S. 268
Okely, J. 271
Olsson, S.E. 109, 110
Olwig, K. Fog 88
Oppong, C. 65
oppression 31, 32, 80n3
Orwell, George 221, 233
Osborne, R.D. 265

Packard, R.P. 71
Pahl, R. 174
Palmer, H. 138
pan-nationalism, cultural 167, 170,
    177, 178, 185
Parkin, D. 18, 60
Parsons, T. 13
Partridge, E. 19
patriotism, non-political, in Canada
    25, 141–59
Patton, C. 59, 62
Pauwels, C. 169, 172, 175, 182
Pear, R. 252
Pearce, A. 46
Peattie, L. 54
people, the see populism
Perrot, Michelle 242
Persson, E. 62
Peters, J. 71
Pheterson, G. 65
Pick, J. 19
Pieterse, J.N. 62
Pittin, R. 65
Plaat, M.V. 67
policing 19, 33, 220, 224–31, 236n10
policy 252, 255–6; anthropology of
    3–10, 261–3 (methodology
    14–18); meaning 19, 239–40
policy documents 15, 18, 20–1,

43–57; hospital 90–1, 92, 93, 102; Sweden 123–6
policy ethnography 7
policy-making: models of 15–16; influence on anthropology 35, 277–8
policy research 20–1, 261–3; case study from Green Revolution 21, 46–53; development policy 21, 43–57; for HIV/AIDS in Africa 78–9; language of 55–6; style of language 44–6, 55; vocabulary and jargon 53–5; *see also* Northern Ireland
policy studies 15–16
political anthropology 6, 12–14, 35
political language 12
political legitimacy *see* legitimacy
political science 271
political technologies, policy as 4, 8–10, 29–34; managing Americans 239–56; reform and resistance in Norway 195–215; tenant management policies in Great Britain 217–36
populism, cultural politics of, and Canadian national identity 25, 136–61
post-structuralism 60
postmodern ethnography 14
postmodernity 167, 243–4
poverty, and housing policy in Britain *see under* housing policies
Power, A. 222
power 30, 60; governance as 6; and housing policy 230–1, 234; language and 12 (discourses in hospital setting 23–4, 88–103); and non-political patriotism and civil society 25, 143–5; policy and 3, 4, 12, 14, 24, 29, 35, 241–4, 246, 252; *see also* political technologies
Preston-Whyte, E. 67, 68
Priority Estates Project (PEP) 236n9
psychology 80n3

public, the 144; *see also* populism

Quebec separatism 138, 139, 155–6, 161n6

Rabinow, P. 8, 9, 30, 221, 242
Rabo, Annika 26
race 59, 60; and national identity in Canada 139
racism 15, 60
Ranger, T. 59, 166
Rappaport, R. 261
Ratey, J. 254
Rathgeber, E.M. 66
rational governance/government 19, 29–34, 196, 204, 209
rationalization process 207, 208–9
Ray, S. 62
Reagan, Ronald 28, 140
Redfield, R. 13
regionalist movements 28
Regner, Åsa 112
Reid, E. 66, 68
Reinhold, S. 14, 20
Rennie, H. 70
resistance 13, 158; Norway 31–2, 195–215
rhetoric, and power 12, 18
Ridley, Nicholas 222
Right *see* New Right
Rispel, L. 70
Rivière, P. 6
Robins, K. 167–8, 175, 180
Rose, N. 9–10, 29, 33, 218–19, 231, 233, 239, 248
Rosendahl, M. 110
Ross, George 170
Ruane, J. 186

Salee, D. 140
Santer, Jacques 185
Satzewic, V. 139
Sayer, D. 207, 208, 214, 215n3
Schein, E.H. 251
Scheper-Hughes, N. 89–90, 99, 100, 102
Schlesinger, P. 166, 174, 175, 176, 180, 186, 187

Schneider, D. 8
Schoepf, B.G. 61, 65, 66
Schopper, P. 63
Schrijvers, J. 68, 79
Schwartz, M. 13
Scott, J. 13, 197–8, 212
Scott, S.J. 72
sectarianism, research in Northern
    Ireland 264, 267, 269
Seeds of Plenty, Seeds of Want
    (Pearce) 46–53
Segal, D.A. 276
Seidel, G. 15, 18, 21–3, 60, 61, 63,
    67, 70, 71, 75, 76
self, techniques of 9, 29, 247; see
    also self-governance; political
    technologies
self-governance: and housing policy
    217–36; see also self-
    management
self-help 231, 233; government
    philosophy of 226
self-improvement 224–31, 233
self-management 229–31; in US 34,
    239–56; see also freedom; self-
    governance
self-rationalization, self-
    streamlining (Mannheim) 249
separatist movements 28
sexism 60
sexual equality, Sweden 26, 107–34
sexuality 59
Shore, C. 11, 26–7, 55, 93, 102, 137,
    166, 168, 173, 187
Silverman, D. 102
Simeon, R. 140
Smallman, M.R. 78
Smith, A.D. 28, 167, 176
Smith, S. 138
social, the, rise of, in Great Britain
    220–4, 233
social cohesion 174
social democratic model 28, 30–1;
    European Union 171, 172, 178,
    186, 187; Sweden 109–11, 114,
    117, 118, 119–23
social deviance see difference
social policy 277

social relations/subject 245–8
social science(s): and HIV/AIDS in
    Africa 78, 174, 176, 262;
    research in Northern Ireland
    265–6, 267; Sweden 109, 110
sociology 13, 271, 277; Sweden 110
Södersten, Bo 133n6
Soledad-Garcia 168
Sontag, S. 60
SOU reports 118, 123–6
South Africa 66, 67, 68–9, 70–1, 72,
    75, 78
Spence, D. 168, 187
Spinelli, Altiero 188n4
Stack, P. 59
Standing, H. 71
Stanley, C. 6
state 2, 108, 131, 166, 183; vs.
    nation 143–5, 204–5; see also
    government, nation states
Stein, Z. 68
Stott, G. 225
Strathern, M. 7
Strauss, A. 90, 92, 95
Strebel, A. 67
studying through (Reinhold) 14
subject/society 245–8
subjectivity 3, 4, 12, 16, 24, 29–35,
    144, 145; as site of governance
    221, 224
supranationalism 167, 168, 177–9,
    186, 187, 188n4
surveillance techniques 9, 228–9; see
    also policing
suspension of disbelief 277–8
Swainson, G. 147
Sweden: gender equality policy 26,
    107–34; national identity 25, 26
symbols, dominant/core, in policy 8

Tabet, P. 65
TASO 63
Taussig, M. 13
Tavernier, Bertrand 175
Taylor, C. 144, 145
television see audiovisual policy of
    European Union
Temmerman, M. 62, 69

tenant management policies in
  Great Britain 32–3, 217–36
Tenants Participatory Advisory
  Service (TPAS) 236n9
Thatcherism 6, 28, 32, 140, 222
Third World 4; *see also*
  development policy research
Thompson, G. 44
Thompson, J.B. 210
Titmuss, R. 5
Tönnies, F. 13
Toubon, M. 181, 183
traditional medicine 71–2, 76–7
traditional societies 12
transactional theory 13
Treaty of Rome 170, 188nn5, 6
Treichler, P. 59, 62
Trend, M.G. 274
Trigger, B.G. 138
Truman Doctrine 8
Tucker, E. 185
Turner, V. 8

Uganda 63
Ulin, P. 73
Underwood, N. 161n7
unemployment research, Northern
  Ireland 267, 268–9
United Nations Beijing Conference
  on Women 66–7
United Nations Development
  Programme 111
United Nations Habitat II
  Conference 80n4
United Nations Research Institute
  for Social Development
  (UNRISD) 21, 46–53
United States: containment policy
  8; and European audiovisual
  policy 27, 169, 171, 172, 175,
  180–3, 185; kinship in 8;
  management policies 34, 239–56;
  multiculturalism 276

Van Dijk, T.E. 60
Van Willigen, J. 7
Vasconcelos, A.-P. 167, 168,
  176, 185

Vidal, L. 21–3, 60–1
Vike, H. 31, 205
Vipond, R.C. 140
Von Hayek, Friedrich 28

Wall Street Journal 182
Wallace, Helen 176
Wallerstein, I. 13
Warnock Report (1984) 6
Watney, S. 59, 62
Watts, C. 65
We are all different report on
  Swedish schools 126–9
Webber, J. 140
Weber, E. 177
Weber, Max 13, 208–9
Weiss, C. 15, 16
welfare benefits, research in
  Northern Ireland 268
welfare state: in Great Britain 31,
  223; in Sweden 26, 107–11,
  114, 123
Welleck, Rene 53
Wellstone, P. 252
Wenders, Wim 181
Whitaker, R. 138
White, A. 3, 5
White, L. 65
Whyte, J. 264
Williams, E.E. 69
Williams, P. 222
Williams, Raymond 18, 19, 45, 53
Wilson, D. 268
Wilson, T.M. 264
Wilson Smith, A. 161n7
Winsor, H. 147, 148
Wodak, R. 60
Wolpe, A. 71
women's studies 118, 124
Wood, L.A. 70
work 239–56
World Bank 79
World Health Organization Global
  AIDS Programme 61, 62; KAP
  questionnaires 63
World Trade Association 27; *see
  also* GATT talks
Worth, D. 69

Wright, S. 4, 11, 15, 18, 20, 55, 90,
     93, 102, 137, 168, 267, 273

xenophobia 25, 139, 175

Yugoslavia 166–7

Zambia 63, 75
Zimbabwe 72
Zwi, A.D. 66